Editor
Eric Migliaccio

Managing Editor
Ina Massler Levin, M.A.

Editor-in-Chief
Sharon Coan, M.S. Ed.

Cover Artist
Denise Bauer

Art Coordinator
Kevin Barnes

Imaging
Rosa C. See

Product Manager
Phil Garcia

Publishers
Mary D. Smith, M.S. Ed.

Key Words for High Achievement

nefarious
regimen
talisman
abate
reputable
queue
grandiose
wan
fatuous
epitaph
pungent
vacillate
punctilious
wraith
panache
dispirit
mélange

Author

R & R FitzGerald

Teacher Created Resources

Teacher Created Resources, Inc.
6421 Industry Way
Westminster, CA 92683
www.teachercreated.com

ISBN-0-7439-3612-4

©2002 Teacher Created Resources, Inc.
Reprinted, 2004
Made in U.S.A.

Table of Contents

Introduction

You will hear it again and again: "The best way to get a good vocabulary is to read a lot." It is true. This book is designed to give you supplemental help in acquiring a good vocabulary. The format of *Key Words for High Achievers* presents you with a diagnostic test and checks on your retention of the words in both the diagnostic and the models. All of the words have been taken from vocabulary expectation lists for honors students and from books on the reading lists for Advanced Placement test in English Language and Composition and English Literature and Composition. Command of the words in this book will provide you with the sophisticated vocabulary that advanced readers, writers, and speakers possess and employ.

Each of the 36 units is whole and independent. Each contains a pre-test, word modeling, a quick match, and pre-test and quick-match answer keys.

How To Use This Book

1. Pre-test yourself on the 32 words in the unit.

2. Check your answers in the pre-test answer key located at the back of each unit.

3. Study the word modeling, which provides the following:

   - correct spelling of the word
     Example: anecdote

   - pronunciation for the word (broken down phonetically by syllables, with the stressed syllable capitalized)
     Example: AN ek dote

   - part of speech identification
     Example: noun

   - definition of the word
     Example: short story; brief narrative

   - context for the word (a sentence demonstrating the proper usage of the word)
     Example: Public speakers often use an *anecdote* to illustrate a point.

   - other forms of the word (if applicable)
     Example: anecdotal (adjective)

4. Re-test yourself with the quick-match review located at the back of each unit.

5. Check your answers in the quick-match answer key.

Good luck with your work, and happy wordsmithing.

Common Word Roots

Root	Meaning	Example
-ambul-	to walk	ambulatory
-anthropo-	humankind	anthropology
-arbor-	tree	arboreal
-arch-	rule, govern	hierarchy
-aristo-	best	aristocracy
-bibl-	book	bibliography
-bio-	life	biography
-ced-, -cess-	move	secede
-chrom-	color	chromatic
-cis-	cut	incision
-cid-	kill	homicide
-cogn-	know	incognito
-corpor-	body	corporation
-cosm-	world	cosmic
-cred-	believe	credible
-crypt-	secret	cryptic
-dem-	people	democracy
-dict-	speak	dictate
-duct-	lead	conduct
-dyn-	power	dynamo
-ego-	self	egomania
-erg-	work	ergonomics
-flect-, -flex-	bend	reflect, reflex
-flor-	flower	floral
-fluct-, -flux-	flow	influx
-gam-	marriage	bigamy
-gen-	to (be) produced	genealogy
-geo-	earth	autograph
-glos-, -glot-	tongue	polyglot
-graph-	write	geography
-gyn-	woman	gynecology
-helio-	sun	heliometry ✓
-hem-, -hemat-	blood	hematoma, hematology
-hydr-	water	hydraulic

Common Word Roots *(cont.)*

Root	Meaning	Example
-ject-	throw	eject
-jud-	judge	judicial
-jur-	law	jury
-kine-	motion	kinetic
-lingu-	tongue	bilingual
-loqu-	speak	eloquence
-merc-	sell	merchant
-meter-	measure	parameter
-morph-	change	metamorphosis
-mort-	dead	mortify
-necro-	corpse	necrophobia
-palp-	feel	palpable
-path-	disease	pathology
-pend-	hang	pending
-petr-	rock	petrology
-phag-	eating	pantophagous
-phon-	sound	telephone
-phil-	love	hemophiliac
-phob-	fear	acrophobia
-phot-	light	photosynthesis
-plut-	wealth	plutocracy
-polis-, -polit	city	metropolis, metropolitan
-roga-	ask	interrogation
-rupt-	break	rupture
-sanct-	holy	sanctify
-sangui-	blood	sanguine
-scop-	see	microscope
-sequ-	follow	sequel
-soma-	body	somatic
-somn-	sleep	somnolence
-tax-, -tact-	order	taxonomy, tactics
-tempor-	time	temporal
-thanas-, -thanat-	death	euthanasia
-theo-	god	theology
-therm-	heat	thermodynamics
-vir-	man	virile
-vol-	will	voluntary
-volv-, volu-	roll	revolve, convolute
-vor-	devour	voracious

Common Prefixes

Prefix	Meaning	Example
ab-	away, away from	aberration
acer-	sharp	acerbic
ad-	to, toward	adjure
ben-	good	beneficent
cen-	center	centrifugal
circum-	around	circumspect
com-	with	complement
con-	with	convivial
contra-	against, opposite	contradict
counter-	against, opposite	countermand
de-	down	deprecate
dis-	not	disavow
eff-	out	efflorescent
em-	within	embroil
en-	within	encroach
equi-	equal, same	equivalent
eu-	good	euphony
ex-	out, out of	exodus
im-	in, into	impel
im-	not	impervious
meta-	beyond	metamorphosis
ob-	in the way	obviate
pre-	before	precipitate
pro-	for	proclivity
pseudo-	false	pseudonym
trans-	across	transmute
un-	not	unequivocal

Prefixes That Denote Negativism

Prefix	Meaning	Example
contra-	against	contradiction
dis-	not	disassociate
il-	not	illicit
im-	not	implausible
in-	not	incompetent
ir-	not	irreplaceable
mis-	not	misrepresent
neg-	not	negligible
un-	not	unmitigated

Common Suffixes

These suffixes tell you the part of speech of a word:

-ion	⟶ is a noun suffix ⟶	as in: nation
-ism	⟶ is a noun suffix ⟶	as in: nationalism
-ic	⟶ is an adjectival suffix ⟶	as in: terrific
-ous	⟶ is an adjectival suffix ⟶	as in: enormous
-al	⟶ is an adjectival suffix ⟶	as in: rational
-fy	⟶ is a verb suffix ⟶	as in: verify
-ize	⟶ is a verb suffix ⟶	as in: nationalize
-cracy	⟶ rule or government ⟶	as in: democracy
-esce, -escent, -esence	⟶ giving off, becoming ⟶	as in: effloresce
-fer, -ferous	⟶ bear, bearing ⟶	as in: conifer
-oid	⟶ like, similar to ⟶	as in: humanoid
-log, -logy	⟶ study of ⟶	as in: biology

Unit 1

Pre-test Yourself

Group 1			
disseminate	interpolate	sordid	renege
cynicism	turgid	proffer	blatant

1. The author was furious when the editor said he would ___interpolate___ new text into the manuscript.

2. ___Blatant___ music disturbed the students who were studying.

3. The missionary will ___proffer___ ~~disseminate~~ information about his religion.

4. An evil reputation preceded the ___sordid___ criminal.

5. She had nothing but ___cynicism___ in her outlook on the hypocritical reformer.

6. The company may ___renege___ on the original offer and substitute another offer.

7. Verbiage, verbosity, and prolix prose can create ___turgid___ writing.

8. Will he ___disseminate___ ~~proffer~~ his hand in an act of friendship?

Group 2			
ruminate	ubiquitous	amuck	preclude
intractable	cryptic	sunder	flag

1. He can ___preclude___ any further damage by acting quickly.

2. Prisoners ran ___amuck___ when the warden cut food rations.

3. The ___ubiquitous___ ~~intractable~~ student refused to sit still in class.

4. He would ___ruminate___ for hours on the meaning of life, even when his roommates threw a loud party.

5. Even an earthquake may not ___sunder___ the old, wooden bridge.

6. He often ran the first 100 yards well, but then he would ___flag___.

7. Danger seemed ___intractable___ ~~ubiquitous~~ when the troops invaded.

8. No one could understand him because he was so ___cryptic___.

Pre-test Yourself *(cont.)*

Group 3

rusticate	synopsis	docile	anachronism
pristine	licentious	crop	gyrate

---

1. The students were asked to write a ___Synopsis___ of what they had read in literature class.

2. At first we feared the animal was aggressive and belonged in the wild, but we later found it to be quite ___docile___.

3. Northern areas in Alaska are still in ___pristine___ condition.

4. We usually ___rusticate___ in Nova Scotia for the summer.

5. Photographers ___crop___ photos so that only what they want to be seen is seen.

6. The faulty compass began to ___gyrate___ in the magnetic storm.

7. The conservative group boycotted the movie on the grounds that it contained ___licentious___ and immoral characters.

8. The Ancient Roman's wearing of a wristwatch was the most obvious ___anachronism___ in the performance.

Group 4

intangible	rift	apocalyptic	dissemble
precis	scintillate	intransigent	corpulent

---

1. A synopsis can also be called a ___(dissemble)___ *precis*.

2. In the second half of the 20th century, many people lived in fear of the ___apocalyptic___ effects of a nuclear war.

3. He was an obdurate, adamant, and ___intransigent___ political enemy.

4. A restaurant's ambiance is often the result of ___(corpulent)___ *intangible* touches in service.

5. The ___rift___ in the political party widened as more people deserted.

6. The ex-convict was known to ___(scintillate)___ *dissemble*, and so his pleas of innocence were met with cynicism.

7. Gourmands tend to be ___(In tangible)___ *corpulent*.

8. Wit peppered the conversation and helped it ___(precis)___ *scintillate*.

Unit 1 *(cont.)*

Words and Definitions

disseminate (di SEM i nate): to spread; to circulate
   Part of Speech: verb
   Example: The group *disseminated* propaganda that disturbed the citizens.
   Other Form(s): dissemination (noun)

sordid (SOR did): filthy; morally degraded
   Part of Speech: adjective
   Example: There were the *sordid* details about their affair.

cynicism (SIN i sizm): (usually scornful) doubtfulness; sneering
   Part of Speech: noun
   Example: The pragmatic man viewed the psychic's claims with *cynicism*.
   Other Form(s): cynic (noun); cynical (adjective)

proffer (PROF fur): to offer; to present (usually humbly)
   Part of Speech: verb
   Example: She *proffered* her hand, and the gallant man kissed it.

interpolate (in TUR po late): to insert; to interject
   Part of Speech: verb
   Example: Her remarks were *interpolated* into the official record.

renege (re NIG): to default; to retract
   Part of Speech: verb
   Example: His honor became suspect after he *reneged* on his promise.

turgid (TUR jid): swollen; polluted
   Part of Speech: adjective
   Example: Certain writers use a *turgid* style that overwhelms the reader.

blatant (BLAY tunt): flagrant; conspicuously offensive
   Part of Speech: adjective
   Example: The video camera recorded the policeman's *blatant* abuse of power.

Words and Definitions *(cont.)*

— **Group 2** —

ruminate (ROO mi nate): to meditate; to contemplate
> **Part of Speech:** verb
> **Example:** Ancient Celtic monks *ruminated* about profound theological problems.
> **Other Form(s):** rumination (noun)

amuck (a MUCK): frenzied; berserk
> **Part of Speech:** adjective
> **Example:** The horse ran *amuck* when the fire started in the barn.

intractable (in TRAK ta bul): uncooperative; disobedient
> **Part of Speech:** adjective
> **Example:** The police found him an *intractable* prisoner who would not listen to reason.

sunder (SUN der): to separate; to divide
> **Part of Speech:** verb
> **Example:** Lightning and severe cold *sundered* many of the trees during the storm.

ubiquitous (yoo BIK wi tus): omnipresent; everywhere at the same time
> **Part of Speech:** adjective
> **Example:** The TV series was so popular that its influence on popular culture seemed *ubiquitous*.

preclude (pre CLUDE): to prevent; to hinder
> **Part of Speech:** verb
> **Example:** Hurricanes *preclude* any sailing from the pier.

cryptic (KRIP tik): mysterious; secretive
> **Part of Speech:** adjective
> **Example:** To prevent being overheard, the spies wrote correspondence in *cryptic* notes.

flag (FLAG): to droop; to become weak
> **Part of Speech:** verb
> **Example:** His energy *flagged*, and he dropped out of the race.

Words and Definitions *(cont.)*

─────────────────── **Group 3** ───────────────────

rusticate (RUS ti kate): to vacation; to sojourn
> **Part of Speech:** verb
> **Example:** I *rusticated* at Brighton-by-the-Sea.

docile (DOSS ul): pliable; manageable
> **Part of Speech:** adjective
> **Example:** *Docile* dogs are easy to train.
> **Other Form(s):** docility (noun)

pristine (PRIS teen): pure; clean; like new
> **Part of Speech:** adjective
> **Example:** The rare collectible was even more valuable due to its *pristine* condition.

crop (CROP): to clip; to cut
> **Part of Speech:** verb
> **Example:** The gardener used large, sharp shears to *crop* the overgrown hedge.

synopsis (sin OP sis): outline; summary
> **Part of Speech:** noun
> **Example:** Instead of going over the report page by page, the speaker gave a *synopsis* of it.

anachronism (uh NAK ro nizm): incongruity in time; obsolete form
> **Part of Speech:** noun
> **Example:** Rotary dial telephones are becoming *anachronisms*.
> **Other Form(s):** anachronistic (adjective)

licentious (lie SEN shus): immoral; sexually undisciplined
> **Part of Speech:** adjective
> **Example:** Chaucer and Rabelais wrote comically about *licentious* characters.
> **Other Form(s):** licentiousness (noun)

gyrate (JY rate): to spin; to revolve
> **Part of Speech:** verb
> **Example:** His invention featured a ball that would *gyrate* at varying speeds.
> **Other Form(s):** gyration (noun)

Words and Definitions *(cont.)*

──────────── **Group 4** ────────────

intangible (in TAN ji bul): incapable of being touched or pinpointed
    Part of Speech: adjective
    Example: Her music had *intangible* qualities that enraptured the listeners.

apocalyptic (uh pok uh LIP tik): doomed; catastrophic
    Part of Speech: adjective
    Example: Certain cults believe that the millennium will bring *apocalyptic* consequences.
    Other Form(s): apocalypse (noun)

precis (PRAY see): summary; synopsis
    Part of Speech: noun
    Example: Students wrote a *precis* of the book to satisfy course requirements.

intransigent (in TRAN si jent): uncompromising; implacable; immovable
    Part of Speech: adjective
    Example: *Intransigent* students are placed in isolation for their bad behavior.
    Other Form(s): intransigence (noun)

rift (RIFT): split; crevice
    Part of Speech: noun
    Example: A *rift* occurred, and the parties agreed to disagree.

dissemble (di SEM bul): to feign; to fake
    Part of Speech: verb
    Example: The fighter *dissembled* injury and caught his opponent off guard.
    Other Form(s): dissembling (verb); dissembling (noun); dissembling (adjective)

scintillate (SIN ti late): to flash; to gleam
    Part of Speech: adjective
    Example: He imagined his performance in the play would *scintillate*, but he stumbled twice and forgot many of his lines.
    Other Form(s): scintillating (adjective)

corpulent (KOR pyoo lent): fat; obese
    Part of Speech: adjective
    Example: Dickens had a peculiar habit of describing *corpulent* people in his books.
    Other Form(s): corpulence (noun)

Unit 1 *(cont.)*

Quick Match

Group 1

A. scorn	C. flagrant	E. polluted	G. degraded
B. default	D. spread	F. interject	H. offer

_____ 1. disseminate

_____ 2. sordid

_____ 3. cynicism

_____ 4. proffer

_____ 5. interpolate

_____ 6. renege

_____ 7. turgid

_____ 8. blatant

Group 2

A. completely hinder	C. divide	E. berserk	G. contemplate
B. secret	D. weaken	F. disobedient	H. omnipresent

_____ 1. ruminate

_____ 2. amuck

_____ 3. intractable

_____ 4. sunder

_____ 5. ubiquitous

_____ 6. preclude

_____ 7. cryptic

_____ 8. flag

Group 3

A. immoral	C. outline	E. incongruity	G. vacation
B. cut	D. spin	F. manageable	H. pure

_____ 1. rusticate

_____ 2. docile

_____ 3. pristine

_____ 4. crop

_____ 5. synopsis

_____ 6. anachronism

_____ 7. licentious

_____ 8. gyrate

Group 4

A. feign	C. crevice	E. flash	G. obese
B. uncompromising	D. untouchable	F. summary	H. catastrophic

_____ 1. intangible

_____ 2. apocalyptic

_____ 3. precis

_____ 4. intransigent

_____ 5. rift

_____ 6. dissemble

_____ 7. scintillate

_____ 8. corpulent

Unit 1 *(cont.)*

Answer Key

Group 1	Group 2	Group 3	Pre-test 4
1. interpolate	1. preclude	1. synopsis	1. precis
2. blatant	2. amuck	2. docile	2. apocalyptic
3. disseminate	3. intractable	3. pristine	3. intransigent
4. sordid	4. ruminate	4. rusticate	4. intangible
5. cynicism	5. sunder	5. crop	5. rift
6. renege	6. flag	6. gyrate	6. dissemble
7. turgid	7. ubiquitous	7. licentious	7. corpulent
8. proffer	8. cryptic	8. anachronism	8. scintillate

Quick Match

Group 1	Group 2	Group 3	Group 4
1. D	1. G	1. G	1. D
2. G	2. E	2. F	2. H
3. A	3. F	3. H	3. F
4. H	4. C	4. B	4. B
5. F	5. H	5. C	5. C
6. B	6. A	6. E	6. A
7. E	7. B	7. A	7. E
8. C	8. D	8. D	8. G

Unit 2

Pre-test Yourself

Group 1

besiege	salacious	diatribe	remonstrate
corollary	polyglot	insuperable	trepidation

---

1. Many members of the United Nations are _____.

2. The professor launched into a _____ at the sassy student.

3. _____ filled the village when the volcano started to erupt.

4. He dealt in _____ jokes, and many decorous people found him distasteful.

5. The mother began to _____ the intractable child.

6. The _____ of the student's dedication to academics was her straight-A report card.

7. The soldiers fought against _____ odds and were driven back.

8. Members of the paparrazzi often _____ celebrities in inappropriate places.

Group 2

analgesic	replicate	garrulous	anathema
probity	estrange	insidious	dichotomy

---

1. While the president's coterie of advisors was under investigation, his personal _____ was never in question.

2. His extreme dislike of the song's lyrics and his unflagging support of First Amendment rights created a _____ within him.

3. Upon waking, the artist tried in vain to _____ a scene from his latest dream.

4. A proper diet proved to be an _____ and was salubrious for him.

5. His iconoclastic views began to _____ some of his more conservative relatives.

6. The judge viewed the criminal's actions as _____, and he was given the maximum sentence allowed by law.

7. People who are lonely can become very _____ when given the chance to speak.

8. Because of his heinous acts, his name was _____ in the small town.

Unit 2 (cont.)

Pre-test Yourself (cont.)

Group 3

languish	didactic	ambiance	inchoate
prescient	cordon	volition	reproach

1. Thousands of political dissidents were forced to_____ in jail during the dictator's reign.

2. Man without _____ is a slave.

3. Plans for the bridge were _____, and a lot of work lay ahead.

4. His oratorical style was stiff and _____.

5. The shortstop seemed _____ because he was always where the ball was hit.

6. The event's organizers used a _____ to keep people from entering the hall early.

7. Special service gave an _____ that would have been lacking otherwise.

8. She found it necessary to _____ him daily for his unwanted attentions.

Group 4

habituate	diurnal	gregarious	quell
enrapture	allocate	saccharine	verdancy

1. _____ people generally enjoy social events.

2. Quartermasters in the army _____ food and clothing to soldiers.

3. When he was finally able to _____ himself to the extreme heat, he started to feel better.

4. The poet's _____ verse soon became unbearable to his captive audience.

5. Diaries record _____ activities and thoughts.

6. The teacher was unable to _____ the students' laughter when the principal tripped in front of the class.

7. Spring brings _____.

8. The great actress was able to _____ her audiences every time she stepped on the stage.

Unit 2 (cont.)

Words and Definitions

──────────── Group 1 ────────────

besiege (bi SEEJ): to surround; to put pressure on
    Part of Speech: verb
    Example: Movie fans *besiege* stars at premieres.

salacious (sa LAY shus): lustful; libidinous
    Part of Speech: adjective
    Example: Strict moralists look down upon *salacious* works of art.

diatribe (DIE uh tribe): tirade; vocal outburst
    Part of Speech: noun
    Example: The teacher was upset by the intractable student and launched into a *diatribe*.

remonstrate (ri MON strate): to argue; to object
    Part of Speech: verb
    Example: An unhappy candidate *remonstrated* with his successful opponent.

corollary (KOR uh lare ee): deduction; result
    Part of Speech: noun
    Example: Geometric principles carry *corollaries* to solve different problems.

polyglot (POL ee glot): of or having several languages
    Part of Speech: adjective
    Example: Most Europeans are *polyglot* out of necessity.

insuperable (in SOO pur a bul): indomitable; unsurpassable
    Part of Speech: adjective
    Example: We felt the odds were *insuperable* and agreed to surrender.

trepidation (trep i DAY shun): alarm; reluctance
    Part of Speech: noun
    Example: The impending journey into danger filled him with *trepidation*.

Words and Definitions *(cont.)*

─────────────── **Group 2** ───────────────

analgesic (an ul JEES ik): pain relieving; pain assuaging
    Part of Speech: adjective
    Example: The drug proved to be an *analgesic* agent that mitigated the agony.

replicate (REP li kate): to repeat; to reproduce
    Part of Speech: verb
    Example: He was asked to *replicate* his most successful performance.
    Other Form(s): replication (noun)

garrulous (GARE uh lus): talkative; verbose
    Part of Speech: adjective
    Example: Lonely people often become *garrulous* when given the opportunity to speak.
    Other Form(s): garrulousness (noun)

anathema (uh NATH uh muh): curse; malediction
    Part of Speech: noun
    Example: The evil sorcerer placed his *anathema* on the town.

probity (PRO bi tee): honesty; uprightness
    Part of Speech: noun
    Example: Everyone trusted her because her *probity* was never questioned.

estrange (eh STRANGE): to alienate; to turn away
    Part of Speech: verb
    Example: His strange habits *estranged* most of his neighbors.

insidious (in SID ee us): wicked; malignant
    Part of Speech: adjective
    Example: The epidemic was caused by an *insidious* virus that nearly decimated the village.

dichotomy (die KOT uh mee): split; contradiction
    Part of Speech: noun
    Example: A philosophical *dichotomy* occurred, and the two sides were estranged.

Words and Definitions (cont.)

─────────────── Group 3 ───────────────

languish (LANG gwish): to weaken; to suffer
Part of Speech: verb
Example: In nineteenth century novels, ladies *languished* for lost lovers.

didactic (die DAK tik): educational; instructive
Part of Speech: adjective
Example: His *didactic* style bored many in the audience.

ambiance (AM bee unts): atmosphere; mood
Part of Speech: noun
Example: Quite often the *ambiance* in a restaurant is better than its food.

inchoate (in KO it): incipient; beginning
Part of Speech: adjective
Example: Their plans were only *inchoate*, and more study was necessary.

prescient (PRESH ent): clairvoyant; prophetic
Part of Speech: adjective
Example: She was *prescient*, and her instincts were unerring.
Other Form(s): prescience (noun)

cordon (COR don): barrier (usually in the form of a rope, etc.)
Part of Speech: noun
Example: Police will place a *cordon* around a crime scene.

volition (vo LI shun): the freedom of choice
Part of Speech: noun
Example: In most instances, the slave was not allowed to exercise his own *volition*.

reproach (re PROACH): to blame; to censure
Part of Speech: verb
Example: The academic dean *reproached* the students during the sit-in.
Other Form(s): reproach (noun); reproachful (adjective)

Words and Definitions *(cont.)*

─────────── **Group 4** ───────────

habituate (ha BIT chu ate): to accustom; to familiarize
    Part of Speech: verb
    Example: She *habituated* herself to the new environment.

diurnal (die URN ul): daily; quotidian
    Part of Speech: adjective
    Example: *Diurnal* animals do not need large eyes.

gregarious (gre GARE ee us): sociable; enjoying company
    Part of Speech: adjective
    Example: He was garrulous and *gregarious*.

quell (KWELL) to suppress; to pacify
    Part of Speech: verb
    Example: The security guards were unable to *quell* the riotous crowd.

enrapture (en RAP chur): to enchant; to fascinate
    Part of Speech: verb
    Example: The dancer's grace *enraptured* the whole assembly.

allocate (AL oh kate): to set apart; to allot
    Part of Speech: verb
    Example: Rescue personnel *allocated* emergency rations to the beleaguered victims.
    Other Form(s): allocation (noun)

saccharine (SAK ur in): overly sweet; artificially sweet; cloying
    Part of Speech: adjective
    Example: The *saccharine* poem written inside the greeting card did not adequately express the man's feelings for his wife.

verdancy (VER dan see): greenness; viridity
    Part of Speech: noun
    Example: Spring brings *verdancy* to my lovely valley.

Unit 2 *(cont.)*

Quick Match

Group 1

A. lustful	C. deduction	E. reluctance	G. argue
B. outburst	D. indomitable	F. surround	H. of many languages

_____ 1. besiege

_____ 2. salacious

_____ 3. diatribe

_____ 4. remonstrate

_____ 5. corollary

_____ 6. polyglot

_____ 7. insuperable

_____ 8. trepidation

Group 2

A. talkative	C. honesty	E. contradiction	G. pain-relieving
B. malignant	D. alienate	F. reproduce	H. curse

_____ 1. analgesic

_____ 2. replicate

_____ 3. garrulous

_____ 4. anathema

_____ 5. probity

_____ 6. estrange

_____ 7. insidious

_____ 8. dichotomy

Group 3

A. choice	C. instructive	E. suffer	G. incipient
B. prophetic	D. censure	F. atmosphere	H. ribbon

_____ 1. languish

_____ 2. didactic

_____ 3. ambiance

_____ 4. inchoate

_____ 5. prescient

_____ 6. cordon

_____ 7. volition

_____ 8. reproach

Group 4

A. fascinate	C. accustom	E. greenness	G. sociable
B. suppress	D. cloyingly sweet	F. daily	H. allot

_____ 1. habituate

_____ 2. diurnal

_____ 3. gregarious

_____ 4. quell

_____ 5. enrapture

_____ 6. allocate

_____ 7. saccharine

_____ 8. verdancy

Unit 2 *(cont.)*

Answer Key

Pre-test Yourself

Group 1	Group 2	Group 3	Group 4
1. polyglot	1. probity	1. languish	1. gregarious
2. diatribe	2. dichotomy	2. volition	2. allocate
3. trepidation	3. replicate	3. inchoate	3. habituate
4. salacious	4. analgesic	4. didactic	4. saccharine
5. remonstrate	5. estrange	5. prescient	5. diurnal
6. corollary	6. insidious	6. cordon	6. quell
7. insuperable	7. garrulous	7. ambiance	7. verdancy
8. besiege	8. anathema	8. reproach	8. enrapture

Quick Match

Group 1	Group 2	Group 3	Group 4
1. F	1. G	1. E	1. C
2. A	2. F	2. C	2. F
3. B	3. A	3. F	3. G
4. G	4. H	4. G	4. B
5. C	5. C	5. B	5. A
6. H	6. D	6. H	6. H
7. D	7. B	7. A	7. D
8. E	8. E	8. D	8. E

Unit 3

Pre-test Yourself

Group 1

polemic	rummage	vent	anecdote
incumbent	maul	disconcert	porcine

---

1. Grizzlies _____ their victims.

2. As presiding officer, it was _____ on her to read the agenda.

3. With his _____ face, he resembled Porky Pig.

4. The congressional debate was full of _____, and the public was left with little knowledge of either candidate's stance on the issues.

5. In primal scream therapy, patients _____ their frustrations in screams.

6. The constantly moving pennants did not _____ him while he was shooting a foul shot.

7. A brief _____ is sometimes better than a full-length explanation.

8. Black bears will often _____ through the county dump in search of food.

Group 2

gainsay	circumspect	indubitable	disengage
postprandial	ukase	amalgamate	sardonic

---

1. The wrestler was caught in a headlock and could not _____ himself.

2. After turkey and all the trimmings, everyone took a _____ walk.

3. Several sour situations made him _____ about getting involved.

4. His probity was _____, and everyone endorsed his honesty.

5. If you _____ someone, you may make an enemy.

6. The two companies will _____ in order to stay in business.

7. The junta issued a _____ that made criticism of the government an act of treason.

8. The sarcastic man had a _____ look on his face.

Pre-test Yourself *(cont.)*

Group 3

buffoon	gravitate	potable	distend
sanction	amenity	fulgent	inimitable

---

1. No one has ever challenged her place among the best because she has an
   _____ style.

2. The white uniform was _____ in the bright moonlight.

3. One of the difficulties in traveling is finding _____ water.

4. There is always one person in a class who plays the _____ for attention.

5. The one _____ the college student insisted on having in his new apartment
   was an electric dishwasher.

6. The NCAA was forced to _____ the university's basketball team for its
   role in a gambling scandal.

7. If you build it, people will come; people _____ toward something new.

8. His stomach would always _____ after a large meal.

Group 4

underscore	commensurate	drudgery	internecine
propinquity	eclectic	rotund	kinetic

---

1. The gourmand was known for his prodigious eating habits and had a
   _____ stomach to show for it.

2. The _____ struggle between the company's two owners led its downfall.

3. The object's _____ energy carried it forward.

4. The program will _____ the need for water conservation during a drought.

5. Assembly line work is _____ for most people.

6. Her _____ taste in furniture was very personal and quiet.

7. The CEO's pay was _____ with the responsibility she bore.

8. Our _____ to the oil refinery caused many illnesses among us.

Unit 3 *(cont.)*

Words and Definitions

─────────────── Group 1 ───────────────

polemic (puh LEM ic): argument; rhetoric
    Part of Speech: noun
    Example: Anger was obvious among those who were involved in the *polemic*.

rummage (RUM ij): to search; to hunt
    Part of Speech: verb
    Example: The space agency sent a mission into space that *rummaged* around the planet.

vent (VENT): to relieve
    Part of Speech: verb
    Example: Discontented citizens *vented* their unhappiness by rebelling.

anecdote (AN ek dote): short story; brief narrative
    Part of Speech: noun
    Example: The professional speaker began the seminar with an *anecdote* about his 4-year-old son.
    Other Form(s): anecdotal (adjective)

incumbent (in KUM bent): obligatory; compelling
    Part of Speech: adjective
    Example: It was *incumbent* on the candidates to express their positions.

maul (MAWL): to beat or bruise; to tear
    Part of Speech: verb
    Example: A huge tiger *mauled* the hunter.

disconcert (dis kon SERT): to unsettle; to agitate
    Part of Speech: verb
    Example: New ideas *disconcert* people who like the status quo.
    Other Form(s): disconcerting (adjective)

porcine (POR seen): piglike; swinish
    Part of Speech: adjective
    Example: His *porcine* behavior offended almost everyone.

Unit 3 *(cont.)*

Words and Definitions *(cont.)*

gainsay (gain SAY): to deny; to dispute
  Part of Speech: verb
  Example: When you *gainsay* falsehood, you may, ironically, dignify it.

circumspect (SIR kum spekt): careful; chary
  Part of Speech: adjective
  Example: He was a timid and *circumspect* person who never took a chance.
  Other Form(s): circumspection (noun)

indubitable (in DOO bi tuh bul): beyond doubt; unquestionable
  Part of Speech: adjective
  Example: She had credentials that were an *indubitable* and forthright testimony to her honor.

disengage (dis en GAGE): to release; to free
  Part of Speech: verb
  Example: When he felt the group no longer represented his views, he *disengaged* himself.

postprandial (post PRAN dee ul): after dinner; after a meal
  Part of Speech: adjective
  Example: In the "old days," men took a *postprandial* smoke and a snifter of brandy.

ukase (yoo KASE): order; proclamation
  Part of Speech: noun
  Example: Fearing rebellion, the tyrant declared a *ukase* to suppress the rebels.

amalgamate (uh MOL guh mate): to mix; to combine
  Part of Speech: verb
  Example: Corporations often *amalgamate* to save money.

sardonic (sar DON ik): scornful; mocking
  Part of Speech: adjective
  Example: Condescension is often accompanied by *sardonic* laughter.

Words and Definitions *(cont.)*

─────────────── **Group 3** ───────────────

buffoon (buh FOON): clown; fool
  Part of Speech: noun
  Example: Every royal court had a *buffoon* to amuse the crowd.
  Other Form(s): buffoonery (noun)

gravitate (GRAV i tate): to be attracted to; to fall toward
  Part of Speech: verb
  Example: Teens *gravitate* to malls because malls provide safe gathering places.

potable (PO tuh bul): drinkable; fit to drink
  Part of Speech: adjective
  Example: When the wells became contaminated, *potable* water was hard to find.
  Other Form(s): potable (noun)

distend (di STEND): to expand; to dilate
  Part of Speech: verb
  Example: He always felt his stomach *distend* after a large meal.

sanction (SANK shun): to authorize; to legitimize
  Part of Speech: verb
  Example: Student governments *sanction* legitimate student clubs.

amenity (uh MEN i tee): pleasantness; refinement
  Part of Speech: noun
  Example: Having a valet is a nice *amenity* that many of us would enjoy.

fulgent (FULL jent): shining; brilliant
  Part of Speech: adjective
  Example: Snow crust becomes *fulgent* in bright moonlight.

inimitable (in IM i tuh bul): matchless; impossible to imitate
  Part of Speech: adjective
  Example: No one ever succeeded at copying his style because it was *inimitable*.

Words and Definitions *(cont.)*

─────────────────────────── **Group 4** ───────────────────────────

underscore (UN der skore): to stress; to emphasize
> **Part of Speech:** verb
> **Example:** The academic dean has issued a letter that will *underscore* his rules on campus activities.

commensurate (kuh MEN sir it): comparable; proportionate
> **Part of Speech:** adjective
> **Example:** His position was *commensurate* with his abilities.

drudgery (DRUJ er ee): tedious work; menial work
> **Part of Speech:** noun
> **Example:** Repetitive behavior on the job makes a *drudgery* of the job.

internecine (in tur NESS een): mutually destructive; pertaining to struggle within a group
> **Part of Speech:** adjective
> **Example:** The team's top two quarterbacks were involved in an *internecine* battle for leadership that proved disruptive and divisive.

propinquity (pro PING kwi tee): proximity; nearness
> **Part of Speech:** noun
> **Example:** His *propinquity* to danger filled him with trepidation.

eclectic (ih KLEK tik): selective; varied
> **Part of Speech:** adjective
> **Example:** She was an *eclectic* interior decorator who purposely mismatched art objects.

rotund (row TUND): corpulent; stout
> **Part of Speech:** adjective
> **Example:** Falstaff was one of Shakespeare's *rotund*, devil-may-care characters.

kinetic (ki NET ik): mobile; moving
> **Part of Speech:** adjective
> **Example:** When he dropped the ball off of the balcony, he made its static energy *kinetic*.

Unit 3 (cont.)

Quick Match

Group 1

A. short story   C. bruise   E. agitate   G. relieve

B. pig-like   D. to search through   F. obligatory   H. argument

_____ 1. polemic   _____ 5. incumbent

_____ 2. rummage   _____ 6. maul

_____ 3. vent   _____ 7. disconcert

_____ 4. anecdote   _____ 8. porcine

Group 2

A. proclamation   C. after dinner   E. combine   G. release

B. unquestionable   D. scornful   F. deny   H. careful

_____ 1. gainsay   _____ 5. postprandial

_____ 2. circumspect   _____ 6. ukase

_____ 3. indubitable   _____ 7. amalgamate

_____ 4. disengage   _____ 8. sardonic

Group 3

A. shining   C. be attracted to   E. matchless   G. authorize

B. expand   D. pleasantness   F. drinkable   H. clown

_____ 1. buffoon   _____ 5. sanction

_____ 2. gravitate   _____ 6. amenity

_____ 3. potable   _____ 7. fulgent

_____ 4. distend   _____ 8. inimitable

Group 4

A. varied   C. stress   E. corpulent   G. mutually destructive

B. mobile   D. nearness   F. menial work   H. proportionate

_____ 1. underscore   _____ 5. propinquity

_____ 2. commensurate   _____ 6. eclectic

_____ 3. drudgery   _____ 7. rotund

_____ 4. internecine   _____ 8. kinetic

Unit 3 *(cont.)*

Answer Key

Pre-test Yourself

Group 1

1. maul
2. incumbent
3. porcine
4. polemics
5. vent
6. disconcert
7. anecdote
8. rummage

Group 2

1. disengage
2. postprandial
3. circumspect
4. indubitable
5. gainsay
6. amalgamate
7. ukase
8. sardonic

Group 3

1. inimitable
2. fulgent
3. potable
4. buffoon
5. amenity
6. sanction
7. gravitate
8. distend

Group 4

1. rotund
2. internecine
3. kinetic
4. underscore
5. drudgery
6. eclectic
7. commensurate
8. propinquity

Quick Match

Group 1

1. H
2. D
3. G
4. A
5. F
6. C
7. E
8. B

Group 2

1. F
2. H
3. B
4. G
5. C
6. A
7. E
8. D

Group 3

1. H
2. C
3. F
4. B
5. G
6. D
7. A
8. E

Group 4

1. C
2. H
3. F
4. G
5. D
6. A
7. E
8. B

Unit 4

Pre-test Yourself

Group 1			
quip	disjointed	proscribe	ambrosia
sinuous	circumscribe	relegate	infringe

1. The leader of the new art movement did not _____ the movement's practitioners with rules.

2. Students' privileges could not _____ on others' rights.

3. Some people ease tension with a _____ or an epigram.

4. His speech was _____ and did not hold our attention.

5. The manager may _____ his ailing star player to pinch-hitting duties.

6. Home cooking often tasted like _____ when compared to the microwave dinners the bachelor was used to eating.

7. Railroads built across the Rockies take _____ routes in their slow climb.

8. The new ordinance will _____ parking near the municipal offices.

Group 2			
enigma	writhe	raucous	bravado
chauvinism	pseudonym	invective	sylvan

1. Strangely, when he broke his ankle, he did not _____ in pain.

2. In order to protect his privacy, the author of romance novels employed the use of a _____.

3. To his dying day, he proclaimed women to be an _____ to him.

4. _____ environments are supposed to calm the nerves.

5. He attacked his opponent and used a lot of _____ in his speech.

6. Saturday nights in college towns are often _____ affairs that bother the locals.

7. When faced with a real problem that had to be solved, his _____ disappeared.

8. No one doubts the place of _____ in starting wars.

Unit 4 (cont.)

Pre-test Yourself (cont.)

Group 3

| foibles | reiterate | disabuse | ovine |
| circumvent | synthesis | betroth | proselytize |

1. Her art mimicked the styles of many artists, and her work was considered a
   _____.

2. On the witness stand, a defendant may _____ her story several times.

3. Missionaries _____ to try to make converts.

4. The couple found most of each other's _____ endearing, and the two
   rarely bickered.

5. If you think you can do what you want, let me _____ you of the idea.

6. A people that never questions its leadership is an _____ people.

7. She will _____ herself to him, and they will be married six months later.

8. In order to frame the suspect, the detective would _____ the law.

Group 4

| trek | nonentity | compliant | prate |
| accommodate | salubrious | duplicity | rife |

1. The thrillseeker began her _____ around the world.

2. In the company of the scholars, the uneducated man felt himself to be a
   _____.

3. The minister would often _____ from his pulpit, and parishioners usually
   fell asleep.

4. He ended their friendship because she often acted with _____ could not be
   trusted.

5. The sign said that the gymnasium would _____ 400 students.

6. Fresh air, clean water, and a healthy diet are _____ for almost anyone.

7. During the French Revolution, the streets were _____ with dissenters.

8. Easily domesticated animals are _____ animals.

Unit 4 *(cont.)*

Words and Definitions

───── **Group 1** ─────

quip (KWIP): joke; jest
   Part of Speech: noun
   Example: Many *quips* were included in her lengthy speech.
   Other Form(s): quip (verb)

disjointed (dis JOINT ed): dislocated; displaced
   Part of Speech: adjective
   Example: Lack of deep thought and organization caused him to write a *disjointed* essay.

proscribe (pro SCRIBE): forbid; denounce
   Part of Speech: verb
   Example: The sign will *proscribe* non-handicapped people from parking in front of the building.

ambrosia (am BRO zhuh): food of the gods; especially delicious food
   Part of Speech: noun
   Example: Whenever they ate at the four-star restaurant, they felt they had eaten *ambrosia*.

sinuous (SIN yoo us): winding; curving
   Part of Speech: adjective
   Example: Mountain roads are often *sinuous* roads.

circumscribe (SIR kum scribe): to limit; to confine
   Part of Speech: verb
   Example: The rules explicitly *circumscribe* behavior in the fraternity houses.

relegate (REL eh gate): to consign; to assign
   Part of Speech: verb
   Example: His superiors *relegated* him to a lower rank because of his many mistakes.

infringe (in FRINJ): to violate; to trespass
   Part of Speech: verb
   Example: Limiting civil rights *infringes* on personal freedoms.

Unit 4 *(cont.)*

Words and Definitions *(cont.)*

enigma (uh NIG muh): mystery; unexplainable phenomenon
Part of Speech: noun
Example: No one could figure him out; he was an *enigma* to everyone.

writhe (RITHE): to squirm; to twist
Part of Speech: verb
Example: The intensive questioning made the captive *writhe* uncomfortably.

raucous (RAW kus): harsh-sounding; rowdy
Part of Speech: adjective
Example: The music was so *raucous* that neighbors called the police.

bravado (bruh VA doe): bragging; false courage
Part of Speech: noun
Example: He was full of *bravado* until he saw the size of his opponent.

chauvinism (SHOW vuh nizm): partisanship; narrowness
Part of Speech: noun
Example: His *chauvinism* blinded him to the rights of other nations.
Other Form(s): chauvinistic (adjective); chauvinist (noun)

pseudonym (SOO doe nim): false name; alias
Part of Speech: noun
Example: Rather than face the public as who he really was, he used a *pseudonym*.

invective (in VEK tiv): denunciation; fulmination
Part of Speech: noun
Example: Her harsh *invective* against the politician convinced many in the audience to vote against him.

sylvan (SILL ven): woody; forested
Part of Speech: adjective
Example: The Adirondack Mountains present a *sylvan* paradise.

Words and Definitions *(cont.)*

──────── **Group 3** ────────

foible (FOY bul): weakness; frailty
    Part of Speech: noun
    Example: Personal *foibles* cost the man respect from his peers.

reiterate (re IT ur ate): to repeat over and over; to restate
    Part of Speech: verb
    Example: He *reiterated* his ideas, and they were finally accepted.

disabuse (dis uh BYOOZ): to disillusion; to disenchant
    Part of Speech: verb
    Example: She quickly *disabused* him of any ideas he might have had about asking her out.

ovine (O vine): sheeplike; easily led
    Part of Speech: adjective
    Example: His *ovine* tendencies made him an easy victim for the con man.

circumvent (sir kum VENT): to bypass; to go around
    Part of Speech: verb
    Example: She *circumvented* the rules by using clever stratagems.

synthesis (SIN thuh sis): integration; unification
    Part of Speech: noun
    Example: Her beautiful music was a *synthesis* of several styles.

betroth (be TROTHE): to engage; to promise to marry
    Part of Speech: verb
    Example: She *betrothed* herself to him, and they were married a short time later.

proselytize (PROS uh li tize): to convert; to win over
    Part of Speech: verb
    Example: Missionaries *proselytize* and accept new members to their religion.

Unit 4 *(cont.)*

Words and Definitions *(cont.)*

trek (TREK): journey; voyage
> **Part of Speech:** noun
> **Example:** Crossing the Himalayas proved to be a lengthy *trek*.
> **Other Form(s):** trek (verb)

prate (PRATE): to babble; to talk foolishly
> **Part of Speech:** verb
> **Example:** A confused man *prated* on the city sidewalk.

nonentity (non EN ti tee): a nobody; insignificant person
> **Part of Speech:** noun
> **Example:** As far as she was concerned, he was a *nonentity* and she ignored him completely.

compliant (com PLY ent): submissive; obedient
> **Part of Speech:** adjective
> **Example:** Ovine people are *compliant* people.

accommodate (uh KOM uh date): to aid; to give assistance
> **Part of Speech:** verb
> **Example:** Good samaritans *accommodate* the needs of others in trouble.

salubrious (sa LOO bree us): healthy; salutary
> **Part of Speech:** adjective
> **Example:** They rusticated in the Bahamas, and the vacation proved to be most *salubrious*.

duplicity (du PLIS i tee): dishonesty; two-facedness
> **Part of Speech:** noun
> **Example:** Several instances of *duplicity* led to the woman's disowning her childhood friend.
> **Other Form(s):** duplicitous (adjective)

rife (RIFE): widespread; prevalent
> **Part of Speech:** adjective
> **Example:** The government was *rife* with corruption, and it eventually collapsed.

Unit 4 (cont.)

Quick Match

Group 1

A. consign	C. delicious food
B. winding	D. violate

E. jest   G. limit
F. forbid   H. dislocated

_____ 1. quip

_____ 2. disjointed

_____ 3. proscribe

_____ 4. ambrosia

_____ 5. sinuous

_____ 6. circumscribe

_____ 7. relegate

_____ 8. infringe

Group 2

A. rowdy   C. denunciation   E. mystery   G. false courage
B. forested   D. alias   F. squirm   H. partisanship

_____ 1. enigma

_____ 2. writhe

_____ 3. raucous

_____ 4. bravado

_____ 5. chauvinism

_____ 6. pseudonym

_____ 7. invective

_____ 8. sylvan

Group 3

A. bypass   C. engage   E. convert   G. sheep-like
B. integration   D. weakness   F. repeat   H. disenchant

_____ 1. foible

_____ 2. reiterate

_____ 3. disabuse

_____ 4. ovine

_____ 5. circumvent

_____ 6. synthesis

_____ 7. betroth

_____ 8. proselytize

Group 4

A. dishonesty   C. aid   E. babble   G. widespread
B. healthy   D. journey   F. submissive   H. nobody

_____ 1. trek

_____ 2. prate

_____ 3. nonentity

_____ 4. compliant

_____ 5. accommodate

_____ 6. salubrious

_____ 7. duplicity

_____ 8. rife

Unit 4 *(cont.)*

Group 1

1. circumscribe
2. infringe
3. quips
4. disjointed
5. relegate
6. ambrosia
7. sinuous
8. proscribe

Group 2

1. writhe
2. pseudonyms
3. enigma
4. sylvan
5. invective
6. raucous
7. bravado
8. chauvinism

Group 3

1. synthesis
2. reiterate
3. proselytize
4. foibles
5. disabuse
6. ovine
7. betroth
8. circumvent

Group 4

1. trekked
2. nonentity
3. prate
4. duplicity
5. accommodate
6. salubrious
7. rife
8. compliant

Quick Math

Group 1

1. E
2. H
3. F
4. C
5. B
6. G
7. A
8. D

Group 2

1. E
2. F
3. A
4. G
5. H
6. D
7. C
8. B

Group 3

1. D
2. F
3. H
4. G
5. A
6. B
7. C
8. E

Group 4

1. D
2. E
3. H
4. F
5. C
6. B
7. A
8. G

Unit 5

Pre-test Yourself

Group 1

specious	alleviate	metaphorical	pragmatic
centrifugal	disparate	revile	enhance

1. Analgesics _____ pain.

2. The _____ force was so strong, the tire flew off the wheel.

3. She could _____ her appearance by wearing colors that complemented her eyes.

4. _____ philosophies caused a rift in the organization.

5. Many people will now _____ the once-beloved actor for his several heinous acts.

6. He gave a _____ and empty argument.

7. The novel was a _____ work that sought to compare modern society to the workings of a machine.

8. Unlike her idealistic husband, she always used _____ thinking to guide her.

Group 2

condone	reciprocate	emulate	gaffe
ply	banter	traumatize	discrete

1. The mother was concerned that witnessing the car accident might _____ her child for life.

2. After completing a course in carpentry, the man will _____ his trade.

3. Once you _____ bad behavior, you give license for future bad behavior.

4. Those close to the family knew that the witty _____ of the siblings was a sign of their closeness.

5. When lightning hit the tree, it split in two _____ halves.

6. Forgetting to tip the waiter was, in that restaurant, a first class _____.

7. States _____ when it comes to extraditing criminals.

8. Young people _____ role models.

Unit 5 *(cont.)*

Pre-test Yourself *(cont.)*

Group 3

agnosticism	reverberate	embodiment	burnish
posit	connive	jargon	dulcet

1. Abe Lincoln has become the _____ of the honest, straight-talking American.

2. From a young age, she would _____ to get what she wanted.

3. Paul's _____ made him feel like an outsider at the church-sponsored charity event.

4. Their _____ and dialect made them difficult to understand.

5. He could _____ his shield until it shone like the sun.

6. Soon, dissent will _____ through the streets of the unhappy town.

7. As an embodiment of calmness, she spoke in _____ tones when she gave instructions.

8. Before he could fully _____ his ideas, the other candidate began rebutted them.

Group 4

inclement	dubious	plenary	breach
metamorphosis	symposium	hazard	aggrieve

1. In anticipation of _____ weather, he packed heavy boots and an umbrella.

2. A _____ was held to discuss the problems facing the community.

3. If water can _____ the levee, the lowlands will flood.

4. Though they disliked their future son-in-law, the woman's parents offered their blessing so they did not wish to _____ their daughter.

5. The symposium included all parties, thus being a _____ session.

6. Experts were _____ about the scientist's claim that he had changed lead to gold.

7. Not really knowing the answer, he could only _____ a guess.

8. A caterpillar's _____ into a butterfly is a natural wonder.

Unit 5 *(cont.)*

Words and Definitions

—————————————— Group 1 ——————————————

specious (SPEE shus): deceptively believable; misleadingly attractive
    Part of Speech: adjective
    Example: The professor calmly and clearly disproved the *specious* argument of the class iconoclast.

alleviate (uh LEE vee ate): to reduce; to mitigate
    Part of Speech: verb
    Example: Nothing could *alleviate* the pain he endured after his dog's death.

metaphorical (met a FOR i kul): symbolic; emblematic
    Part of Speech: adjective
    Example: His poetry was rife with *metaphorical* devices.

pragmatic (prag MAT iK): practical; utilitarian
    Part of Speech: adjective
    Example: Successful businesspeople are often *pragmatic* people.
    Other Form(s): pragmatism (noun)

centrifugal (cen TRI fyoo gul): away from the center; outward motion
    Part of Speech: adjective
    Example: *Centrifugal* force threw the space vehicle into an erratic orbit.

disparate (DI spare ut): distinct; dissimilar
    Part of Speech: adjective
    Example: Their ideas were *disparate*, and they had to separate.

revile (re VILE): to hate; to vituperate
    Part of Speech: verb
    Example: An orator *reviled* the assembled dignitaries for their unconcern.

enhance (en HANCE): to add; to enrich
    Part of Speech: verb
    Example: A new wing on the building *enhanced* its appearance.

Words and Definitions *(cont.)*

─────────── **Group 2** ───────────

condone (kun DOHN): to tolerate; to excuse
   Part of Speech: verb
   Example: If you *condone* bad behavior, you encourage it.

reciprocate (re SIP ro kate): to return; to give back
   Part of Speech: verb
   Example: She *reciprocated* his love, and they were married.

emulate (EM yoo late): to imitate; to copy
   Part of Speech: verb
   Example: Students who want to excel *emulate* students who have excelled.

gaffe (GAF): social blunder; faux pas
   Part of Speech: noun
   Example: He committed a *gaffe* at dinner when he drank the water in the fingerbowl.

ply (PLY): to practice; to employ
   Part of Speech: verb
   Example: He *plies* his trade as a carpenter skillfully and is much sought after.

banter (BAN tur): to tease; to twit
   Part of Speech: verb
   Example: The two *bantered* at first, but then began to argue in earnest.
   Other Form(s): banter (noun)

traumatize (TRAW muh tize): to wound; to injure
   Part of Speech: verb
   Example: Her cruel statements *traumatized* the would-be suitor.

discrete (dis CREET): separate; distinct
   Part of Speech: adjective
   Example: When the storm hit, the pier was broken into *discrete* sections.

--- **Group 3** ---

agnosticism (ag NOS ti sizm): uncertainty; doubt (usually about the existence of a higher power)
Part of Speech: noun
Example: His many questions about the hereafter revealed his *agnosticism*.

reverberate (re VUR bur ate): to echo; to resound
Part of Speech: verb
Example: The scandalous facts *reverberated* through all levels of government.
Other Form(s): reverberation (noun)

embodiment (em BOD ee ment): incarnation; representation
Part of Speech: noun
Example: Julius Caesar was the *embodiment* of all men who think they are invulnerable.
Other Form(s): embody (verb)

burnish (BUR nish): to polish; to buff
Part of Speech: verb
Example: The jeweler *burnished* the gold setting for the ring.

posit (POS it): to postulate; to take for granted without proof
Part of Speech: verb
Example: She *posited* her belief that her husband was the nicest man who ever lived.

connive (cuh NIVE): to plot; to scheme
Part of Speech: verb
Example: The conspirators *connived* to overthrow their leader.

jargon (JAR gun): specific language; gibberish
Part of Speech: noun
Example: Computer specialists have their own *jargon* that many outsiders do not understand.

dulcet (DUL set): melodious; musical
Part of Speech: adjective
Example: Great and distinctive singers often have *dulcet* tones in their voices.

Unit 5 (cont.)

Words and Definitions (cont.)

──────────── **Group 4** ────────────

inclement (in KLEM unt): rainy or stormy; showing no mercy
Part of Speech: adjective
Example: Due to the *inclement* weather, the referees decided to postpone the game until tomorrow.

dubious (DOO bee us): doubtful; questionable
Part of Speech: adjective
Example: His reasons for doing what he did were *dubious* and suspect.

plenary (PLE nuh ree): full; entire
Part of Speech: adjective
Example: The ruling group called a *plenary* session, and everyone had to attend.

breach (BREECH): to break through; to open
Part of Speech: verb
Example: Water *breached* the levee and flooded the city.

metamorphosis (met a MORE fuh sis): transformation; complete change
Part of Speech: noun
Example: Solid counseling in a controlled environment led to his personal *metamorphosis*.

symposium (sim PO zee um): conference; panel discussion
Part of Speech: noun
Example: A plenary session was planned for the literature *symposium*.

hazard (HAZ urd): to volunteer; to proffer
Part of Speech: verb
Example: She knew nothing about the possible outcome but *hazarded* a guess anyway.

aggrieve (uh GREEV): to mistreat; to abuse
Part of Speech: verb
Example: Constant losses *aggrieve* even the hardiest souls.

Unit 5 *(cont.)*

Quick Match

Group 1

A. distinct	C. enrich	E. vituperate	G. outward motion
B. practical	D. misleading	F. lessen	H. symbolic

_____ 1. specious   _____ 5. centrifugal

_____ 2. alleviate   _____ 6. disparate

_____ 3. metaphorical   _____ 7. revile

_____ 4. pragmatic   _____ 8. enhance

Group 2

A. practice	C. wound	E. tolerate	G. distinct
B. tease	D. give back	F. blunder	H. copy

_____ 1. condone   _____ 5. ply

_____ 2. reciprocate   _____ 6. banter

_____ 3. emulate   _____ 7. traumatize

_____ 4. gaffe   _____ 8. discrete

Group 3

A. plot	C. postulate	E. uncertainty	G. polish
B. melodious	D. gibberish	F. representation	H. echo

_____ 1. agnosticism   _____ 5. posit

_____ 2. reverberate   _____ 6. connive

_____ 3. embodiment   _____ 7. jargon

_____ 4. burnish   _____ 8. dulcet

Group 4

A. transformation	C. upset	E. stormy	G. entire
B. conference	D. volunteer	F. doubtful	H. break through

_____ 1. inclement   _____ 5. metamorphosis

_____ 2. dubious   _____ 6. symposium

_____ 3. plenary   _____ 7. hazard

_____ 4. breach   _____ 8. aggrieve

Unit 5 _(cont.)_

Answer Key

Pre-test Yourself

Group 1
1. alleviate
2. centrifugal
3. enhance
4. disparate
5. revile
6. specious
7. metaphorical
8. pragmatic

Group 2
1. traumatize
2. ply
3. condone
4. banter
5. discrete
6. gaffe
7. reciprocate
8. emulate

Group 3
1. embodiment
2. connive
3. agnosticism
4. jargon
5. burnish
6. reverberate
7. dulcet
8. posit

Group 4
1. inclement
2. symposium
3. breach
4. aggrieve
5. plenary
6. dubious
7. hazard
8. metamorphosis

Quick Match

Group 1
1. D
2. F
3. H
4. B
5. G
6. A
7. E
8. C

Group 2
1. E
2. D
3. H
4. F
5. A
6. B
7. C
8. G

Group 3
1. E
2. H
3. F
4. G
5. C
6. A
7. D
8. B

Group 4
1. E
2. F
3. G
4. H
5. A
6. B
7. D
8. C

Unit 6

Pre-test Yourself

Group 1

garner	precipitous	contumely	swathe
anomaly	elegy	misconstrue	rarefied

---

1. It was a violent and _____ change in his lifestyle.

2. His vicious speech fairly dripped with _____.

3. When you become involved in nuclear physics, you enter a _____ atmosphere.

4. It took him a long time to meet all the voters, but he will _____ quite a few votes for his efforts.

5. He merely wants to be friends, but the woman might _____ his intentions.

6. Mothers _____ their children with soft and warm blankets.

7. The isolated incident in his life was considered an _____ and not part of a behavior pattern.

8. His " _____ to a Pigeon" is considered a satire on graveside speeches.

Group 2

ineptitude	portend	dissonance	canon
effervescent	terse	aggregate	rouse

---

1. The coalition believed that the accepted _____ did not take into account the experiences of all groups.

2. The superstitious man worried that the crack in his mirror might _____ a troubling future.

3. Many members disagreed with the chairman, and there was a great deal of _____.

4. Her remarks were laconic, _____, and directly to the point.

5. He whispered her name, hoping it would _____ her from her sleep.

6. It took some time, but we finally proved that his _____ and incompetence were real.

7. _____ people are always welcome at social gatherings.

8. The _____ of the two groups proved large enough to change the course of the election.

Unit 6 *(cont.)*

Pre-test Yourself *(cont.)*

Group 3

coquetry	regale	aggrandize	meretricious
swath	eclipse	parlay	dowdy

---

1. Las Vegas is known for its _____ ways.

2. Lightning cut a _____ right through the trees.

3. After dinner, the great storyteller began to _____ us with a wonderful tale.

4. He was very jealous when she practiced her _____ on anyone else but him.

5. His clothes were timeworn and _____.

6. He hopes he can _____ the money he won on the first race into a whole day of gambling.

7. With this one success, she will _____ all her failures.

8. Greedy people _____ their own fortunes at the expense of others.

Group 4

apprise	friable	collateral	inimical
befuddle	laconic	neural	hone

---

1. _____ philosophies caused a wide rift in the organization.

2. Extreme heat made the cup _____ and extremely delicate.

3. The disease attacked his _____ system, and treatment seemed useless.

4. He must _____ the membership of the shortfall in funds as was his responsibility.

5. Many professional athletes _____ their skills in minor league play.

6. Their ideas were _____, and both scientists were awarded a Nobel prize.

7. The American cowboy was always known for his _____ speech and bowed legs.

8. Too many people speaking at once would often _____ and confuse him.

Unit 6 *(cont.)*

Words and Definitions

────────── **Group 1** ──────────

garner (GAR nur): to gather; to collect
    Part of Speech: verb
    Example: Pollsters *garner* answers to questions.

precipitous (pre SIP i tus): severe; sudden
    Part of Speech: adjective
    Example: *Precipitous* actions can result in dangerous situations.

contumely (KON too muh lee): reproach; disgrace
    Part of Speech: noun
    Example: The speaker's *contumely* aggrieved everyone present.
    Other Form(s): contumelious (adjective)

swathe (SWAWTH): to wrap; to bind
    Part of Speech: verb
    Example: Rescuers *swathed* the injured person in heavy blankets.

anomaly (uh NOM uh lee): aberration; abnormality
    Part of Speech: noun
    Example: The irresponsible action was an *anomaly* in his case.
    Other Form(s): (adjective) anomalous

elegy (EL uh jee): lament; mournful poem
    Part of Speech: noun
    Example: The poet read an *elegy* at the graveside.

misconstrue (mis kun STREW): to misinterpret; to misunderstand
    Part of Speech: verb
    Example: She *misconstrued* what he said and was quite angry.

rarefied (RARE uh fide): lofty; elevated
    Part of Speech: adjective
    Example: Life as a multimillionaire is a *rarefied* existence.

Words and Definitions *(cont.)*

─────────────── **Group 2** ───────────────

ineptitude (in EP ti tood): incompetence; unfitness
    Part of Speech: noun
    Example: Critics blamed the collapse of the project on the *ineptitude* of the managers.
    Other Form(s): ineptness (noun)

portend (pore TEND): to foreshadow; to augur
    Part of Speech: verb
    Example: Certain weather fronts *portend* severe storms.
    Other Form(s): portent (noun); portentous (adjective)

dissonance (DIS uh nence): discordance; disagreement
    Part of Speech: noun
    Example: His ideas created *dissonance* among his fellow planners.
    Other Form(s): dissonant (adjective)

canon (CAN un): standard; criterion
    Part of Speech: noun
    Example: The *canon* in Western literature has been attacked by multiculturalists.
    Other Form(s): canonical (adjective)

effervescent (ef ur VES ent): enthusiastic; bubbling
    Part of Speech: adjective
    Example: She was an *effervescent* young lady who delighted everyone.
    Other Form(s): effervescence (noun)

terse (TURS): laconic; concise
    Part of Speech: adjective
    Example: His remarks were *terse* and directly to the point.

aggregate (AG gruh get): combined; all together
    Part of Speech: adjective
    Example: The *aggregate* effect of their investments was felt by the entire financial world.
    Other Form(s): aggregate (noun)

rouse (ROWZ): to stimulate; to awaken
    Part of Speech: verb
    Example: He *roused* the sleepy students with a lively dance in front of the room.

Unit 6 (cont.)

Words and Definitions (cont.)

Group 3

coquetry (CO ket tree): dalliance; flirtation
Part of Speech: noun
Example: *Coquetry* was a refined art in nineteenth century France.
Other Form(s): coquettish (adjective); coquette (noun)

regale (ri GALE): to honor; to entertain
Part of Speech: verb
Example: Old timers *regaled* the youngsters with stories about pioneer days.
Other Form(s): regalement (noun)

aggrandize (ag GRAN dize): to increase; to augment
Part of Speech: verb
Example: The sly broker *aggrandized* his own commissions by "churning" accounts.
Other Form(s): aggrandizement (noun)

meretricious (mare eh TRI shus): superficially attractive; gaudy
Part of Speech: adjective
Example: The actor's *meretricious* clothing made the audience gasp.

swath (SWOTH): path; track
Part of Speech: noun
Example: Storms cut a wide *swath* through Florida and caused widespread destruction.

eclipse (ee KLIPS): to obscure; to darken
Part of Speech: verb
Example: Her reputation was so great it *eclipsed* the reputations of all the other people.

parlay (PAR lay): to maneuver; to manipulate
Part of Speech: verb
Example: The bettor *parlayed* his winnings had eventually won a lot of money.

dowdy (DOW dee): old fashioned; shabby
Part of Speech: adjective
Example: The beggar's clothing was *dowdy* and disheveled.

Unit 6 *(cont.)*

Words and Definitions *(cont.)*

apprise (a PRIZE): to notify; to tell
>   **Part of Speech:** verb
>   **Example:** Deans *apprised* the students of the rules, but they paid little attention to them.
>   **Other Form(s):** appraisal (noun)

friable (FRY uh bul): brittle; easily crumbled
>   **Part of Speech:** adjective
>   **Example:** Cast-iron furniture becomes quite *friable* if left out in sub-zero weather.

collateral (cuh LAT ur ul): security for an obligation; a loan
>   **Part of Speech:** noun
>   **Example:** The man used his gold watch as *collateral* for the money he owed.

inimical (in IM i kul): harmful; hostile
>   **Part of Speech:** adjective
>   **Example:** He had several unhealthy eating habits that were *inimical* to his physical well-being.

befuddle (bee FUD ul): to confuse; to muddle
>   **Part of Speech:** verb
>   **Example:** When thoughts are expressed in too abstract a way, the abstraction *befuddles* me.

laconic (luh KON ik): concise; succinct
>   **Part of Speech:** adjective
>   **Example:** He spoke in terse and *laconic* sentences.

neural (NUHR ul): of the nervous system
>   **Part of Speech:** adjective
>   **Example:** Electric shock can cause severe *neural* damage.

hone (HONE): to sharpen; to whet
>   **Part of Speech:** verb
>   **Example:** Many professional ballplayers *hone* their skills in the minor leagues.

Unit 6 *(cont.)*

Quick Match

Group 1

A. bind	C. misunderstand	E. sudden	G. gather
B. lament	D. lofty	F. abnormality	H. insult

_____ 1. garner

_____ 2. precipitous

_____ 3. contumely

_____ 4. swathe

_____ 5. anomaly

_____ 6. elegy

_____ 7. misconstrue

_____ 8. rarefied

Group 2

A. bubbling	C. concise	E. discordance	G. foreshadow
B. combined	D. awaken	F. incompetence	H. criterion

_____ 1. ineptitude

_____ 2. portend

_____ 3. dissonance

_____ 4. canon

_____ 5. effervescent

_____ 6. terse

_____ 7. aggregate

_____ 8. rouse

Group 3

A. superficial	C. manipulate	E. flirtation	G. increase
B. path	D. shabby	F. entertain	H. obscure

_____ 1. coquetry

_____ 2. regale

_____ 3. aggrandize

_____ 4. meretricious

_____ 5. swath

_____ 6. eclipse

_____ 7. parlay

_____ 8. dowdy

Group 4

A. confuse	C. brittle	E. sharpen	G. harmful
B. concise	D. of the nerves	F. notify	H. security

_____ 1. apprise

_____ 2. friable

_____ 3. collateral

_____ 4. inimical

_____ 5. befuddle

_____ 6. laconic

_____ 7. neural

_____ 8. hone

Unit 6 *(cont.)*

Answer Key

Pre-test Yourself

Group 1

1. precipitous
2. contumely
3. rarefied
4. garner
5. misconstrue
6. swathe
7. anomaly
8. elegy

Group 2

1. canon
2. portend
3. dissonance
4. terse
5. rouse
6. ineptitude
7. effervescent
8. aggregate

Group 3

1. meretricious
2. swath
3. regale
4. coquetry
5. dowdy
6. parlay
7. eclipse
8. aggrandize

Group 4

1. inimical
2. friable
3. neural
4. apprise
5. hone
6. collateral
7. laconic
8. befuddle

Quick Match

Group 1

1. G
2. E
3. H
4. A
5. F
6. B
7. C
8. D

Group 2

1. F
2. G
3. E
4. H
5. A
6. C
7. B
8. D

Group 3

1. E
2. F
3. G
4. A
5. B
6. H
7. C
8. D

Group 4

1. F
2. C
3. H
4. G
5. A
6. B
7. D
8. E

Unit 7

Pre-test Yourself

Group 1

disheveled	putrid	fraught	vapid
clandestine	apothegm	sententious	bilk

---

1. He had always been a firm believer in the _____ that said that the early bird always gets the worm.

2. The battlefield carnage gave off a _____ smell.

3. His speech was spurious and _____.

4. The C.I.A. is involved in _____ matters.

5. Empty talk is _____ talk.

6. His clothing became _____ when he fell off the train.

7. His fall from the train was _____ with danger.

8. Confidence men _____ the unwary and run with the money.

Group 2

harp	antedate	indomitable	coiffure
scrofulous	outmoded	effrontery	mesmerize

---

1. The hero had an _____ will, but the words weakened his body.

2. He would always _____ on his failures, and his friends grew tired of listening.

3. He grew excited when he realized that the fossil he had unearthed might _____ all other fossils found at the excavation site.

4. He was a leering, salacious, and _____ villain.

5. The holographs at the World's Fair always _____ the gawking crowd.

6. She did not put on a hat, and the wind ruined her _____.

7. The student's _____ did not go unnoticed by the dean of discipline.

8. Young people always complain about the _____ methods their elders use.

Group 3

amenable	bivouac	drone	frangible
interface	predisposed	rook	sporadic

---

1. Some nights, he would _____ on and on, and the audience would grow impatient.

2. Both sides were _____ to the agreement and signed it.

3. The waterboard was _____ and had to be handled carefully.

4. Con men _____ the unsuspecting.

5. The soldiers will _____ for the night on the high hill.

6. Having grown up in Southern California, he was _____ to liking warm weather.

7. They should _____ the computer systems in order to expedite communication between the two companies.

8. _____ rainstorms struck the area; they came and went quickly.

Group 4

rollick	drawl	inure	sedulous
anneal	candor	guffaw	void

---

1. His _____ was appreciated by those who wanted the truth.

2. She was an assiduous and _____ student who did her work in a punctilious manner.

3. He would _____ slowly with a Southern accent.

4. The CEO may _____ the contract because it does her company no good.

5. Even constant disappointment could not _____ him to failure.

6. The horses will surely _____ in the grassy meadow.

7. His loud _____ showed his contempt for his opponent.

8. Steel manufacturers _____ their product to make it tougher.

Unit 7 *(cont.)*

Words and Definitions *(cont.)*

——————————————— Group 1 ———————————————

disheveled (di SHEV uld): unkempt; disorderly
  Part of Speech: adjective
  Example: When he started to wrestle with the other student, his clothes became *disheveled*.
  Other Form(s): dishevel (verb)

putrid (PYOO trid): rotten; decaying
  Part of Speech: adjective
  Example: Unrefrigerated meat will become *putrid* after a few days.

fraught (FRAWT): full of; charged
  Part of Speech: adjective
  Example: The descent down the ice face was *fraught* with danger.

vapid (VAP id): flat; insipid
  Part of Speech: adjective
  Example: The play failed because of its *vapid* dialogue.

clandestine (clan DEH stine): secret; covert
  Part of Speech: adjective
  Example: It was a *clandestine* group that planned the rebellion.

apothegm (AP uh them): maxim; aphorism
  Part of Speech: noun
  Example: He spoke in *apothegms* that revealed his lack of profound thinking.

sententious (sen TEN chus): preachy; bombastic
  Part of Speech: adjective
  Example: Hypocrites often use *sententious* phrases.

bilk (BILK): to swindle; to cheat
  Part of Speech: verb
  Example: The con man *bilked* older people out of their life savings.

Unit 7 *(cont.)*

Words and Definitions *(cont.)*

harp (HARP): to dwell on; to persist
> **Part of Speech:** verb
> **Example:** The politician *harped* on the problem, and the public said "Enough is enough."

antedate (AN ti date): to precede; to forerun
> **Part of Speech:** verb
> **Example:** Their efforts initiated and *antedated* all other efforts.

indomitable (in DOM ih tuh bul): invincible; unconquerable
> **Part of Speech:** adjective
> **Example:** Her spirit was *indomitable*, and she persisted in her crusade.

coiffure (kwa FYOOR): hairdo; hairstyle
> **Part of Speech:** noun
> **Example:** The salon specialized in *coiffures* and manicures for the wealthy.

scrofulous (SCROF yoo lus): degenerate; corrupt
> **Part of Speech:** adjective
> **Example:** Caligula was a *scrofulous* and hedonistic ruler who brought shame on his empire.

outmoded (owt MODE ed): out of fashion; obsolete
> **Part of Speech:** adjective
> **Example:** Methods that are *outmoded* are discarded and replaced.

effrontery (eh FRUNT ur ee): audacity; nerve
> **Part of Speech:** noun
> **Example:** Colette's sauciness and *effrontery* scandalized and amused Paris.

mesmerize (MEZ mur ize): to hypnotize; to stupefy
> **Part of Speech:** verb
> **Example:** Magicians *mesmerize* their audiences with amazing performances.
> **Other Form(s):** mesmerization (noun)

Unit 7 *(cont.)*

Words and Definitions *(cont.)*

amenable (uh MEE nuh bul): agreeable; reasonable
   Part of Speech: adjective
   Example: The interested parties were *amenable* to mutually agreed-upon solutions.

interface (IN tur face): to coordinate; to join
   Part of Speech: verb
   Example: The computer networks *interfaced* and provided quick answers to complex equations.

bivouac (BIV oo ak): to camp; to encamp temporarily
   Part of Speech: verb
   Example: Troops *bivouaced* in the valley while awaiting orders.
   Other Form(s): bivouac (noun)

predisposed (pree dis POSED): inclined; partial to
   Part of Speech: adjective
   Example: Biased people are *predisposed* to the adoption of certain positions.
   Other Form(s): predispose (verb)

drone (DRONE): to buzz; to murmur
   Part of Speech: verb
   Example: The orator *droned* on and on while his listeners dozed in the sun.

rook (ROOK): to swindle; to cheat
   Part of Speech: verb
   Example: Many charlatans *rook* the elderly over the telephone.

frangible (FRAN ji bul): breakable; fragile
   Part of Speech: adjective
   Example: No one realized how *frangible* her feelings were.
   Other Form(s): frangibility (noun)

sporadic (spuh RAD ik): occasional; intermittent
   Part of Speech: adjective
   Example: His efforts at getting good grades were *sporadic* and inconsistent.

Words and Definitions *(cont.)*

———————————— **Group 4** ————————————

rollick (RAUL ik): to romp; to revel
Part of Speech: verb
Example: Revelers *rollick* in the streets of New Orleans during Mardi Gras.

drawl (DRAWL): to prolong syllables; to lengthen syllables
Example: By the way she *drawled*, we knew she was from the South.

inure (in YOOR): accustom; take effect
Part of Speech: verb
Example: His Antarctic exposure *inured* him to the coldest temperatures anywhere else in the world.

sedulous (SED yoo lus): diligent; assiduous
Part of Speech: adjective
Example: *Sedulous* detectives solved the difficult crime.

anneal (uh NEEL): to strengthen; to toughen
Part of Speech: verb
Example: All great swordsmiths *anneal* their swords with great care.

candor (KAN dor): frankness; honesty
Part of Speech: noun
Example: Is it too much to expect *candor* from our elected leaders?

guffaw (guh FAW): hoarse laugh; belly laugh
Part of Speech: verb
Example: People *guffawed* when the dishonest speaker asked to be believed.
Other Form(s): guffaw (noun)

void (VOYD): to cancel; to retract
Part of Speech: verb
Example: The authorities *voided* his license after fraud was proven.

Unit 7 *(cont.)*

Quick Match

Group 1

A. secret	C. swindle	E. preachy	G. unkempt
B. maxim	D. full	F. rotten	H. insipid

_____ 1. disheveled   _____ 5. clandestine

_____ 2. putrid   _____ 6. apothegm

_____ 3. fraught   _____ 7. sententious

_____ 4. vapid   _____ 8. bilk

Group 2

A. degenerate	C. persist	E. invincible	G. hairstyle
B. hypnotize	D. audacity	F. precede	H. obsolete

_____ 1. harp   _____ 5. scrofulous

_____ 2. antedate   _____ 6. outmoded

_____ 3. indomitable   _____ 7. effrontery

_____ 4. coiffure   _____ 8. mesmerize

Group 3

A. breakable	C. murmur	E. coordinate	G. occasional
B. inclined to	D. agreeable	F. encamp	H. swindle

_____ 1. amenable   _____ 5. drone

_____ 2. interface   _____ 6. rook

_____ 3. bivouac   _____ 7. frangible

_____ 4. predisposed   _____ 8. sporadic

Group 4

A. accustom	C. belly laugh	E. frankness	G. assiduous
B. strengthen	D. cancel	F. romp	H. prolong syllables

_____ 1. rollick   _____ 5. anneal

_____ 2. drawl   _____ 6. candor

_____ 3. inure   _____ 7. guffaw

_____ 4. sedulous   _____ 8. void

Unit 7 *(cont.)*

Answer Key

Pre-test Yourself

Group 1	**Group 2**	**Group 3**	**Group 4**
1. apothegm	1. indomitable	1. drone	1. candor
2. putrid	2. harp	2. amenable	2. sedulous
3. sententious	3. antedate	3. frangible	3. drawl
4. clandestine	4. scrofulous	4. rook	4. void
5. vapid	5. mesmerize	5. bivouack	5. inure
6. disheveled	6. coiffure	6. predisposed	6. rollick
7. fraught	7. effrontery	7. interface	7. guffaw
8. bilk	8. outmoded	8. sporadic	8. anneal

Quick Match

Group 1	**Group 2**	**Group 3**	**Group 4**
1. G	1. C	1. D	1. F
2. F	2. F	2. E	2. H
3. D	3. E	3. F	3. A
4. H	4. G	4. B	4. G
5. A	5. A	5. C	5. B
6. B	6. H	6. H	6. E
7. E	7. D	7. A	7. C
8. C	8. B	8. G	8. D

Unit 8

Pre-test Yourself

Group 1

animus	recrimination	inveigle	sophistry
misanthropic	ebullience	blandishment	paroxysm

---

1. She was always effervescent and full of _____.

2. Her editorial was full of _____ toward her opponent in the upcoming election.

3. A depression in South America caused a _____ on the New York Stock Exchange.

4. His _____ fulfill her dreams, and they eloped.

5. The fast-talking entrepeneur would often _____ the new recruits into doing his work for him.

6. One does not expect _____ from a real scholar.

7. When spots carry _____, little can be done to save a relationship.

8. His speeches revealed a _____ man who had nothing nice to say about anyone.

Group 2

simile	ingratiate	charisma	expurgate
renascence	animadversion	parody	blithe

---

1. She used a _____ to compare the musician's hair to the mane of a lion.

2. People with attractive cachets about them carry a _____ to be envied.

3. Government censors may _____ passages of the group's manifesto.

4. Students who are _____ about academic work usually do not succeed.

5. The _____ of his work angered him because he thought it unfair.

6. He expressed his _____ of the play by writing a parody of it.

7. New people and new ideas precede a _____ in any field.

8. Seeking favor from his boss, he would _____ himself by doing extra work.

Unit 8 (cont.)

Pre-test Yourself (cont.)

Group 3

convoke	plaintive	dissidence	ingenuous
bohemian	anterior	sullen	extrapolate

---

1. The leader of the group will _____ a plenary session of its members.

2. Radar was positioned _____ to the mast rather than behind it.

3. She was could _____ the cost of the jewels by comparing them to jewels sold in the past.

4. When she was told that she could not take the course she needed, she put on a _____ face.

5. He acted in all candor because he was _____.

6. The mourners let out _____ cries of loss.

7. _____ on a large scale split the church into sects.

8. She was content to live a _____life on a commune with several other out-of-work artists.

Group 4

plethora	serendipity	accost	mendacity
fractious	cant	redress	disquiet

---

1. Only through _____ was he lucky enough to win the main prize.

2. Several disgruntled employees will _____ the manager in his office.

3. _____ has no bounds where self-aggrandizement is concerned.

4. Ancient people thought that a _____ of ills was punishment of the gods.

5. His _____ and intractable behavior attracted the principal's attention.

6. The politician's familiar _____ did not please the citizens.

7. The director of the horror film thought he could _____ his audience by having the scene take place in a dark closet.

8. Involved nations will probably _____ the damage they have done, but many of the victims feel it is too late.

Unit 8 *(cont.)*

Words and Definitions

––––––––––––––––––––– Group 1 –––––––––––––––––––––

animus (AN i mus): ill will; hostility
Part of Speech: noun
Example: Enemies expressed their *animus* in heated speeches.

recrimination (re krim i NAY shun): counter charge; retaliation
Part of Speech: noun
Example: Opposing politicians often traffic in *recrimination* and bitter accusation.
Other Form(s): recriminate (verb); recriminatory (adjective)

inveigle (in VAY gul): to entangle; to catch
Part of Speech: verb
Example: Her special charms *inveigled* him, and he was soon an emotional wreck.

sophistry (SOF iss tree): equivocation; prevarication
Part of Speech: noun
Example: Ethics teachers have to avoid any semblance of *sophistry*.
Other Form(s): sophist (noun); sophistic (adjective)

misanthropic (mis an THROP ik): scorning or hating humanity; antisocial
Part of Speech: adjective
Example: The electorate disapproved of the senator's *misanthropic* views on social welfare.
Other Form(s): misanthropy (noun); misanthrope (noun)

ebullience (eh BOOL yence): high spirits; exhilaration
Part of Speech: noun
Example: Victory at the last moment brought on a great *ebullience* in the crowd.
Other Form(s): ebullient (adjective)

blandishment (BLAN dish ment): cajolery; flattery
Part of Speech: noun
Example: She enjoyed his *blandishment* and promised him special consideration.

paroxysm (PARE uks siz um): convulsion; fit
Part of Speech: noun
Example: Electric charges brought on *paroxysms* and uncontrollable spasms.
Other Form(s): paroxysmal (adjective)

Unit 8 *(cont.)*

Words and Definitions *(cont.)*

─────────────── **Group 2** ───────────────

simile (SIM i lee): analogy; type of comparison
    Part of Speech: noun
    Example: Poets construct *similes* to explain phenomena to readers.

ingratiate (in GRAY shee ate): to win favor; to gain influence
    Part of Speech: verb
    Example: He *ingratiated* himself to her with constant blandishment.

charisma (kuh RIZ muh): personal magnetism; special charm
    Part of Speech: noun
    Example: Eva Peron's *charisma* captured the Argentinean people.
    Other Form(s): charismatic (adjective)

expurgate (EX pur gate): to purge; to censor
    Part of Speech: verb
    Example: Governmental overseers *expurgated* offensive passages from the legislation.

renascence (rih NAY sense): renaissance; rebirth
    Part of Speech: noun
    Example: His writing is seeing a *renascence* after years of neglect.

animadversion (an i mad VUR zhun): hostile criticism; censorious remark
    Part of Speech: noun
    Example: Her *animadversion* was clear from her caustic and acerbic attacks.
    Other Form(s): animadvert (verb)

parody (PAR oh dee): spoof; satire
    Part of Speech: noun
    Example: The *parody* was so incisive that everyone laughed at its object.
    Other Form(s): parody (verb)

blithe (BLYTHE): cheerful; devil-may-care
    Part of Speech: adjective
    Example: His cavalier style showed him to be a *blithe* and effervescent spirit.

Words and Definitions *(cont.)*

─────────────────────── **Group 3** ───────────────────────

convoke (con VOKE): to assemble; to call together
  Part of Speech: verb
  Example: The leader *convoked* his ruling ministers for an important council.
  Other Form(s): convocation (noun)

plaintive (PLAIN tiv): mournful; melancholy
  Part of Speech: adjective
  Example: The lost child spoke in *plaintive* tones about his missing family.

dissidence (DIS i dense): disagreement; dispute
  Part of Speech: noun
  Example: *Dissidence* was so rampant that no agreement could be reached.
  Other Form(s): dissident (adjective)

ingenuous (in JEN yoo us): sincere; genuine
  Part of Speech: adjective
  Example: Everyone praised him for his *ingenuous* stand on the issue.
  Other Form(s): ingenuousness (noun)

bohemian (boh HEE mee an): uncommon; unorthodox
  Part of Speech: adjective
  Example: Artists supposedly live *bohemian* lives.
  Other Form(s): bohemian (noun)

anterior (an TEER ee or): forward; in front
  Part of Speech: adjective
  Example: The insect in question had *anterior*, and not posterior, antennae.

sullen (SULL en): morose; resentful
  Part of Speech: adjective
  Example: Children show their disapproval by giving *sullen* looks when displeased.
  Other Form(s): sullenness (noun)

extrapolate (ex TRAP uh late): to infer; to estimate
  Part of Speech: verb
  Example: Actuaries *extrapolate* life-expectancy from collected demographic data.
  Other Form(s): extrapolation (noun)

Words and Definitions *(cont.)*

--- **Group 4** ---

plethora (PLETH ur uh): superabundance; surfeit
Part of Speech: noun
Example: Hypochondriacs suffer from a *plethora* of feigned illnesses.

serendipity (ser en DIP i tee): chance; happenstance
Part of Speech: noun
Example: Lottery participants hope *serendipity* favors them.
Other Form(s): serendipitous (adjective)

accost (uh KOST): to assault; to confront
Part of Speech: verb
Example: Thieves *accosted* the man and robbed him of all his goods.

mendacity (men DAS i tee): duplicity; disingenuousness
Part of Speech: noun
Example: The speaker's *mendacity* became obvious when he reversed his position.
Other Form(s): mendacious (adjective)

fractious (FRAK shus): peevish; cranky
Part of Speech: adjective
Example: He became *fractious* when various people criticized him.
Other Form(s): fractiousness (noun)

cant (KANT): empty talk; sanctimony
Part of Speech: noun
Example: Hypocrites spew *cant* and sophistry.

redress (re DRESS): to set right; to rectify
Part of Speech: verb
Example: He *redressed* his errors and repaid his clients.

disquiet (dis KWY ut): to worry; to deprive of peace
Part of Speech: verb
Example: His pencil tapping *disquieted* the teacher, and she asked him to stop.
Other Form(s): disquietude (noun); disquieting (adjective)

Unit 8 *(cont.)*

Quick Match

Group 1

A. people-hating	C. convulsion	E. exhileration	G. hostility
B. cajolery	D. countercharge	F. false arguments	H. persuade

_____ 1. animus

_____ 2. recrimination

_____ 3. inveigle

_____ 4. sophistry

_____ 5. misanthropic

_____ 6. ebullience

_____ 7. blandishment

_____ 8. paroxysm

Group 2

A. criticism	C. rebirth	E. cheerful	G. purge
B. satirize	D. special charm	F. analogy	H. win favor

_____ 1. simile

_____ 2. ingratiate

_____ 3. charisma

_____ 4. expurgate

_____ 5. renascence

_____ 6. animadversion

_____ 7. parody

_____ 8. blithe

Group 3

A. sincere	C. call together	E. forward	G. mournful
B. unorthodox	D. infer	F. dispute	H. morose

_____ 1. convoke

_____ 2. plaintive

_____ 3. dissidence

_____ 4. ingenuous

_____ 5. bohemian

_____ 6. anterior

_____ 7. sullen

_____ 8. extrapolate

Group 4

A. duplicity	C. rectify	E. empty talk	G. cranky
B. surfeit	D. confront	F. chance	H. worry

_____ 1. plethora

_____ 2. serendipity

_____ 3. accost

_____ 4. mendacity

_____ 5. fractious

_____ 6. cant

_____ 7. redress

_____ 8. disquiet

Unit 8 *(cont.)*

Answer Key

Pre-test Yourself

Group 1	Group 2	Group 3	Group 4
1. ebullience	1. simile	1. convoke	1. serendipity
2. recrimination	2. charisma	2. anterior	2. accost
3. paroxysm	3. expurgate	3. extrapolate	3. mendacity
4. blandishment	4. blithe	4. sullen	4. plethora
5. inveigle	5. parody	5. ingenuous	5. fractious
6. sophistry	6. animadversion	6. plaintive	6. cant
7. animus	7. renascence	7. dissidence	7. disquiet
8. misanthropic	8. ingratiate	8. bohemian	8. redress

Quick Match

Group 1	Group 2	Group 3	Group 4
1. G	1. F	1. C	1. B
2. D	2. H	2. G	2. F
3. H	3. D	3. F	3. D
4. F	4. G	4. A	4. A
5. A	5. C	5. B	5. G
6. E	6. A	6. E	6. E
7. B	7. B	7. H	7. C
8. C	8. E	8. D	8. H

Unit 9

Pre-test Yourself

Group 1

| acerbic | prosaic | ineffable | draconian |
| soporific | unimpeachable | consign | empirical |

1. Artists often _____ their work to art galleries in the hope that they will be bought.

2. _____ laws and edicts were considered the impetus for the rebellions.

3. People become _____ when a speaker drones on and on.

4. She had a quality in her voice that was _____ and enchanting.

5. Good researchers restrict themselves to observing _____ evidence.

6. His teaching credentials were _____, and he was hired on the spot.

7. Her _____ remarks cut right through her opponent.

8. Life is _____ when you are caught in a rut.

Group 2

| elicit | purport | dross | salient |
| calumny | harbinger | acquisitive | lassitude |

1. Impostors _____ to be what they are not.

2. The low-budget movie did _____ high praise from several film critics.

3. Robber barons of the nineteenth century were avaricious and _____.

4. Tabloids deal quite often in _____.

5. His ideas proved to be _____, and his plan was followed.

6. The sailors felt that the bird was a _____ of bad weather.

7. The team's _____ contributed to its losing record.

8. He thought he could make money from the _____ and tried to sell the leftovers.

Unit 9 (cont.)

Pre-test Yourself (cont.)

Group 3

| proclivity | acuity | rancid | unregenerate |
| efflorescent | iniquity | connote | senescent |

1. When he became _____, his children put him in a nursing home.

2. The serial killer was full of _____.

3. Storing the butter in the sunlight made it into a _____ and oleaginous pile.

4. Friends kept him away from the racetrack because he has a _____ for gambling.

5. Plantings become _____ in the spring.

6. Alertness and _____ warned him of an approaching problem.

7. Recidivist prisoners are _____ criminals.

8. Her body language might _____ agreement, even though she clearly said the word "No."

Group 4

| ostracize | efficacy | misogyny | adulate |
| hallowed | dogmatic | prolix | cynosure |

1. The _____ of rest on many illnesses is undeniable.

2. _____ teachers rarely gain rapport with their students.

3. His _____ prevented him from voting for women's suffrage.

4. At 6' 8", he became a _____ wherever he went.

5. Teenagers _____ movie stars and athletes.

6. The club would _____ those who came from lower-income families.

7. The lecture was so _____ that many left the auditorium before it was over.

8. Graumann's Theater in Hollywood is a _____ place for actors.

Words and Definitions

Group 1

acerbic (a SUR bik): bitter; sour
Part of Speech: adjective
Example: An *acerbic* attitude will rarely receive a happy welcome.

prosaic (proh ZAY ik): commonplace; ordinary
Part of Speech: adjective
Example: Drudgery is *prosaic* and repetitive labor.

ineffable (in EF uh bul): inexpressible; indescribable
Part of Speech: adjective
Example: The music had an *ineffable* effect on the audience.

draconian (dra KO nee en): exceedingly harsh; rigorous
Part of Speech: adjective
Example: The emperor's laws were *draconian*, and the people rebelled.

soporific (sop uh RIF ik): sleepy; drowsy
Part of Speech: adjective
Example: Lots of verbiage will make any class *soporific*.

unimpeachable (un im PEACH a bul): beyond doubt; beyond reproach
Part of Speech: adjective
Example: She had *unimpeachable* credentials for the position.

consign (con SINE): to give over; to deposit with
Part of Speech: verb
Example: They *consigned* their art works with the gallery owner.

empirical (em PEER i kul): experimental; observed
Part of Speech: adjective
Example: A scientist must depend upon *empirical* evidence to make a finding.

Words and Definitions *(cont.)*

――――――――――――――― **Group 2** ―――――――――――――――

elicit (uh LIS it): to evoke; to educe
  Part of Speech: verb
  Example: Successful comedians *elicit* laughter from their listeners.

purport (pur PORT): to claim; to contend
  Part of Speech: verb
  Example: People who *purport* to be experts have to prove it over long periods of time.

dross (DROSS): worthless material; trivial matter
  Part of Speech: noun
  Example: Alchemists purported to make gold out of *dross*.

salient (SAY lee ent): prominent; conspicuous
  Part of Speech: adjective
  Example: His arguments proved *salient* and utterly convincing.

calumny (CAL um nee): slander; libel
  Part of Speech: noun
  Example: Sleazy magazines often use *calumny* to attract attention and sales.
  Other Form(s): calumnious (adjective)

harbinger (HAR bin jer): forerunner; omen
  Part of Speech: noun
  Example: Asters are *harbingers* of frosty weather in the north.

acquisitive (ah KWI zi tiv): greedy; materialistic
  Part of Speech: adjective
  Example: He indulged in *acquisitive* behavior and soon became both rich and disliked.

lassitude (LASS i tude): languor; indolence
  Part of Speech: noun
  Example: The widespread *lassitude* of the team proved its downfall.

Words and Definitions *(cont.)*

───────────────────── **Group 3** ─────────────────────

proclivity (pro KLIV i tee): inclination; propensity
    Part of Speech: noun
    Example: As a youth she showed a *proclivity* towards music and became a fine cellist.

acuity (uh Q i tee): keenness; mental alertness
    Part of Speech: noun
    Example: Her *acuity* made her a much desired mathematician.

rancid (RAN sid): fetid; stinking
    Part of Speech: adjective
    Example: When the power failed, the food soon became *rancid* and putrid.

unregenerate (un ri JEN ur it): unrepentant; without qualm
    Part of Speech: adjective
    Example: The gangster was an *unregenerate* and evil man.

efflorescent (ef luh RES ent): flowering; growing
    Part of Speech: adjective
    Example: Plants became *efflorescent* in the temperate climate.
    Other Form(s): efflorescence (noun)

iniquity (in IK wi tee): wickedness; sin
    Part of Speech: noun
    Example: The unregenerate gangster was accused of great and widespread *iniquity*.
    Other Form(s): iniquitous (adjective)

connote (cuh NOTE): to suggest; to imply
    Part of Speech: verb
    Example: Her tone of voice *connoted* her uneasiness about the outcome.
    Other Form(s): connotation (noun)

senescent (se NES ent): old; aging
    Part of Speech: adjective
    Example: As he became *senescent*, his mental acuity began to wane.
    Other Form(s): senescence (noun)

Words and Definitions *(cont.)*

─────────────────── **Group 4** ───────────────────

ostracize (OS truh size): to exclude; to shun
> **Part of Speech:** verb
> **Example:** Society *ostracizes* people who do not take baths.

efficacy (EF fi kuh see): effectiveness; capability
> **Part of Speech:** noun
> **Example:** Her *efficacy* as a leader was hurt by her inexperience.
> **Other Form(s):** efficacious (adjective)

misogyny (mi SOJ i nee): hatred of women
> **Part of Speech:** noun
> **Example:** Widespread *misogyny* alienated many women.
> **Other Form(s):** misogynist (noun); misogynistic (adjective)

adulate (AD yoo late): to worship; to idolize
> **Part of Speech:** verb
> **Example:** Teenagers often *adulate* rock musicians.
> **Other Form(s):** adulation (noun)

hallowed (HAL ode): sacred; holy
> **Part of Speech:** adjective
> **Example:** Colleges refer to their quadrangles as *hallowed* and scholarly places.

dogmatic (dog MAT ik): authoritarian; emphatic
> **Part of Speech:** adjective
> **Example:** He expressed his opinions in a *dogmatic* fashion and would not listen to reason.
> **Other Form(s):** dogma (noun)

prolix (pro LIKS): verbose; garrulous
> **Part of Speech:** adjective
> **Example:** His speeches were *prolix* and interminable.
> **Other Form(s):** prolixity (noun)

cynosure (SY no sure): focal point; center of attention
> **Part of Speech:** noun
> **Example:** Her acerbic wit made her the *cynosure* at most soirees.

Unit 9 (cont.)

Quick Match

Group 1

A. beyond reproach C. deposit with E. experimental G. commonplace
B. sleepy D. indescribable F. bitter H. harsh

_____ 1. acerbic _____ 5. soporific

_____ 2. prosaic _____ 6. unimpeachable

_____ 3. ineffable _____ 7. consign

_____ 4. draconian _____ 8. empirical

Group 2

A. conspicuous C. claim E. greedy G. forerunner
B. slander D. indolence F. evoke H. worthless material

_____ 1. elicit _____ 5. calumny

_____ 2. purport _____ 6. harbinger

_____ 3. dross _____ 7. acquisitive

_____ 4. salient _____ 8. lassitude

Group 3

A. growing C. evil E. imply G. inclination
B. unrepentant D. keenness F. aging H. fetid

_____ 1. proclivity _____ 5. efflorescent

_____ 2. acuity _____ 6. iniquity

_____ 3. rancid _____ 7. connote

_____ 4. unregenerate _____ 8. senescent

Group 4

A. hatred of women C. shun E. authoritarian G. idolize
B. holy D. verbose F. capability H. center of attention

_____ 1. ostracize _____ 5. hallowed

_____ 2. efficacy _____ 6. dogmatic

_____ 3. misogyny _____ 7. prolix

_____ 4. adulate _____ 8. cynosure

Unit 9 (cont.)

Answer Key

Group 1	Group 2	Group 3	Group 4
1. consign	1. purport	1. senescent	1. efficacy
2. draconian	2. elicit	2. iniquity	2. dogmatic
3. soporific	3. acquisitive	3. rancid	3. misogyny
4. ineffable	4. calumny	4. proclivity	4. cynosure
5. empirical	5. salient	5. efflorescent	5. adulate
6. unimpeachable	6. harbinger	6. acuity	6. ostracize
7. acerbic	7. lassitude	7. unregenerate	7. prolix
8. prosaic	8. dross	8. connote	8. hallowed

Quick Match

Group 1	Group 2	Group 3	Group 4
1. F	1. F	1. G	1. C
2. G	2. C	2. D	2. F
3. D	3. H	3. H	3. A
4. H	4. A	4. B	4. G
5. B	5. B	5. A	5. B
6. A	6. G	6. C	6. E
7. C	7. E	7. E	7. D
8. E	8. D	8. F	8. H

Unit 10

Pre-test Yourself

Group 1

inveterate	desiccate	surreptitious	mendicant
advent	pariah	conjecture	fastidious

1. After the stock market crashed, he became a _____ and spent his days begging for change.

2. Since he was an _____ liar, he could never be trusted.

3. His clothes came from the best men's shops because he was a _____ man.

4. Winds continued to sweep across the veldt and _____ everything in their path.

5. As someone who was an inveterate liar, he became a _____ in his small community.

6. Spy agencies deal in _____ matters.

7. During the meeting, she may _____ about the possible progress of the project.

8. The _____ of desiccating winds marked the beginning of the dry season.

Group 2

recumbent	perigee	doggerel	ostensive
quibble	craven	sycophant	adventitious

1. The office _____ always supported his boss's decisions.

2. His verse was considered second-rate and just a touch above _____.

3. Couch potatoes can often be found in _____ positions.

4. His reasons for accepting a position with the prosperous company were _____.

5. When the planet reached its _____, definite rock formations could be seen.

6. His lack of principle in the face of danger showed him to be a _____ man.

7. His personal fortune was the result of an _____ discovery of a winning lottery ticket.

8. Pettifoggers who want to confuse issues _____ over minor items.

Pre-test Yourself *(cont.)*

Group 3

bamboozle	malediction	peripatetic	aesthetic
rue	succor	embroil	conundrum

---

1. The voters' _____ was whether to vote solid incumbent or the young upstart.

2. Slick talkers and tricksters _____ people into believing almost anything.

3. Nurses give _____ to their patients.

4. Johnny Appleseed was a _____ mythological hero who forested America.

5. The conspiracy could _____ a lot of well-known people who do not want publicity.

6. In the movie, the warlock cast a _____ on the protagonist.

7. Her _____ sensibility was highly developed with regards to music.

8. He will _____ the day he had perjured himself.

Group 4

gravamen	empathy	recrudescence	affluence
insular	dormant	parsimony	chimera

---

1. The judge directed the prosecution to present the _____ of its case.

2. Many felt that the jury's verdict was directly influenced by the _____ and social prominence of the defendant.

3. His poem about her loss showed he had _____ for her.

4. The cult's _____ was the direct result of a new and charismatic leader.

5. Biased opinions mark the _____ mind.

6. Hostility remained _____ until the new tax reawakened the citizenry's ire.

7. Mists over the water created a _____ for the imaginative.

8. Misers are known for their _____.

Words and Definitions

Group 1

inveterate (in VET ur it): chronic; habitual
  Part of Speech: adjective
  Example: His smoking was *inveterate* and uncontrolled.

desiccate (DES i kate): to dry out; to deprive of spirit
  Part of Speech: verb
  Example: Westerly winds *desiccate* the foliage on the windward side of the mountain.
  Other Form(s): dessication (noun); dessicatory (adjective)

surreptitious (sur ep TI shus): covert; clandestine
  Part of Speech: adjective
  Example: He made *surreptitious* plans to overthrow the government.

mendicant (MEN di kant): beggar; supplicator
  Part of Speech: noun
  Example: Medieval highways were crowded with *mendicants* who pestered travelers for alms.
  Other Form(s): mendicancy (noun); mendicant (adjective)

advent (AD vent): arrival; beginning
  Part of Speech: noun
  Example: The *advent* of the computer signaled the demise of the typewriter.

pariah (pa RY uh): outcast; undesirable person
  Part of Speech: noun
  Example: His viciousness marked him as a societal *pariah*.

conjecture (con JEK chure): to guess; to surmise
  Part of Speech: verb
  Example: Professional gamblers rarely *conjecture*; they carefully play the odds.
  Other Form(s): conjecture (noun)

fastidious (fas TID ee us): critical; hard to please
  Part of Speech: adjective
  Example: His *fastidious* standards estranged many people.
  Other Form(s): fastidiousness (noun)

Words and Definitions *(cont.)*

───────────────── **Group 2** ─────────────────

recumbent (re CUM bent): reclining; lying down
    Part of Speech: adjective
    Example: A *recumbent* lion is the trademark of a major movie studio.

perigee (PER i jee): closest to a planet
    Part of Speech: noun
    Example: When the space station reached its *perigee*, it could be seen clearly from Earth.

doggerel (DOG gur ul): worthless poetry; trivial verse
    Part of Speech: noun
    Example: He wrote *doggerel*, but thought himself a great poet.

ostensive (aw STEN siv): manifest; directly demonstrative
    Part of Speech: adjective
    Example: Dogs are able to learn commands only through their repeated and *ostensive* use.

quibble (KWIB ul): to be trivial; to make a petty objection
    Part of Speech: verb
    Example: The judge told the defendant's lawyer not to *quibble* about words.
    Other Form(s): quibble (noun); quibbling (adjective)

craven (CRAY ven): cowardly; abject
    Part of Speech: adjective
    Example: *Craven* men die many deaths, but the brave die only once.

sycophant (SIK oh fant): toady; flatterer
    Part of Speech: noun
    Example: Kings surrounded themselves with *sycophants*, who curried favor with the court.
    Other Form(s): sycophantic (adjective); sycophancy (noun)

adventitious (ad ven TI shus): accidental; not inherent
    Part of Speech: adjective
    Example: Unexpected and *adventitious* events led to his promotion within the company.

Words and Definitions (cont.)

─────────────────────── **Group 3** ───────────────────────

bamboozle (bam BOO zull): to deceive; to mislead
Part of Speech: verb
Example: Disingenuous salesmen *bamboozle* customers and sell them dross.

malediction (mal eh DIK shun): curse; execration
Part of Speech: noun
Example: Sorcerers cast *maledictions* on those they wanted to doom.

peripatetic (per i pu TET ik): itinerant; walking from place to place
Part of Speech: adjective
Example: Nomads are *peripatetic* people.

aesthetic (az THET ik): concerning beauty; appreciation of beauty
Part of Speech: adjective
Example: The art critic had a refined *aesthetic* sense and was much in demand.

rue (ROO): to regret; to grieve
Part of Speech: verb
Example: He *rued* the day had she entered his life.

succor (SUK ur): to give aid; to assist
Part of Speech: noun
Example: Good samaritans *succor* those who require help.

embroil (em BROIL): involve in conflict; make confused
Part of Speech: verb
Example: She was concerned that her nascent relationship with her best friend's ex-boyfriend would *embroil* her in an unpleasant situation.

conundrum (kuh NUN drum): riddle; puzzle
Part of Speech: noun
Example: She had difficulty living in the *conundrum* he had made of her life.

Unit 10 (cont.)

Words and Definitions (cont.)

gravamen (gruh VAY men): most important part; essence
   Part of Speech: noun
   Example: The judge asked the lawyer to address the *gravamen* of the case.

empathy (EM puh thee): identification; similarity of feeling
   Part of Speech: noun
   Example: Sensitive people show *empathy* for those who suffer.
   Other Form(s): empathize (verb); empathetic (adjective)

recrudescence (ree kroo DES ense): reactivation; renewal
   Part of Speech: noun
   Example: A *recrudescence* of the ancient conundrum disturbed modern philosophers.
   Other Form(s): recrudesce (verb)

affluence (AH flu ense): wealth; riches
   Part of Speech: noun
   Example: Magnanimous acts of kindness were her thanks for the *affluence* she attained.
   Other Form(s): affluent (adjective)

insular (IN su lur): isolated; provincial
   Part of Speech: adjective
   Example: *Insular* thinking results in shortsighted policies.

dormant (DOR mant): asleep; inert
   Part of Speech: adjective
   Example: His talents lay *dormant* until he was inspired by one of his teachers.
   Other Form(s): dormancy (noun)

parsimony (PAR si mo nee): miserliness; cautiousness with money
   Part of Speech: noun
   Example: The venture failed because of the *parsimony* of the developers.
   Other Form(s): parsimonious (adjective)

chimera (ky MER uh): a fantastic product of the imagination; imaginative creation
   Part of Speech: noun
   Example: The child's imagination created a *chimera* out of the shadows of the trees on his window.
   Other Form(s): chimerical (adjective)

Unit 10 *(cont.)*

Quick Match

Group 1

A. beginning	C. dry out	E. chronic	G. beggar
B. fussy	D. outcast	F. covert	H. surmise

_____ 1. inveterate

_____ 2. desiccate

_____ 3. surreptitious

_____ 4. mendicant

_____ 5. advent

_____ 6. pariah

_____ 7. conjecture

_____ 8. fastidious

Group 2

A. flatterer	C. lying down	E. closest point	G. crude poetry
B. manifest	D. to be petty	F. accidental	H. cowardly

_____ 1. recumbent

_____ 2. perigee

_____ 3. doggerel

_____ 4. ostensive

_____ 5. quibble

_____ 6. craven

_____ 7. sycophant

_____ 8. adventitious

Group 3

A. itinerant	C. involve	E. aid	G. riddle
B. grieve	D. deceive	F. curse	H. concerning beauty

_____ 1. bamboozle

_____ 2. malediction

_____ 3. peripatetic

_____ 4. aesthetic

_____ 5. rue

_____ 6. succor

_____ 7. embroil

_____ 8. conundrum

Group 4

A. renewal	C. asleep	E. most important part	G. identification
B. provincial	D. miserliness	F. wealth	H. product of the imagination

_____ 1. gravamen

_____ 2. empathy

_____ 3. recrudescence

_____ 4. affluence

_____ 5. insular

_____ 6. dormant

_____ 7. parsimony

_____ 8. chimera

Unit 10 *(cont.)*

Answer Key

——— Pre-test Yourself ———

Group 1

1. mendicant
2. inveterate
3. fastidious
4. desiccate
5. pariah
6. surreptitious
7. conjecture
8. advent

Group 2

1. sycophant
2. doggerel
3. recumbent
4. ostensive
5. perigee
6. craven
7. adventitious
8. quibble

Group 3

1. conundrum
2. bamboozle
3. succor
4. peripatetic
5. embroil
6. malediction
7. aesthetic
8. rued

Group 4

1. gravamen
2. affluence
3. empathy
4. recrudescence
5. insular
6. dormant
7. chimera
8. parsimony

——— Quick Match ———

Group 1

1. E
2. C
3. F
4. G
5. A
6. D
7. H
8. B

Group 2

1. C
2. E
3. G
4. B
5. D
6. H
7. A
8. F

Group 3

1. D
2. F
3. A
4. H
5. B
6. E
7. C
8. G

Group 4

1. E
2. G
3. A
4. F
5. B
6. C
7. D
8. H

Unit 11

Pre-test Yourself

Group 1

disgruntled	vituperate	purloin	canard
subterfuge	rudiments	acclimate	tangential

---

1. It seemed that the newspaper columnist would _____ any newly elected official.

2. Before one can be expert at anything, one must learn its _____.

3. _____ students gathered in the quadrangle to voice their disapproval.

4. In a few moments, the swimmer will _____ himself to the temperature of the water.

5. Many intelligence agencies use _____ to find out what other nations are doing.

6. The boy would _____ small amounts of money so that no one would notice the theft.

7. Tabloids spread the _____ about the well-known actor so as to ruin him.

8. Her _____ ideas were rarely considered because they were not pertinent.

Group 2

liaison	enjoin	bibulous	russet
accede	disavow	peregrinate	context

---

1. Peripatetic people, like Johnny Appleseed, _____.

2. Concerned parents often _____ their children to work harder in school.

3. When statements are taken out of _____, reputations can be ruined.

4. She wore a deep-brown dress to complement her _____ hair.

5. If both sides _____ to the terms, an armistice can ensue.

6. It was too late, but the defendant did _____ his earlier statement.

7. Legates are _____ personnel who smooth the way for true ambassadors.

8. AA was a place where the _____ person tried to solve his problem.

Pre-test Yourself *(cont.)*

Group 3

disrepute	travesty	cumbersome	efface
rapport	acclamation	peremptory	garish

---

1. His _____ tone made the students move quickly.

2. The equipment was _____ and slowed the mountain climber down.

3. Teachers look for immediate _____ with their pupils.

4. In an act meant to instigate war, the revolutionary group will _____ the city's famous landmark.

5. Many view the gambling casinos in Las Vegas as meretricious and _____.

6. Critics found the play so bad that they labeled it a _____ rather than a tragedy.

7. All members voted for her, and she was elected with _____ for her good deeds.

8. The bureau investigating the crime fell into _____ when it was found to be corrupt.

Group 4

banal	mercenary	abscond	spurious
cadence	perfidy	despoil	harry

---

1. Cliches in his musical pieces made them _____.

2. Some people saw the casino owner as a _____ who was simply concerned with making lots of money.

3. Before the thief could _____ with the jewels, the police arrived on the scene.

4. Vandals may _____ the museum.

5. Soldiers must march to a certain _____ on the parade grounds.

6. Soldiers arrested the man because he offered them a _____ passport.

7. She would often _____ and pester him to do some repairs around the house.

8. His _____ alarmed and disgusted everyone he came in contact with.

Unit 11 (cont.)
Words and Definitions

─────────────── Group 1 ───────────────

disgruntled (dis GRUN tuld): discontent; unhappy
   Part of Speech: adjective
   Example: Many citizens were *disgruntled* about the outcome and rampaged through the streets.
   Other Form(s): disgruntlement (noun)

vituperate (vy TOO pur ate): to berate; to reproach
   Part of Speech: verb
   Example: Disgruntled members of the opposing party *vituperated* their opponents.
   Other Form(s): vituperative (adjective); vituperation (noun)

purloin (pur LOIN): to pilfer; to steal
   Part of Speech: verb
   Example: Kleptomaniacs are people who have an obsessive to desire to *purloin* items for which they have no real need.

canard (kuh NARD): false story; unfounded rumor
   Part of Speech: noun
   Example: The *canard* was widespread and adversely affected a lot of workers.

subterfuge (SUB tur fyooj): deception; blame avoidance
   Part of Speech: noun
   Example: Spies use *subterfuge* to gather information.

rudiments (ROO di ments): fundamental elements; first principles
   Part of Speech: noun
   Example: She taught her students the *rudiments*, and they progressed from there.
   Other Form(s): rudimentary (adjective)

acclimate (a KLI mate): to adapt; to get used to
   Part of Speech: verb
   Example: He *acclimated* himself to the cold conditions and managed to survive.
   Other Form(s): acclimation (noun)

tangential (tan JEN chul): divergent; peripheral
   Part of Speech: adjective
   Example: The remarks had a *tangential* and unimportant effect on the outcome.
   Other Form(s): tangent (noun)

Unit 11 *(cont.)*

Words and Definitions *(cont.)*

liaison (lee AY zon): connection; nexus
Part of Speech: noun
Example: Legates act as *liaisons* between countries with diplomatic relations.

enjoin (en JOIN): to command; to order
Part of Speech: verb
Example: The coach *enjoined* his team to play with more intensity.

bibulous (BIB yoo lus): drunken; inebriated; given to drinking liquor
Part of Speech: adjective
Example: He was quite *bibulous* after the victory celebration.

russet (RUS et): copper-colored; auburn
Part of Speech: adjective
Example: Autumn brings a *russet* tint to the mountainsides of the Adirondacks.

accede (ek SEED): to assent to; to consent to
Part of Speech: verb
Example: Agreement was reached when the last holdouts *acceded* to the terms offered.

disavow (dis uh VOW): to deny; to disclaim
Part of Speech: verb
Example: The defendant *disavowed* any knowledge of the conspiracy.
Other Form(s): disavowal (noun)

peregrinate (PER eh gri nate): to travel; to roam
Part of Speech: verb
Example: Nomads *peregrinate* through the region every year at the same time.
Other Form(s): peregrination (noun); peregrinator (noun)

context (KON text): relevant circumstances; relationship
Part of Speech: noun
Example: He said his words were taken out of *context* and therefore misinterpreted.
Other Form(s): contextual (adjective)

Words and Definitions *(cont.)*

───────────── **Group 3** ─────────────

disrepute (dis re PYOOT): disgrace; dishonor
    Part of Speech: noun
    Example: *Disrepute* followed the man's embezzlement of funds.

travesty (TRAV es tee): misrepresentation; grotesque imitation
    Part of Speech: noun
    Example: The play was a *travesty* of the art form; it was awful.

cumbersome (CUM bur sum): clumsy; awkward
    Part of Speech: adjective
    Example: The old methods were considered *cumbersome*, and new methods were adopted.

efface (e FACE): to obliterate; to wipe out
    Part of Speech: verb
    Example: The flood *effaced* what was once a thriving village.

rapport (ra PORE): connection; relationship
    Part of Speech: noun
    Example: Good teachers establish healthy *rapport* with their classes.

acclamation (a kluh MAY shun): ovation; assent
    Part of Speech: noun
    Example: The hero answered the crowd's *acclamation* with a grand salute.

peremptory (per EMP to ree): imperious; dictatorial
    Part of Speech: adjective
    Example: His *peremptory* attitude alienated many of his colleagues.
    Other Form(s): peremptoriness (noun)

garish (GARE ish): flashy; gaudy
    Part of Speech: adjective
    Example: The movie star wore *garish* clothing to attract attention.

Words and Definitions *(cont.)*

─────────────────────────── **Group 4** ───────────────────────────

banal (buh NAL): common; ordinary
   Part of Speech: adjective
   Example: His ideas were boring because they were *banal*.
   Other Form(s): banality (noun)

mercenary (MUR se nare ee): greedy; avaricious
   Part of Speech: adjective
   Example: Acquisitiveness marked him as a *mercenary* man.
   Other Form(s): mercenary (noun)

abscond (ab SKOND): to flee; to make off with
   Part of Speech: verb
   Example: Invaders *absconded* with great works of art from the city's museum.

spurious (SPYUR ee us): fraudulent; bogus
   Part of Speech: adjective
   Example: Arguments that are *spurious* should be disregarded.

cadence (KAY dense): rhythm; inflection
   Part of Speech: noun
   Example: The *cadence* of the music was broken when the cymbalist dropped the cymbals.

perfidy (PER fi dee): treachery; betrayal
   Part of Speech: noun
   Example: Arnold's *perfidy* almost turned the tide of the Revolutionary War.
   Other Form(s): perfidious (adjective)

despoil (de SPOIL): to plunder; to pillage
   Part of Speech: verb
   Example: Clear cut loggers *despoiled* the Adirondack Mountains in the nineteenth century.

harry (HAR ee): to harass; to annoy
   Part of Speech: noun
   Example: Wasps *harried* the diners in the outdoor café.

Unit 11 *(cont.)*

Quick Match

Group 1

A. false story   C. berate   E. steal   G. discontent
B. basic principles   D. adapt   F. peripheral   H. deception

_____ 1. disgruntled   _____ 5. subterfuge
_____ 2. vituperate   _____ 6. rudiments
_____ 3. purloin   _____ 7. acclimate
_____ 4. canard   _____ 8. tangential

Group 2

A. consent   C. relevant circumstances   E. nexus   G. command
B. travel   D. deny   F. auburn   H. inebriated

_____ 1. liaison   _____ 5. accede
_____ 2. enjoin   _____ 6. disavow
_____ 3. bibulous   _____ 7. peregrinate
_____ 4. russet   _____ 8. context

Group 3

A. wipe out   C. grotesque imitation   E. flashy   G. clumsy
B. relationship   D. ovation   F. disgrace   H. imperious

_____ 1. disrepute   _____ 5. rapport
_____ 2. travesty   _____ 6. acclamation
_____ 3. cumbersome   _____ 7. peremptory
_____ 4. efface   _____ 8. garish

Group 4

A. to make off with   C. treachery   E. bogus   G. annoy
B. rhythm   D. trivial   F. greedy   H. plunder

_____ 1. banal   _____ 5. cadence
_____ 2. mercenary   _____ 6. perfidy
_____ 3. abscond   _____ 7. despoil
_____ 4. spurious   _____ 8. harry

Unit 11 *(cont.)*

Answer Key

─────────────── **Pre-test Yourself** ───────────────

Group 1	**Group 2**	**Group 3**	**Group 4**
1. vituperate	1. peregrinate	1. peremptory	1. banal
2. rudiments	2. enjoin	2. cumbersome	2. mercenary
3. disgruntled	3. context	3. rapport	3. abscond
4. acclimate	4. russet	4. efface	4. despoil
5. subterfuge	5. accede	5. garish	5. cadence
6. purloin	6. disavow	6. travesty	6. spurious
7. canard	7. liaison	7. acclamation	7. harry
8. tangential	8. bibulous	8. disrepute	8. perfidy

─────────────── **Quick Match** ───────────────

Group 1	**Group 2**	**Group 3**	**Group 4**
1. G	1. E	1. F	1. D
2. C	2. G	2. C	2. F
3. E	3. H	3. G	3. A
4. A	4. F	4. A	4. E
5. H	5. A	5. B	5. B
6. B	6. D	6. D	6. C
7. D	7. B	7. H	7. H
8. F	8. C	8. E	8. G

Unit 12

Pre-test Yourself

Group 1

cachet	mellifluous	jaundiced	rancor
dilatory	paramour	feral	abrogate

1. Despite being thrashed by their opponents, the players showed no _____ or ill-will.

2. The engaged aristocrat secretly pined for his _____, not his fiance.

3. An arbitrator might _____ the contract on the grounds of fraud.

4. There are certain animals that cannot be tamed and are perpetually _____.

5. _____ sounds came from the voice-training halls.

6. The basketball team's _____ tactics led to a low-scoring game.

7. There was a certain _____ in being cast in one of the famous director's films.

8. His _____ view of society made him a true misanthrope.

Group 2

glower	dissipate	rococo	cajole
predilection	echelon	aborigine	skulk

1. He had a _____ for sweets even though he was diabetic.

2. Idlers _____ about town and frightened ordinary citizens.

3. The _____ chief—the ruler of the original people—asked for certain favors from the new rulers.

4. Anger made him _____ at the people who bothered him.

5. Ludwig of Bavaria, "Mad Ludwig," built elaborate, _____ castles.

6. Profligate people _____ themselves at will.

7. The manipulative director could _____ fine performances out of his actors.

8. As a full professor, he enjoyed the perquisites given to members of the highest academic _____.

Unit 12 (cont.)

Pre-test Yourself (cont.)

Group 3

grandiose	dispirit	abate	closure
solidarity	prognosticate	incursion	recidivism

1. Relatives of the victims wanted some certainty and _____ for their losses.

2. The gambler banked his financial future on his ability to accurately _____ the outcome of the Super Bowl.

3. During their less-successful years, losses would _____ the team and its manager.

4. The brothers had been breaking the law since they were young and were prone to _____.

5. The members of the union felt a steadfast _____ existed among them.

6. Commandos made an _____ onto the beach, and then the main force arrived.

7. With the application of balms, the pain will usually _____.

8. The Las Vegas entrepeneur's latest _____ idea involved building a casino modeled after our solar system.

Group 4

abase	solicitous	malinger	rankle
cliche	insolvency	truncate	pastiche

1. Hatred at his betrayal by his friend will surely _____ his heart.

2. The overthrown dictator must _____ himself in front of the new regime.

3. When she needed him to offer real advice, he would usually spout some trite _____ instead.

4. Her quilts were a _____ of several classical styles.

5. The nurse was a _____ caregiver.

6. Spendthrift and dissolute habits often lead to _____.

7. Soldiers who _____ are thrown into the brig or sent to the front lines.

8. Police may _____ a demonstration by firing water cannons at the crowd.

Unit 12 *(cont.)*

Words and Definitions

―――――――――――――――― **Group 1** ――――――――――――――――

cachet (ca SHAY): mark of distinction; prestige
    Part of Speech: noun
    Example: Tattoos give people a kind of *cachet* within certain social groups.

mellifluous (me LIF loo us): musical; harmonious
    Part of Speech: adjective
    Example: Spring birds filled the meadow with *mellifluous* twirping.

jaundiced (JON dist): jealous; resentful
    Part of Speech: adjective
    Example: The man's *jaundiced* views caused him to root for the downfall of anyone who happened to be rich or famous.

rancor (RANG kur): resentment; malice
    Part of Speech: noun
    Example: He forgave them and showed no *rancor* toward them.
    Other Form(s): rancorous (adjective)

dilatory (DILE uh tor ee): delaying; postponing
    Part of Speech: adjective
    Example: After failing to complete his assignment on time, the student attempted to use *dilatory* tactics on his teacher.

paramour (PAR uh moor): beloved; sweetheart
    Part of Speech: noun
    Example: The queen had many *paramours* and was often a source of scandal.

feral (FEER ul): untamed; wild
    Part of Speech: adjective
    Example: *Feral* animals are difficult to domesticate.

abrogate (AB ro gate): to repeal; to revoke
    Part of Speech: verb
    Example: Congress *abrogated* the old laws and replaced them with new legislation.
    Other Form(s): abrogation (noun)

Words and Definitions *(cont.)*

―――――――――――――――――― **Group 2** ――――――――――――――――――

glower (GLAUW ur): to scowl; to frown
    Part of Speech: verb
    Example: Disappointed voters *glowered* at the election board members.

dissipate (DIS i pate): to scatter; to diffuse
    Part of Speech: verb
    Example: Strong westerly winds *dissipated* what few clouds there were.
    Other Form(s): dissipation (noun)

rococo (ro KO ko): ornate; overdecorated
    Part of Speech: adjective
    Example: Arabesque and *rococo* architecture has always fascinated travelers.

cajole (cuh JOLE): to persuade (by flattery, deceit, etc.); to beguile
    Part of Speech: verb
    Example: She *cajoled* the child into going to bed early.
    Other Form(s): cajolery (noun); cajolement (noun)

predilection (pred i LEK shun): tendency; inclination
    Part of Speech: noun
    Example: His *predilection* toward red sportscars might be one reason for his regular visits to traffic court.

echelon (ESH eh lon): command level; hierarchal level
    Part of Speech: noun
    Example: As a general, he belonged to the highest army *echelon*.

aborigine (ab uh RIJ i nee): original people; native
    Part of Speech: noun
    Example: He was an *aborigine* whose family dated back to the beginnings of time.
    Other Form(s): aboriginal (adjective)

skulk (SKULK): to lurk; to move stealthily
    Part of Speech: verb
    Example: The suspicious character *skulked* and loitered near the bank.

Words and Definitions *(cont.)*

───────────── **Group 3** ─────────────

grandiose (GRAN dee ose): magnificent; imposing
 Part of Speech: adjective
 Example: His dreams were *grandiose* and not of the usual scope.
 Other Form(s): grandiosity (noun)

dispirit (di SPIR it): to discourage; to demoralize
 Part of Speech: verb
 Example: Injuries and withdrawals *dispirited* the whole team.

abate (uh BATE): to decrease; to lessen
 Part of Speech: verb
 Example: When the storm *abated*, they continued their journey.
 Other Form(s): abatement (noun)

closure (CLO zhur): conclusion; termination
 Part of Speech: noun
 Example: *Closure* followed the minister's eulogy at the gravesite.

solidarity (sah li DARE i tee): unity; fellowship
 Part of Speech: noun
 Example: The genuine feeling of *solidarity* among the teammates gave the team an air of invincibility.

prognosticate (prog NOS ti kate): to predict; to prophesy
 Example: He *prognosticated* what was going to happen.
 Other Form(s): prognosticator (noun); prognostication (noun)

incursion (in KUR zhun): raid; attack
 Part of Speech: noun
 Example: The soldiers' *incursion* caught the town by surprise.

recidivism (ree SID i vizm): relapse into crime; reversion
 Part of Speech: noun
 Example: *Recidivism* is a major reason for high prison populations.
 Other Form(s): recidivist (noun); recidivistic (adjective)

Unit 12 *(cont.)*

Words and Definitions *(cont.)*

――――――――――――― **Group 4** ―――――――――――――

abase (uh BASE): to degrade; to disgrace
> **Part of Speech:** verb
> **Example:** The guard's attempts to *abase* the political prisoner were later brought before a military court.
> **Other Form(s):** abasement (noun)

solicitous (suh LIS i tus): concerned; anxious
> **Part of Speech:** adjective
> **Example:** Good nurses are *solicitous* caregivers.

malinger (muh LING gur): to shirk; to avoid
> **Part of Speech:** verb
> **Example:** Dismissal from the factory is certain when workers *malinger*.

rankle (RANG kul): to fester; to vex
> **Part of Speech:** verb
> **Example:** Old misgivings *rankle* in his heart, and he cannot give his trust.

cliché (klee SHAY): worn-out expressions; commonplace
> **Part of Speech:** noun
> **Example:** People who speak in *clichés* are avoiding deep thought.

insolvency (in SOL ven see): bankruptcy; indigence
> **Part of Speech:** noun
> **Example:** The bank's *insolvency* caused a riot in the streets.
> **Other Form(s):** insolvent (adjective)

truncate (TRUNG kate): to cut short; to abbreviate
> **Part of Speech:** verb
> **Example:** The chairperson *truncated* the meeting so people could get home in the storm.
> **Other Form(s):** truncation (noun)

pastiche (pas TEESH): hodgepodge; melange
> **Part of Speech:** noun
> **Example:** The artist's work was a *pastiche* of many styles.

Unit 12 *(cont.)*

Quick Match

Group 1

A. postponing	C. repeal	E. sweetheart	G. musical
B. untamed	D. mark of quality	F. jealous	H. malice

_____ 1. cachet

_____ 2. mellifluous

_____ 3. jaundiced

_____ 4. rancor

_____ 5. dilatory

_____ 6. paramour

_____ 7. feral

_____ 8. abrogate

Group 2

A. inclination	C. frown	E. ornate	G. scatter
B. original person	D. hierarchic level	F. lurk	H. coax

_____ 1. glower

_____ 2. dissipate

_____ 3. rococo

_____ 4. cajole

_____ 5. predilection

_____ 6. echelon

_____ 7. aborigine

_____ 8. skulk

Group 3

A. decrease	C. predict	E. magnificent	G. discourage
B. unity	D. relapse into crime	F. raid	H. conclusion

_____ 1. grandiose

_____ 2. dispirit

_____ 3. abate

_____ 4. closure

_____ 5. solidarity

_____ 6. prognosticate

_____ 7. incursion

_____ 8. recidivism

Group 4

A. shirk	C. disgrace	E. hodgepodge	G. commonplace
B. fester	D. cut short	F. concerned	H. bankruptcy

_____ 1. abase

_____ 2. solicitous

_____ 3. malinger

_____ 4. rankle

_____ 5. cliché

_____ 6. insolvency

_____ 7. truncate

_____ 8. pastiche

Unit 12 *(cont.)*

Answer Key

Pre-test Yourself

Group 1	**Group 2**	**Group 3**	**Group 4**
1. rancor	1. predilection	1. closure	1. rankle
2. paramour	2. skulked	2. prognosticate	2. abase
3. abrogate	3. aborigine	3. dispirit	3. cliché
4. feral	4. glower	4. recidivism	4. pastiche
5. mellifuous	5. rococo	5. solidarity	5. solicitous
6. dilatory	6. dissipate	6. incursion	6. insolvency
7. cachet	7. cajole	7. abate	7. malinger
8. jaundiced	8. echelon	8. grandiose	8. truncate

Quick Match

Group 1	**Group 2**	**Group 3**	**Group 4**
1. D	1. C	1. E	1. C
2. G	2. G	2. G	2. F
3. F	3. E	3. A	3. A
4. H	4. H	4. H	4. B
5. A	5. A	5. B	5. G
6. E	6. D	6. C	6. H
7. B	7. B	7. F	7. D
8. C	8. F	8. D	8. E

Unit 13

Pre-test Yourself

Group 1

archive	minutiae	devoid	stanch
insipid	overt	recompense	coddle

---

1. The teacher would often _____ her favorite students.

2. A solicitous nurse will _____ the flow of blood by pressing on the wound.

3. The manager of the pizza parlor did not give _____ to the trainees.

4. Documents and memorabilia from the history of the sport could be found in the _____.

5. The hungry boy was dismayed to find the refrigerator _____ of food.

6. The inventor considered the state of his wardrobe to be among the _____ that he did not concern himself with.

7. The orator had an _____ style that verged on the ultra-banal.

8. After a while, sneaky theft was abandoned, and workers were _____ in their thievery.

Group 2

antipathy	recondite	douse	stultify
broach	emend	taunt	clique

---

1. She felt her critics might _____ her creative output.

2. The professor felt that the textbook was too _____ for her intermediate students.

3. Whenever she would _____ the subject of marriage, her boyfriend seemed to develop a stomachache.

4. After losing his home and business to the flood, the man felt great _____ toward the river.

5. He might _____ the horrible things he has done and still be met with skepticism.

6. As a member of a particularly popular _____ in school, Bob was invited to most social events.

7. One should never _____ an electrical fire with water.

8. A crowd will _____ an outfielder after a third fielding error.

Unit 13 *(cont.)*

Pre-test Yourself *(cont.)*

Group 3

vindicate	stigma	imbibe	aver
rogue	disarray	perfunctory	transpire

---

1. Certain events must _____ in order for the plan to be fully implemented.

2. When the planning went wrong, the staff was confused and in _____.

3. Though he was found guilty, he knew that the evidence would eventually _____ him.

4. The broker turned out to be a _____ who bilked his customers.

5. He gave it a _____ perusal and then quickly discarded it.

6. People avoided him because he bore the _____ of his evil past.

7. Despite evidence to the contrary, he will _____ that he was telling the truth.

8. Because of his history of alcohol-related problems, he would not _____ the champagne at the ceremonial toast.

Group 4

fetish	actuate	sublimate	nexus
jettison	censure	paragon	extol

---

1. She was a _____ of virtue, and everyone praised her for her probity.

2. The school board may _____ the teacher for his unseemly behavior.

3. He became obsessed with the _____ and claimed it protected him from evil.

4. She could _____ her love after her child's death by bestowing it on orphans.

5. Firebrands _____ causes.

6. The crew will _____ some of its catch to stabilize the boat.

7. She acted as a _____ between the two corporations.

8. The successful storeowner could not help but _____ the virtues of hard work to his employees.

Unit 13 *(cont.)*

Words and Definitions

———— Group 1 ————

archive (AR kive): record; historical document
  Part of Speech: noun
  Example: Records of all of the students who have matriculated at the college were located in the school *archive*.
  Other Form(s): archival (adjective); archive (verb)

minutiae (my NOO shuh): trivial details; particulars
  Part of Speech: noun
  Example: Trivia and *minutiae* interested him the most.

devoid (di VOID): barren; completely lacking
  Part of Speech: adjective
  Example: Heartless people are *devoid* of true feelings.

stanch (STANCH): to stop; to thwart
  Part of Speech: verb
  Example: Tourniquets *stanch* the flow of blood from a wound.

insipid (in SIP id): uninteresting, lifeless
  Part of Speech: adjective
  Example: His *insipid* style bored readers.

overt (oh VERT): explicit; visible
  Part of Speech: adjective
  Example: His reasons were *overt* and clearly expressed.

recompense (REK um pents): payment; amends
  Part of Speech: noun
  Example: The injured driver expected *recompense* from the other driver's insurance carrier.

coddle (COD ul): to pamper; to spoil
  Part of Speech: verb
  Example: Some mothers *coddle* children who have temper tantrums.

Words and Definitions *(cont.)*

─────────────── **Group 2** ───────────────

antipathy (an TIP uh thee): loathing; hatred
 Part of Speech: noun
 Example: He despised the man and could not hide his *antipathy*.

recondite (REK un dite): little known; obscure
 Part of Speech: adjective
 Example: Philosophers often express themselves in *recondite* terms.

douse (DOUSE): to drench; to saturate
 Part of Speech: verb
 Example: Firemen attempted to *douse* the flames before they spread to other houses.

stultify (STUL ti fy): to neutralize; to render useless
 Part of Speech: verb
 Example: Conformist policies *stultify* creative thought.

broach (BROACH): to suggest; to mention
 Part of Speech: verb
 Example: When she *broached* the subject, he quickly changed it.

emend (e MEND): to edit; to revise
 Part of Speech: verb
 Example: Publishers *emend* raw manuscripts to make them more salable.
 Other Form(s): emendable (adjective); emendation (noun)

taunt (taunt): to jeer at; to deride
 Part of Speech: verb
 Example: Boxers are not permitted to pummel spectators who *taunt* them.

clique (KLIK): select group; small society
 Part of Speech: noun
 Example: The elite club formed a *clique* that opposed any policy change.

Unit 13 *(cont.)*

Words and Definitions *(cont.)*

Group 3

vindicate (VIN di kate): to acquit; to find blameless
  Part of Speech: verb
  Example: The man's testimony will finally *vindicate* him, and he will walk out a free man.
  Other Form(s): vindication (noun)

stigma (STIG muh): mark of disgrace; blemish
  Part of Speech: noun
  Example: He forever bore the *stigma* of his heinous crime.

imbibe (im BIBE): to drink; to quaff
  Part of Speech: verb
  Example: Students *imbibe* too much when they binge drink.

aver (uh VUR): to assert; to affirm
  Part of Speech: verb
  Example: The unconscious victim may yet *aver* the guilt of his attacker.

rogue (ROAG): scoundrel; unprincipled person
  Part of Speech: noun
  Example: *Rogues* are found wherever money changes hands.

disarray (dis uh RAY): disorder; disarrangement
  Part of Speech: noun
  Example: A key player's injury sent the team into *disarray*, and they lost the game.

perfunctory (per FUNK to ree): superficial; cursory
  Part of Speech: adjective
  Example: Professors should give thesis papers more than a *perfunctory* glance.

transpire (tran SPIRE): to happen; to occur
  Part of Speech: verb
  Example: Events *transpired* that could not be controlled.

Words and Definitions (cont.)

――――――――― **Group 4** ―――――――――

fetish (FET ish): an object believed to have magical powers; talisman
  Part of Speech: noun
  Example: The captain's *fetish* unnerved his officers.

actuate (AK choo ate): to incite; to inspire
  Part of Speech: verb
  Example: Local firebrands *actuated* the rebellion.

sublimate (SUB li mate): to redirect; to transform
  Part of Speech: verb
  Example: She *sublimated* all of her passion to her work after her love affair ended abruptly.
  Other Form(s): sublimation (noun)

nexus (NEKS us): link; tie
  Part of Speech: noun
  Example: A superhighway proved the *nexus* between the two countries.

jettison (JET i sun): to throw overboard; to expel
  Part of Speech: verb
  Example: Disabled airplanes *jettison* fuel before trying to land.

censure (SEN shure): to rebuke; to reprimand
  Part of Speech: verb
  Example: Members of the committee could *censure* the wayward member.

paragon (PARE uh gon): ideal; model
  Part of Speech: noun
  Example: Her exemplary behavior marked her as a *paragon* of decorousness.

extol (ex TOLE): to praise; to eulogize
  Part of Speech: verb
  Example: Speaker after speaker *extolled* the merits of the outstanding scholar.

Unit 13 (cont.)

Quick Match

Group 1

A. thwart	C. uninteresting	E. amends	G. pamper
B. explicit	D. record	F. particulars	H. barren

_____ 1. archive

_____ 2. minutiae

_____ 3. devoid

_____ 4. stanch

_____ 5. insipid

_____ 6. overt

_____ 7. recompense

_____ 8. coddle

Group 2

A. obscure	C. hatred	E. drench	G. neutralize
B. mention	D. deride	F. select group	H. edit

_____ 1. antipathy

_____ 2. recondite

_____ 3. douse

_____ 4. stultify

_____ 5. broach

_____ 6. emend

_____ 7. taunt

_____ 8. clique

Group 3

A. affirm	C. scoundrel	E. happen	G. drink
B. acquit	D. blemish	F. superficial	H. disorder

_____ 1. vindicate

_____ 2. stigma

_____ 3. imbibe

_____ 4. aver

_____ 5. rogue

_____ 6. disarray

_____ 7. perfunctory

_____ 8. transpire

Group 4

A. link	C. rebuke	E. inspire	G. magical object
B. redirect	D. praise	F. expel	H. ideal

_____ 1. fetish

_____ 2. actuate

_____ 3. sublimate

_____ 4. nexus

_____ 5. jettison

_____ 6. censure

_____ 7. paragon

_____ 8. extol

Unit 13 *(cont.)*

Answer Key

─────────────── **Pre-test Yourself** ───────────────

Group 1
1. coddle
2. stanch
3. recompense
4. archive
5. devoid
6. minutiae
7. insipid
8. overt

Group 2
1. stultify
2. recondite
3. broach
4. antipathy
5. emend
6. clique
7. douse
8. taunt

Group 3
1. transpire
2. disarray
3. vindicate
4. rogue
5. perfunctory
6. stigma
7. aver
8. imbibe

Group 4
1. paragon
2. censure
3. fetish
4. sublimate
5. actuate
6. jettison
7. nexus
8. extol

─────────────── **Quick Match** ───────────────

Group 1
1. D
2. F
3. H
4. A
5. C
6. B
7. E
8. G

Group 2
1. C
2. A
3. E
4. G
5. B
6. H
7. D
8. F

Group 3
1. B
2. D
3. G
4. A
5. C
6. H
7. F
8. E

Group 4
1. G
2. E
3. B
4. A
5. F
6. C
7. H
8. D

Unit 14

Pre-test Yourself

Group 1

ascribe	sable	demure	conflagration
pedagogy	imbroglio	bandy	revere

---

1. The great _____ was apparently started by a cow kicking over a lantern.

2. His pupils did very well on standardized tests, and no one questioned his
   _____.

3. The crimes that the prosecutor could _____ to the rogue were actually committed by someone else.

4. Her _____ and wistful manner captivated her audience.

5. After listening to a blues compilation record, the young guitarist began to _____ several of the old blues masters.

6. In dime romances, the heroine is described as having _____ hair and limpid eyes.

7. When standup comedians _____ words with customers, they are involving the customers in the show.

8. The _____ between the three nations led to worldwide tension.

Group 2

riposte	maxim	comport	patriarchy
deploy	goad	supple	bawdy

---

1. He gave a good _____ and scored against his opponent's advance.

2. The coach will _____ his players in a zone defense.

3. By the end of the evening, the bar was brimming with _____ folk.

4. Contortionists must have very _____ bodies.

5. The _____ may have been hackneyed, but there was some truth in it.

6. Suffragists fought for the right for a woman's voice to be heard in the
   _____.

7. Detectives may _____ the suspect into admitting damaging facts.

8. When the students show that they can _____ themselves well on the trip, they will be promised another trip as reward.

Unit 14 (cont.)

Pre-test Yourself (cont.)

Group 3

victuals	depredate	rabid	august
supercilious	orthodoxy	flagellate	carnage

1. Townspeople started hoarding _____ before the onset of the blizzard.

2. His _____ attitude towards his co-workers created a hostile officeplace environment.

3. The therapist's _____ prevented him from correctly diagnosing the patient.

4. Football fans who remove their shirts in freezing weather are _____.

5. The vandals were caught before they could _____ the premises.

6. Don't _____ yourself for minor errors.

7. Royalty's _____ presence caused a stir among the worshipers.

8. Caesar took no prisoners and left _____ on the battlefields.

Group 4

sanctimony	malleable	quest	contiguous
immutable	pedantry	transitory	radiate

1. Hypocrites and spurious reformers spout _____.

2. His _____ was obvious from his use of polysyllabic words to explain simple things.

3. The Irish found gold to be _____ and became the first people in the West to shape it.

4. The martyr's principles were _____, and this resulted in his death.

5. During his long and arduous _____ for success, the man alienated most of his closest friends.

6. The coughing spells were _____ and not considered a chronic condition.

7. The crack in the windshield appeared to start from a central point and _____ outward.

8. Their properties were _____, and so they shared certain chores.

Unit 14 (cont.)

Words and Definitions

─────────────── **Group 1** ───────────────

ascribe (uh SKRIBE): to attribute; to assign
    Part of Speech: verb
    Example: Researchers *ascribe* the writings to an ancient poet.

sable (SAY bul): black; somber
    Part of Speech: adjective
    Example: Mourners wore *sable* clothing at the requiem.

imbroglio (im BROH glee oh): complicated situation; confusion
    Part of Speech: noun
    Example: An *imbroglio* caused the cancellation of the event.

conflagration (con fluh GRAY shun): holocaust; uncontrolled fire
    Part of Speech: noun
    Example: Strong winds created a *conflagration* out of a landfill's spontaneous combustion.

pedagogy (PED uh go gee): science of teaching
    Part of Speech: noun
    Example: Universities are involved with *pedagogy*.
    Other Form(s): pedagogical (adjective)

demure (de MYOOR): shy; modest
    Part of Speech: adjective
    Example: She was a *demure* young lady who charmed just about everyone.

bandy (BAN dee): to toss about; to exchange
    Part of Speech: verb
    Example: When you *bandy* words, you are involved in word play.

revere (ri VEER): to worship; to venerate
    Part of Speech: verb
    Example: Worshippers *revere* the words of the prophet.
    Other Form(s): revered (adjective); reverence (noun)

Unit 14 *(cont.)*

Words and Definitions *(cont.)*

riposte (ri POST): retort; retaliatory action
Part of Speech: noun
Example: When he was confronted with hostility, he made a quick *riposte*.

maxim (MAX im): proverb; apothegm
Part of Speech: noun
Example: He spoke in *maxims* and reminded me of Aesop.

comport (kom PORT): to behave; to conduct
Part of Speech: verb
Example: The teacher told her that she must *comport* herself well under stress.
Other Form(s): comportment (noun)

patriarchy (PAY tree ar kee): male-led government
Part of Speech: noun
Example: Women resented the *patriarchy* because it ignored their needs.
Other Form(s): patriarchal (adjective)

deploy (de PLOY): to station; to place systematically
Part of Speech: verb
Example: Sherman *deployed* his troops in such a way that the enemy couldn't escape.
Other Form(s): deployment (noun)

goad (GOAD): to poke; to prompt
Part of Speech: verb
Example: His enemy's incitement *goaded* him into action.

supple (SUP ul): flexible; pliant
Part of Speech: adjective
Example: Gymnasts need *supple* bodies to do what they do.

bawdy (BAW dee): vulgar; obscene
Part of Speech: adjective
Example: Choristers sang *bawdy* songs that offended some in the audience.

Words and Definitions *(cont.)*

─────────────────── **Group 3** ───────────────────

victuals (VIT uls): edibles; food supplies
> **Part of Speech:** noun
> **Example:** Cowboys dined on *victuals* prepared by the camp chef.

depredate (DEP re date): to plunder; to rob
> **Part of Speech:** verb
> **Example:** Invading forces *depredated* the town and then burned it.

rabid (RA bid): extreme; fanatical
> **Part of Speech:** adjective
> **Example:** Sports mania creates *rabid* spectators.

august (aw GUST): redoubtable; majestic
> **Part of Speech:** adjective
> **Example:** His *august* presence required all to kneel and ask for mercy.

supercilious (soo per SILL ee us): haughty; condescending
> **Part of Speech:** adjective
> **Example:** He scoffed at them with a *supercilious* air.
> **Other Form(s):** superciliousness (noun)

orthodoxy (OR tho dox ee): custom; norm
> **Part of Speech:** noun
> **Example:** *Orthodoxy* required that certain steps, and only those steps, should be taken.
> **Other Form(s):** orthodox (adjective)

flagellate (FLAJ eh late): to flog; to scourge
> **Part of Speech:** verb
> **Example:** Ancient ascetics *flagellated* themselves to atone for their sins.

carnage (CAR nej): slaughter; butchery
> **Part of Speech:** noun
> **Example:** The train wreck caused considerable *carnage* and death.

Words and Definitions *(cont.)*

--- **Group 4** ---

sanctimony (SANK ti mo nee): hypocrisy; false piety
  Part of Speech: noun
  Example: Beware the reformer who is full of *sanctimony*.
  Other Form(s): sanctimonious (adjective)

malleable (MAL ee uh bul): pliable; flexible
  Part of Speech: adjective
  Example: Precious *malleable* metals are shaped into jewelry.

quest (KWEST): search; pursuit
  Part of Speech: noun
  Example: Each year, the teams in the National Football league are involved in a *quest* to win the Super Bowl.

contiguous (kon TIG yoo us): touching; connecting
  Part of Speech: adjective
  Example: Semi-detached houses are *contiguous* and share a common wall.

immutable (i MYOO tuh bul): unchangeable; enduring
  Part of Speech: adjective
  Example: Through all the years, he remained *immutable* and true to his tenets.

pedantry (PED un tree): pretension; affectation
  Part of Speech: noun
  Example: *Pedantry* has no place in a classroom.
  Other Form(s): pedantic (adjective); pedant (noun); pedantize (verb)

transitory (TRANS i tor ee): temporary; evanescent
  Part of Speech: adjective
  Example: Life is *transitory*; death is not.

radiate (RAY dee ate): to send out; to scatter
  Part of Speech: verb
  Example: Streets in Washington, D.C., *radiate* around the Capitol.

Unit 14 (cont.)

Quick Match

Group 1

A. complicated situation   C. exchange   E. holocaust   G. modest
B. assign   D. teaching   F. venerate   H. black

_____ 1. ascribe   _____ 5. pedagogy
_____ 2. sable   _____ 6. demure
_____ 3. imbroglio   _____ 7. bandy
_____ 4. conflagration   _____ 8. revere

Group 2

A. retort   C. conduct   E. vulgar   G. flexible
B. male government   D. prompt   F. apothegm   H. station

_____ 1. riposte   _____ 5. deploy
_____ 2. maxim   _____ 6. goad
_____ 3. comport   _____ 7. supple
_____ 4. patriarchy   _____ 8. bawdy

Group 3

A. fanatical   C. edibles   E. plunder   G. flog
B. haughty   D. redoubtable F. slaughter   H. norm

_____ 1. victuals   _____ 5. supercilious
_____ 2. depredate   _____ 6. orthodoxy
_____ 3. rabid   _____ 7. flagellate
_____ 4. august   _____ 8. carnage

Group 4

A. search   C. touching   E. unchangeable   G. send out
B. affectation D. temporary   F. pliable   H. hypocrisy

_____ 1. sanctimony   _____ 5. immutable
_____ 2. malleable   _____ 6. pedantry
_____ 3. quest   _____ 7. transitory
_____ 4. contiguous   _____ 8. radiate

Unit 14 (cont.)

Answer Key

Pre-test Yourself

Group 1	Group 2	Group 3	Group 4
1. conflagration	1. riposte	1. victuals	1. sanctimony
2. pedagogy	2. deploy	2. supercilious	2. pedantry
3. ascribe	3. bawdy	3. orthodoxy	3. malleable
4. demure	4. supple	4. rabid	4. immutable
5. revere	5. maxim	5. depredate	5. quest
6. sable	6. patriarchy	6. flagellate	6. transitory
7. bandy	7. goad	7. august	7. radiate
8. imbroglio	8. comport	8. carnage	8. contiguous

Quick Match

Group 1	Group 2	Group 3	Group 4
1. B	1. A	1. C	1. H
2. H	2. F	2. E	2. F
3. A	3. C	3. A	3. A
4. E	4. B	4. D	4. C
5. D	5. H	5. B	5. E
6. G	6. D	6. H	6. B
7. C	7. G	7. G	7. D
8. F	8. E	8. F	8. G

Unit 15

Pre-test Yourself

Group 1			
attenuate	rampant	glean	debunk
choreograph	incipient	sate	extrude

1. After hours of boundless enthusiasm, the toddler's energy finally began to
_____.

2. The grinder will _____ meat for the sausage casings.

3. Dandelions were _____ in his fields in the spring.

4. Even after finishing the entire pint of ice cream, he could not _____ his appetite.

5. His problems were _____ and could be handled at their source.

6. When the farmers were finished harvesting, the poor would _____ whatever lay in the fields.

7. He may _____ the board's finding but be met with obstinence.

8. Flight leaders _____ the low flight patterns.

Group 2			
retribution	disburse	scenario	masochism
translucent	balk	parameter	celerity

1. Since he seemed to intentionally cause most of his problems, many said he was engaged in
_____.

2. Before the assignment was given, the leader described each _____ within which the attack was to be carried out.

3. When his car was vandalized by his former friend, the teenager sought
_____.

4. The soldier knew that he would _____ at the drill sergeant's orders and be punished harshly.

5. Pursers on ships _____ money.

6. Had he not acted with _____, the problem would have been worse.

7. She described the _____ to attentive students so that they could act on it.

8. Some gemstones are _____, while others are opaque.

Unit 15 (cont.)

Pre-test Yourself (cont.)

Group 3

protract	implacable	vicarious	kudos
exhume	stymie	charlatan	resurgent

1. Despite all of the employee's efforts, the boss appeared _____; and he fired her within the first month.

2. They will _____ the body if new evidence suggests foul play.

3. He was a mountebank, a quack, and a _____.

4. The networks may _____ the halftime break in order to air the news conference in its entirety.

5. The father derived a _____ pleasure from watching his son hit the game-winning home run in the state finals.

6. Art deco, the popular style of the '20s and '30s, became _____ in the '80s.

7. The defense could _____ the other team's attempts to score the game-winning touchdown.

8. The winning team received _____ from the crowd.

Group 4

matriarchy	chortle	pallor	exhort
appurtenance	transcribe	disparity	stolid

1. Stenographers _____ from their shorthand into longhand.

2. The decoration was an _____ that could easily be done away with.

3. More than one student may _____ if the austere teacher trips and falls.

4. He is a _____ individual who never complains.

5. When a queen rules, a country is a _____.

6. The _____ between what was collected and what was handed in caused suspicion.

7. At least 20 people will _____ the home team to victory.

8. Since he was incarcerated 24 hours a day, he soon developed a deathly _____.

Unit 15 (cont.)

Words and Definitions

─────── Group 1 ───────

attenuate (uh TEN yoo ate): to thin out; to extend
Part of Speech: verb
Example: A child's self-absorption should *attenuate* as he matures.

rampant (RAM pent): unchecked; flourishing
Part of Speech: adjective
Example: Virulent strains of the toxin were *rampant* in the lower township.

glean (GLEEN): to gather; to collect
Part of Speech: verb
Example: The students might *glean* valuable information from the substitute teacher.

debunk (de BUNK): to expose falseness; to discredit
Part of Speech: verb
Example: Although he tried, the columnist could not *debunk* the honesty and righteousness of the televangelist.

choreograph (KOR ee oh graf): to create a dance; to plan out
Part of Speech: verb
Example: She will *choreograph* her first feature film when she is just 23 years old.
Other Form(s): choreography (noun); choreographer (noun)

incipient (in SIP ee ent): commencing; inceptive
Part of Speech: adjective
Example: Plans for the festival were in their *incipient* stages and had to be modified later on.
Other Form(s): incipience (noun)

sate (SATE): to satisfy fully; to fill to the point of excess
Part of Speech: verb
Example: Some gourmands are not happy unless they *sate* themselves.

extrude (ex TRUDE): to force out; to expel
Part of Speech: verb
Example: Workers *extruded* the pipe and pushed it into the conduit.

Words and Definitions *(cont.)*

_____ **Group 2** _____

retribution (reh tri BYOO shen): repayment; revenge
   Part of Speech: noun
   Example: He was financially hurt by the fiasco and wanted *retribution* from those responsible.

disburse (dis BURS): to distribute; to mete out
   Part of Speech: noun
   Example: Cashiers *disburse* tickets to movie-goers.
   Other Form(s): disbursement (noun)

scenario (suh NARE ee o): situation; outline
   Part of Speech: noun
   Example: Before making any decisions, he always considered the worst possible *scenario* that could result from his actions.

masochism (MAS uh kizm): enjoyment of pain; self-destruction
   Part of Speech: noun
   Example: Accident-prone people may suffer from *masochism*.
   Other Form(s): masochistic (adjective)

translucent (trans LOO sent): permitting light to pass through but diffusing it so that personsor objects on the other side are not clearly visible.
   Part of Speech: adjective
   Example: The window glass in some rooms is *translucent* rather than transparent.

balk (BALK): to draw back initially; to false start
   Part of Speech: verb
   Example: When she was asked to lead the parade, she *balked* at first but finally agreed.
   Other Form(s): balk (noun)

parameter (puh RAM eh tur): limit; boundary
   Part of Speech: noun
   Example: The *parameters* for the new sport were published in a rulebook.

celerity (se LARE i tee): swiftness; rapidity
   Part of Speech: noun
   Example: He reacted with great *celerity* when he saw the flames approaching.
   Other Form(s): celeritous (adjective)

Words and Definitions *(cont.)*

─────────────── **Group 3** ───────────────

protract (pro TRAKT): to lengthen; to drag out
  Part of Speech: verb
  Example: Unfortunately, he *protracted* his speech and bored everyone.
  Other Form(s): protracted (adjective)

implacable (im PLAK uh bul): unforgiving; unpleasable
  Part of Speech: adjective
  Example: His need for revenge was *implacable*, and no one could talk him out of his mood.

vicarious (vy CARE ee us): empathetic; substitutive
  Part of Speech: adjective
  Example: The lonely man got a *vicarious* enjoyment from watching groups of people in the park.

kudos (KOO doze): praise; acclaim
  Part of Speech: noun
  Example: *Kudos* were given to the successful candidate.

exhume (ex OOM): to dig up; to disinter
  Part of Speech: verb
  Example: Coroners *exhume* bodies when questions arise about the cause of death.
  Other Form(s): exhumation (noun)

stymie (STY mee): to block; to thwart
  Part of Speech: verb
  Example: The platoon used snipers hidden in strategic locations in order to *stymie* the enemy's advances.

charlatan (SHAR luh ten): quack; impostor
  Part of Speech: noun
  Example: The doctor was a *charlatan* who misdiagnosed many of his patients.

resurgent (ree SUR jent): rising again; re-emergent
  Part of Speech: adjective
  Example: Certain styles become *resurgent* years after becoming dated.
  Other Form(s): resurgence (noun)

Unit 15 *(cont.)*

Words and Definitions *(cont.)*

───────────── **Group 4** ─────────────

matriarchy (MAY tree ar kee): female authority; female dominance
   Part of Speech: noun
   Example: Queens rule in a matriarchy.
   Other Form(s): *matriarchal* (adjective)

chortle (CHOR tul): to chuckle; to guffaw
   Part of Speech: verb
   Example: When the teacher's teeth slipped out, students in the front row *chortled*.

pallor (PAL ur): extreme paleness; pallidness
   Part of Speech: noun
   Example: Lengthy illness left him with a ghostly *pallor*.

disparity (dih SPARE i tee): variance; difference
   Part of Speech: noun
   Example: The prosecuting attorney made numerous mentions of the *disparity* between the defendant's initial statement and her testimony on the witness stand.

appurtenance (a PUR te nance): auxiliary; accessory
   Part of Speech: noun
   Example: He felt as if he were an *appurtenance* and that his work was no longer needed.

transcribe (tran SKRIBE): to copy; to transliterate
   Part of Speech: verb
   Example: Her secretary *transcribed* her notes and made a permanent record of them.
   Other Form(s): transcription (noun)

exhort (ex ORT): to urge; to encourage
   Part of Speech: verb
   Example: Home fans *exhorted* the team and cheered it on to victory.

stolid (STAHL id): unemotional; stoical
   Part of Speech: adjective
   Example: He had a wooden and *stolid* personality that prevented him from smiling.
   Other Form(s): stolidity (noun); stolidness (noun)

Unit 15 (cont.)

Quick Match

Group 1

A. discredit   C. plan out   E. thin out   G. gather

B. force out   D. unchecked   F. satisfy   H. commencing

_____ 1. attenuate   _____ 5. choreograph

_____ 2. rampant   _____ 6. incipient

_____ 3. glean   _____ 7. sate

_____ 4. debunk   _____ 8. extrude

Group 2

A. self-abuse   C. refuse   E. situation   G. distribute

B. payment   D. swiftness   F. clear   H. boundary

_____ 1. retribution   _____ 5. translucent

_____ 2. disburse   _____ 6. balk

_____ 3. scenario   _____ 7. parameter

_____ 4. masochism   _____ 8. celerity

Group 3

A. acclaim   C. impostor   E. thwart   G. rising again

B. substitutive   D. disinter   F. unpleasable   H. drag out

_____ 1. protract   _____ 5. exhume

_____ 2. implacable   _____ 6. stymie

_____ 3. vicarious   _____ 7. charlatan

_____ 4. kudos   _____ 8. resurgent

Group 4

A. auxiliary   C. female rule   E. variance   G. paleness

B. stoical   D. urge   F. guffaw   H. copy

_____ 1. matriarchy   _____ 5. appurtenance

_____ 2. chortle   _____ 6. transcribe

_____ 3. pallor   _____ 7. exhort

_____ 4. disparity   _____ 8. stolid

Unit 15 (cont.)

Answer Key

Pre-test Yourself

Group 1

1. attenuate
2. extrude
3. rampant
4. sate
5. incipient
6. glean
7. debunk
8. choreograph

Group 2

1. masochism
2. parameter
3. retribution
4. balk
5. disburse
6. celerity
7. scenario
8. translucent

Group 3

1. implacable
2. exhume
3. charlatan
4. protract
5. vicarious
6. resurgent
7. stymie
8. kudos

Group 4

1. transcribe
2. appurtenance
3. chortle
4. stolid
5. matriarchy
6. disparity
7. exhort
8. pallor

Quick Match

Group 1

1. E
2. D
3. G
4. A
5. C
6. H
7. F
8. B

Group 2

1. B
2. G
3. E
4. A
5. F
6. C
7. H
8. D

Group 3

1. H
2. F
3. B
4. A
5. D
6. E
7. C
8. G

Group 4

1. C
2. F
3. G
4. E
5. A
6. H
7. D
8. B

Unit 16

Pre-test Yourself

Group 1

| mutate | crone | wrangle | proximity |
| asperity | séance | exigency | recalcitrant |

---

1. He wasn't happy with the circumstances and voiced his dislike with _____.

2. _____ requires quick thinking and actions.

3. That drug can _____ the cellular makeup of the laboratory rats.

4. His _____ to the radiation caused his mutation.

5. In the mirror, she saw a _____ and not the vibrant young woman she had once been.

6. He is an intractable nuisance who takes pride in being _____.

7. The medium conducted a _____ in an attempt to channel the widow's recently deceased husband.

8. The woman knew that if she left her sons unsupervised they would _____ incessantly.

Group 2

| axiom | providence | gerontology | increment |
| nettle | stint | reprobate | discomfit |

---

1. Most of the family viewed the cousin as a _____ incapable of accomplishing anything positive.

2. Under the agreement, she received a salary _____ each year.

3. He knew the insult would _____ him.

4. Descartes' famous _____ translates to "I think, therefore I am."

5. The fans feared that the shattering defeat would _____ the home team.

6. I love turkey, so please do not _____ on giving me a lot.

7. Her promotion came through _____ alone, because she didn't deserve it.

8. As life-expectancy becomes longer and longer, _____ becomes more important.

Unit 16 (cont.)

Pre-test Yourself (cont.)

Group 3

gesticulate	simian	mete	ignominy
asseverate	pallid	balmy	remit

---

1. As he left the country for exile, he was heaped with _____ and vituperation.

2. The artist gave the caveman in his drawing many _____ characteristics.

3. We looked forward to _____ weather after the storm.

4. He warned us by _____ wildly and jumping up and down.

5. He will _____ his innocence in the matter.

6. The company would not _____ the rebate for several months.

7. The queen will _____ out justice to each and every reprobate.

8. Fear turned his complexion _____.

Group 4

loathe	scurry	narcissism	transfix
paucity	inane	cataclysm	requisite

---

1. The highway billboard was deemed dangerous because it could _____ passing drivers and distract them from the road.

2. In retrospect, she was able to see that the breakup with her fiance was not the _____ she had initially felt it to be.

3. She handed in the _____ forms and got her real estate license.

4. He could see a field mouse _____ before the mowing machine.

5. _____ dialogue doomed the play to failure.

6. His _____ estranged him from most people he became acquainted with.

7. After several negative experiences, she will _____ the taste of meatloaf.

8. His paper contained a _____ of ideas, and the professor gave it an "F."

Unit 16 *(cont.)*

Words and Definitions

――――――― **Group 1** ―――――――

mutate (MYOO tate): to change; to alter
Part of Speech: verb
Example: When cells *mutate*, birth defects can result.
Other Form(s): mutation (noun); mutational (adjective)

crone (KRONE): hag; withered woman
Part of Speech: noun
Example: In the fairy tale, the ancient *crone* became a beautiful young woman.

wrangle (RANG gul): to argue; to quarrel
Part of Speech: verb
Example: It is uncomfortable to watch a married couple *wrangle* in public.

proximity (prox IM i tee): nearness; closeness
Part of Speech: noun
Example: The *proximity* of the oil spill to the reservoir caused great alarm.
Other Form(s): proximate (adjective)

asperity (as PARE i tee): bitterness; acrimony
Part of Speech: noun
Example: The *asperity* in her voice sent chills up his spine.

séance (SAY onse): session; meeting
Part of Speech: noun
Example: Several crones sat in a *séance* and conjured the dead.

exigency (EX i jen see): urgency; crisis
Part of Speech: noun
Example: In times of *exigency*, rapid response is necessary.
Other Form(s): exigent (adjective)

recalcitrant (re KAL si trant): unmanageable; intractable
Part of Speech: adjective
Example: The students proved *recalcitrant* and learned little.
Other Form(s): recalcitrance (noun)

─────────────────── **Group 2** ───────────────────

axiom (AX ee um): widely accepted principle; self-evident truth
  Part of Speech: noun
  Example: It is an *axiom* that food is necessary for survival.
  Other Form(s): axiomatic (adjective)

providence (PROV i dence): fate; destiny
  Part of Speech: noun
  Example: She believed that *providence* was on her side and that she would become famous.
  Other Form(s): provident (adjective)

gerontology (jer on TOL uh gee): study of old age
  Part of Speech: noun
  Example: He began to study *gerontology* when he realized he had come to old age.
  Other Form(s): gerontologist (noun)

reprobate (REH pro bate): miscreant; immoral person
  Part of Speech: noun
  Example: He is an untrustworthy *reprobate* who should be incarcerated.
  Other Form(s): reprobation (noun); reprobate (adjective)

nettle (NET ul): to irk; to irritate
  Part of Speech: verb
  Example: His annoying habits *nettled* and generally unsettled his coworkers.

discomfit (dis KUM fit): to thwart; to baffle
  Part of Speech: verb
  Example: When the armies met, one thoroughly *discomfited* the other.
  Other Form(s): discomfiture (noun)

stint (STINT): to restrict; to limit
  Part of Speech: verb
  Example: Misers *stint* on spending money.

increment (IN kreh ment): addition; supplement
  Part of Speech: noun
  Example: Her pay went up in *increments* of three percent for each year of service.
  Other Form(s): incremental (adjective)

———————————— **Group 3** ————————————

gesticulate (jes TIK yoo late): to make gestures; to express (with gestures)

Part of Speech: verb

Example: He would often *gesticulate* wildly when he lectured, and it annoyed some members of his audience.

Other Form(s): gesticulation (noun); gesticulative (adjective)

simian (SIM ee un): like an ape; like a monkey

Part of Speech: adjective

Example: The famous cartoon character was drawn to have a *simian* look to his face.

Other Form(s): simian (noun)

mete (MEAT): to distribute; to deal out

Part of Speech: verb

Example: The judge *meted* out justice with an even hand.

ignominy (IG naw mi nee): dishonor; disgrace

Part of Speech: noun

Example: He carried the stigma of his *ignominy* with him for the rest of his life.

Other Form(s): ignominious (adjective)

asseverate (a SEV ur ate): to assert; to affirm

Part of Speech: verb

Example: Lawyers for the defendant *asseverated* the defendant's innocence.

pallid (PAL id): pale; ashen

Part of Speech: adjective

Example: In the movie, the man became *pallid* when he saw the ghost.

balmy (BALM ee): mild; soothing

Part of Speech: adjective

Example: Temperature climates produce some *balmy* days.

Other Form(s): balminess (noun)

remit (re MIT): to send payment; to transmit

Part of Speech: verb

Example: He *remitted* the funds when the bank called for them.

Other Form(s): remittance (noun)

Unit 16 (cont.)

Words and Definitions (cont.)

———————— Group 4 ————————

loathe (LOWTH): hate; detest
Part of Speech: verb
Example: Although the actors *loathe* the smell of French fries, they continue to film fast-food commercials.

scurry (SKUR ee): to scamper; to move hurriedly
Part of Speech: verb
Example: Meadow voles *scurried* away as the mower came closer.

narcissism (NAR si sizm): self-love; egocentricity
Part of Speech: noun
Example: He loved himself to the point of *narcissism.*
Other Form(s): narcissistic (adjective); narcissist (noun)

transfix (trans FIX): to stun; to overawe
Part of Speech: verb
Example: The speaker's sudden outburst *transfixed* the crowd.

paucity (PAW si tee): scarcity; sparsity
Part of Speech: noun
Example: Drought often leads to a *paucity* of food.

inane (in ANE): silly; absurd
Part of Speech: adjective
Example: Remarks made to the tribunal were so *inane* that they were immediately dismissed.
Other Form(s): inanity (noun)

cataclysm (KAT uh klizm): upheaval; a great change
Part of Speech: noun
Example: The hurricane created a *cataclysm* in the tiny coastal village.
Other Form(s): cataclysmic (adjective)

requisite (REK wi sit): required; necessary
Part of Speech: adjective
Example: Courses in philology are *requisite* for future language scholars.

Unit 16 (cont.)

Quick Match

Group 1

| A. unmanageable | C. quarrel | E. crisis | G. change |
| B. closeness | D. hag | F. bitterness | H. meeting to contact spirits |

_____ 1. mutate   _____ 5. asperity

_____ 2. crone   _____ 6. séance

_____ 3. wrangle   _____ 7. exigency

_____ 4. proximity   _____ 8. recalcitrant

Group 2

| A. thwart | C. self-evident truth | E. restrict | G. study of old age |
| B. fate | D. irritate | F. addition | H. miscreant |

_____ 1. axiom   _____ 5. nettle

_____ 2. providence   _____ 6. discomfit

_____ 3. gerontology   _____ 7. stint

_____ 4. reprobate   _____ 8. increment

Group 3

| A. ape-like | C. make payment | E. disgrace | G. assert |
| B. pale | D. mild | F. gesture | H. distribute |

_____ 1. gesticulate   _____ 5. asseverate

_____ 2. simian   _____ 6. pallid

_____ 3. mete   _____ 7. balmy

_____ 4. ignominy   _____ 8. remit

Group 4

| A. self-love | C. sparseness | E. detest | G. scamper |
| B. upheaval | D. necessary | F. overawe | H. absurd |

_____ 1. loathe   _____ 5. paucity

_____ 2. scurry   _____ 6. inane

_____ 3. narcissism   _____ 7. cataclysm

_____ 4. transfix   _____ 8. requisite

Unit 16 *(cont.)*

Answer Key

Pre-test Yourself

Group 1	Group 2	Group 3	Group 4
1. asperity	1. reprobate	1. ignominy	1. transfix
2. exigency	2. increment	2. simian	2. cataclysm
3. mutate	3. nettle	3. balmy	3. requisite
4. proximity	4. axiom	4. gesticulating	4. scurry
5. crone	5. discomfit	5. asseverate	5. inane
6. recalcitrant	6. stint	6. remit	6. narcissism
7. séance	7. providence	7. mete	7. loathe
8. wrangle	8. gerontology	8. pallid	8. paucity

Quick Match

Group 1	Group 2	Group 3	Group 4
1. G	1. C	1. F	1. E
2. D	2. B	2. A	2. G
3. C	3. G	3. H	3. A
4. B	4. H	4. E	4. F
5. F	5. D	5. G	5. C
6. H	6. A	6. B	6. H
7. E	7. E	7. D	7. B
8. A	8. F	8. C	8. D

Unit 17

Pre-test Yourself

Group 1

sumptuous	centripetal	vexatious	autonomy
refractory	educe	parley	macabre

1. The tiny island nation finally achieved political _____ in 1926.

2. Her probing questions often _____ responses from the audience.

3. The _____ force of a massive black hole is what causes the Milky Way to spin.

4. He was an intransigent, intractable, and _____ young man.

5. Dark tales of the _____ were popular in Victorian times.

6. For the vacationing couple, several minor annoyances proved to be _____.

7. Silk draperies and velvet upholstery gave the room a _____ look.

8. Politicians in the caucus held a formal _____.

Group 2

rampart	incongruous	badger	suffrage
expunge	mordant	castigate	periphery

1. The dean of discipline would often _____ the fraternity house for its wild parties.

2. Ironically, women had to fight for _____ in a democratic society.

3. Tanks rolled right over the _____ and swept into the town.

4. His explanations were _____ with the evidence, and the jury pronounced him guilty.

5. He was told that he would have to wait two years before the court would _____ the crime from his record.

6. Centrifugal force pushed the ball bearing out to the _____ of the wheel.

7. H.L. Mencken, the astute and acerbic writer, had a _____ wit.

8. Students continually _____ the administration for a students' lounge.

Unit 17 *(cont.)*

Pre-test Yourself *(cont.)*

Group 3

| perturb | augur | randy | impeach |
| satire | denigrate | cache | tenuous |

1. _____ tendencies led him into salacious situations.

2. He had a shaky and _____ hold on delegates to the convention.

3. Senators may _____ a president but then vote to acquit him.

4. Adventurers hunted for the legendary pirate's _____.

5. The _____ lampooned the new and growing society of cellular-phone users.

6. When you _____ a person, you attempt to lower the person in everyone's esteem.

7. A broken shoelace early in the morning may _____ bad luck for the day ahead.

8. Catastrophes did not daunt him, but minor problems _____ him no end.

Group 4

| engender | nihilism | disperse | assiduous |
| rescind | visceral | saunter | berserk |

1. He followed his _____ feeling, and it turned out that his intuition was correct.

2. Police will usually _____ the crowd at an accident scene.

3. _____ attention to detail was his trademark.

4. Riot squads dispersed the _____ crowds rioting in the streets.

5. The legislature could _____ the old act and replace it with new legislation.

6. The nervous boy may _____ past the group of cheerleaders, but his anxiety is evident.

7. The drama might _____ a catharsis in the audience.

8. The musician was known for his iconoclastic ideals and his espousal of _____.

Unit 17 *(cont.)*

Words and Definitions

―――――――――――― Group 1 ――――――――――――

sumptuous (SUMP choo us): rich; lavish
   Part of Speech: adjective
   Example: Roman emperors held *sumptuous* banquets and were generally hedonistic.

centripetal (sen TRIP e tul): spiraling inward; spinning toward the center
   Part of Speech: adjective
   Example: Water going down a drain has *centripetal* motion.

vexatious (vex AY shus): bothersome; pestering
   Part of Speech: adjective
   Example: Everyone but her husband found high-pitched laugh to be *vexatious*.
   Other Form(s): vexation (noun)

autonomy (au TAWN o mee): self-rule; independence
   Part of Speech: noun
   Example: Repression usually follows a small area's quest for *autonomy*.
   Other Form(s): autonomous (adjective)

refractory (re FRAKT uh ree): uncooperative; unmanageable
   Part of Speech: adjective
   Example: *Refractory* students learn little in school.

educe (i DOOS): to elicit; to evoke
   Part of Speech: verb
   Example: A good teacher *educes* answers from students.

parley (PAR lay): discussion; conference
   Part of Speech: noun
   Example: All concerned parties in the autonomy negotiations met at a general *parley*.
   Other Form(s): parley (verb)

macabre (muh KAH bruh): gruesome; grim
   Part of Speech: adjective
   Example: Stephen King delights in the *macabre*.

Unit 17 *(cont.)*

Words and Definitions *(cont.)*

───────────── **Group 2** ─────────────

rampart (RAM part): fortification; embankment
    Part of Speech: noun
    Example: The *rampart* separated the town from the outside world.

incongruous (in KON groo us): inconsistent; out of place
    Part of Speech: adjective
    Example: Anyone under six feet tall looks *incongruous* in an NBA game.
    Other Form(s): incongruity (noun)

castigate (KAS ti gate): to punish; to chastise
    Part of Speech: verb
    Example: The judge *castigated* the defendant, sentencing him to jail.
    Other Form(s): castigation (noun); castigator (noun); castigatory (adjective)

suffrage (SUF rij): right to vote
    Part of Speech: noun
    Example: Susan B. Anthony was a seminal figure for women's *suffrage* in the United States.
    Other Form(s): suffragist (noun)

expunge (ex PUNJ): to erase; to remove
    Part of Speech: verb
    Example: When she was found innocent, the court *expunged* any record of her appearance.

mordant (MOR dant): caustic; corrosive
    Part of Speech: adjective
    Example: The critic's savage review contained many *mordant* observations.

badger (BADJ ur): to provoke; to harass
    Part of Speech: verb
    Example: He told the teacher another student *badgered* him into fracas.

periphery (pe RIF er ee): edge; perimeter
    Part of Speech: noun
    Example: Hermits live on the *periphery* of society.
    Other Form(s): peripheral (adjective)

Unit 17 *(cont.)*

Words and Definitions *(cont.)*

───────────── **Group 3** ─────────────

perturb (pur TURB): to disturb; to fluster
> **Part of Speech:** verb
> **Example:** He *perturbed* many present with his intransigent behavior.

augur (AW gur): to predict; to prophesy
> **Part of Speech:** verb
> **Example:** Red skies at night supposedly *augur* a good day ahead.
> **Other Form(s):** augury (noun)

randy (RAN dee): lascivious; lustful
> **Part of Speech:** adjective
> **Example:** She accused him of *randy* behavior and showed him to the door.

impeach (im PEACH): to accuse; to charge
> **Part of Speech:** verb
> **Example:** The lawyer *impeached* his own witness and lost the case.
> **Other Form(s):** impeachable (noun)

satire (SA tire): caricature; parody
> **Part of Speech:** noun
> **Example:** *Satire* is often the best weapon against tyranny.
> **Other Form(s):** satirical (adjective); satirist (noun)

denigrate (DEN i grate): to defame; to vilify
> **Part of Speech:** verb
> **Example:** He *denigrated* his opponent in public debate.

cache (KASH): hiding place; repository
> **Part of Speech:** noun
> **Example:** Pirates of old stored their treasure in out-of-the-way *caches*.

tenuous (TEN yoo us): slight; insubstantial
> **Part of Speech:** adjective
> **Example:** She garnered only a *tenuous* grasp of the professor's lecture, and so she hired a tutor.

Unit 17 *(cont.)*

Words and Definitions *(cont.)*

——————————— Group 4 ———————————

engender (en JEN dur): to cause; to produce
Part of Speech: verb
Example: Good behavior should *engender* good behavior.

nihilism (NY il izm): the rejection of moral authority
Part of Speech: noun
Example: *Nihilism* is incongruous with religion.
Other Form(s): nihilist (noun); nihilistic (adjective)

disperse (dis PURS): to scatter; to disseminate
Part of Speech: verb
Example: The police *disperse* the crowd by using tear gas.
Other Form(s): dispersal (noun)

assiduous (uh SID joo us): attending closely; persevering
Part of Speech: adjective
Example: Her *assiduous* efforts resulted in a successful campaign.

rescind (re SIND): to revoke; to abrogate
Part of Speech: verb
Example: The dean *rescinded* his regulation on smoking.

visceral (VIS ur al): intuitive; of or from the gut
Part of Speech: adjective
Example: She had a *visceral* feeling that tragedy would result from the situation.

saunter (SAUN tur): to stroll; to promenade
Part of Speech: verb
Example: When he *sauntered* into the room late, the instructor chastised him.

berserk (bur SURK): frenzied; hysterical
Part of Speech: adjective
Example: Loss after loss drove her into *berserk* behavior.

Unit 17 *(cont.)*

Quick Match

Group 1

A. pestering	C. lavish	E. unmanageable	G. self-rule
B. gruesome	D. conference	F. spiraling inward	H. evoke

_____ 1. sumptuous

_____ 2. centripetal

_____ 3. vexatious

_____ 4. autonomy

_____ 5. refractory

_____ 6. educe

_____ 7. parley

_____ 8. macabre

Group 2

A. chastise	C. harass	E. edge	G. right to vote
B. fortification	D. erase	F. inconsistent	H. caustic

_____ 1. rampart

_____ 2. incongruous

_____ 3. castigate

_____ 4. suffrage

_____ 5. expunge

_____ 6. mordant

_____ 7. badger

_____ 8. periphery

Group 3

A. lustful	C. disturb	E. vilify	G. parody
B. slight	D. prophesy	F. accuse	H. hiding place

_____ 1. perturb

_____ 2. augur

_____ 3. randy

_____ 4. impeach

_____ 5. satire

_____ 6. denigrate

_____ 7. cache

_____ 8. tenuous

Group 4

A. persevering	C. frenzied	E. renunciation	G. revoke
B. scatter	D. intuitive	F. promenade	H. produce

_____ 1. engender

_____ 2. nihilism

_____ 3. disperse

_____ 4. assiduous

_____ 5. rescind

_____ 6. visceral

_____ 7. saunter

_____ 8. berserk

Unit 17 *(cont.)*

Answer Key

Pre-test Yourself

Group 1
1. autonomy
2. educe
3. centripetal
4. refractory
5. macabre
6. vexatious
7. sumptuous
8. parley

Group 2
1. castigate
2. suffrage
3. rampart
4. incongruous
5. expunge
6. periphery
7. mordant
8. badger

Group 3
1. randy
2. tenuous
3. impeach
4. cache
5. satire
6. denigrate
7. augur
8. perturb

Group 4
1. visceral
2. disperse
3. assiduous
4. berserk
5. rescind
6. saunter
7. engender
8. nihilism

Quick Match

Group 1
1. C
2. F
3. A
4. G
5. E
6. H
7. D
8. B

Group 2
1. B
2. F
3. A
4. G
5. D
6. H
7. C
8. E

Group 3
1. C
2. D
3. A
4. F
5. G
6. E
7. H
8. B

Group 4
1. H
2. E
3. B
4. A
5. G
6. D
7. F
8. C

Unit 18

Pre-test Yourself

Group 1

sibilant	adjudge	tepid	incredulous
digress	requiem	chicanery	voracity

1. Steam escaping from the valve gave off a _____ sound.

2. Mourners wore somber clothing at the _____.

3. His rash remarks left listeners _____.

4. If she does _____ from the script, the result may be a powerful extempore speech.

5. Her feelings for him were _____ and noncommittal.

6. The prosecutor may _____ the defendant sane enough to stand trial.

7. Grizzlies attack with great _____ and force when defending their cubs.

8. The election's loser claimed the winner won by _____.

Group 2

transcendent	immolation	disparage	ravage
stricture	categorical	protagonist	acumen

1. There was no doubt about his _____ answer.

2. Many primitive societies believed that _____ appeased the gods.

3. Experience and _____ made her a most valuable member of the team.

4. The farmer used pesticides to control the insects before they had a chance to _____ the entire crop.

5. Babe Ruth's abilities as a baseball player were _____, and many think of him of more as a mythological figure than a real person.

6. A severe _____ was imposed on the college basketball program.

7. Nick Adams is the name of the _____ in many of Hemingway's stories.

8. It seemed that the critic would _____ and belittle the author's entire body of work.

Unit 18 *(cont.)*

Pre-test Yourself *(cont.)*

Group 3

aphorism	redoubtable	verisimilitude	stipulate
discern	inadvertent	chary	pique

---

1. Once she could _____ what the problem was, she quickly remedied it.

2. Having been the victim of several burglaries made him _____ about letting anyone have the keys.

3. The advisor spouted an _____ when he could have offered more personalized advice.

4. Her talents were _____, and few would challenge her reputation.

5. The athlete insisted that his contract _____ that he was entitled to use the team's private jet.

6. The high-budget commercial will _____ the public's interest in the movie.

7. Some artists are known for their realism and _____.

8. No one hinted that his actions were anything but _____ and unpremeditated.

Group 4

captious	indigence	semantic	dispassionate
vanguard	respite	cogent	plebeian

---

1. Scientists must remain _____ about their experiments and see the results objectively.

2. The three-day trek was so tiring that a _____ had to be taken at mid-journey.

3. The problem was not in substance but in _____ interpretation.

4. Poor harvests drove the farm families into _____ and squalor.

5. _____ remarks by prejudiced critics upset the novelist.

6. He was an active person who often appeared in the _____ of a movement.

7. The lawyer's arguments were _____ and well received by the judicial panel.

8. His tastes were _____ and certainly not the tastes of a connoisseur.

Unit 18 (cont.)

Words and Definitions

————————— Group 1 —————————

sibilant (SIB i lant): hissing; whistling
   Part of Speech: adjective
   Example: A faulty radiator gave off *sibilant* sounds.
   Other Form(s): sibilance (noun)

adjudge (ad JUDGE): to ordain; to pronounce
   Part of Speech: verb
   Example: He was *adjudged* competent to stand trial.

tepid (TEP id): moderately warm; unenthusiastic
   Part of Speech: adjective
   Example: His responses were weak and *tepid*.

incredulous (in KRED yoo lus): disbelieving; distrusting
   Part of Speech: adjective
   Example: Onlookers were *incredulous* as the acrobat did his loops in the air.

digress (di GRESS): to deviate; to depart (from the main subject)
   Part of Speech: verb
   Example: It is difficult to get a point across if you *digress*.
   Other Form(s): digression (noun); digressive (adjective)

requiem (REK wee um): mass for the dead; hymn for the dead
   Part of Speech: noun
   Example: Sable was the color required for the *requiem*.

chicanery (shi KAY nuh ree): trickery; deception
   Part of Speech: noun
   Example: His great fortune was the result of his *chicanery* in the stock market.

voracity (vuh RAS i tee): ravenousness; great eagerness
   Part of Speech: noun
   Example: The scholar's great learning came from the *voracity* of her reading.
   Other Form(s): voracious (adjective); voraciousness (noun)

Words and Definitions *(cont.)*

―――――――――――― **Group 2** ――――――――――――

transcendent (tran SEN dent): exceeding; unique
  Part of Speech: surpassing
  Example: Music can make *transcendent* changes in people.
  Other Form(s): transcendental (adjective)

immolation (im o LAY shun): sacrifice; sacrificial offer
  Part of Speech: noun
  Example: Mayans used the *immolation* of young women as a way of pleasing the gods.
  Other Form(s): immolate (verb); immolator (noun)

disparage (di SPARE udj): to belittle; to deprecate
  Part of Speech: verb
  Example: Teachers who *disparage* a student in class risk losing the respect of the other students.
  Other Form(s): disparaging (adjective)

ravage (RA vidj): to destroy; to lay waste
  Part of Speech: verb
  Example: Floods *ravaged* the valley and destroyed the crops.

stricture (STRIK chur): restriction; restraint
  Part of Speech: noun
  Example: Government *stricture* prevented business from flourishing.

categorical (kat e GORE i kul): inclusive; encompassing
  Part of Speech: adjective
  Example: She had *categorical* knowledge in the music field.

protagonist (pro TAG uh nist): principal figure; leader (of a cause, etc.)
  Part of Speech: noun
  Example: Hemingway's *protagonists* are usually macho men.

acumen (a CUE men): keen insight; penetration
  Part of Speech: noun
  Example: Great *acumen* is required in order to master any field of study.

Words and Definitions (*cont.*)

--- Group 3 ---

aphorism (AF or izm): proverb; apothegm
  Part of Speech: noun
  Example: Pretentious people often speak in *aphorisms*.
  Other Form(s): aphoristic (adjective); aphorist (noun); aphorize (verb)

redoubtable (re DOWT uh bul): formidable; worthy of respect
  Part of Speech: adjective
  Example: Babe Ruth's ability to hit home runs was *redoubtable*.

verisimilitude (ver i si MIL i tood): appearance of reality; seeming truth
  Part of Speech: noun
  Example: The best zoos recreate their animals' natural habitats with great *verisimilitude*.

stipulate (STIP yoo late): to specify; to determine
  Part of Speech: verb
  Example: College registrars *stipulate* when money is due for registration.
  Other Form(s): stipulation (noun); stipulator (noun)

discern (di SERN): to see; to perceive
  Part of Speech: verb
  Example: She could *discern* the need for improvement and went right to work.
  Other Form(s): discernment (noun); discernible (adjective)

inadvertent (in ad VUR tent): accidental; mistaken
  Part of Speech: adjective
  Example: The referee decided that the contact was *inadvertent*, and so he did not call a penalty.

chary (CHAIR ee): careful; cautious
  Part of Speech: adjective
  Example: She was *chary* of making new acquaintances.

pique (PEEK): to arouse; to interest
  Part of Speech: verb
  Example: Intellectual inquiry *piqued* his mind.

Unit 18 *(cont.)*

Words and Definitions *(cont.)*

captious (CAP shus): nagging; fault-finding
    Part of Speech: adjective
    Example: *Captious* people picked on everything she said.

indigence (IN di jents): poverty; destitution
    Part of Speech: noun
    Example: Unemployment caused *indigence* throughout the entire valley.
    Other Form(s): indigent (adjective)

semantic (se MAN tik): pertaining to meaning in language
    Part of Speech: adjective
    Example: Linguists are interested in *semantic* investigation.
    Other Form(s): semantics (noun)

dispassionate (dis PA shin it): calm; impartial
    Part of Speech: adjective
    Example: How he could remain *dispassionate* in the face of tragedy puzzled everyone.

vanguard (VAN gawrd): leading position; forefront
    Part of Speech: noun
    Example: Pablo Picasso was in the *vanguard* of abstract painters.

respite (REH spit): intermission; rest
    Part of Speech: noun
    Example: They took few *respites* during the long trek across the mountains.

cogent (CO jent): convincing; compelling
    Part of Speech: adjective
    Example: The chairperson indicated that only *cogent* arguments were welcome.

plebeian (plih BEE un): common; ignoble
    Part of Speech: adjective
    Example: His taste in art was *plebeian* and provincial.
    Other Form(s): plebeian (noun); plebeianism (noun)

Unit 18 (cont.)

Quick Match

Group 1

A. slightly warm   C. disbelieving   E. pronounce   G. hissing
B. trickery   D. death mass   F. deviate   H. ravenousness

_____ 1. sibilant   _____ 5. digress

_____ 2. adjudge   _____ 6. requiem

_____ 3. tepid   _____ 7. chicanery

_____ 4. incredulous   _____ 8. voracity

Group 2

A. belittle   C. encompassing   E. devastate   G. sacrifice
B. leading figure   D. insight   F. exceeding   H. restraint

_____ 1. transcendent   _____ 5. stricture

_____ 2. immolation   _____ 6. categorical

_____ 3. disparage   _____ 7. protagonist

_____ 4. ravage   _____ 8. acumen

Group 3

A. see   C. determine   E. formidable   G. appearance of reality
B. apothegm   D. mistaken   F. cautious   H. arouse

_____ 1. aphorism   _____ 5. discern

_____ 2. redoubtable   _____ 6. inadvertent

_____ 3. verisimilitude   _____ 7. chary

_____ 4. stipulate   _____ 8. pique

Group 4

A. meaning (in language)   C. fault-finding   E. rest   G. common
B. compelling   D. impartial   F. poverty   H. forefront

_____ 1. captious   _____ 5. vanguard

_____ 2. indigence   _____ 6. respite

_____ 3. semantic   _____ 7. cogent

_____ 4. dispassionate   _____ 8. plebeian

Unit 18 *(cont.)*

Answer Key

——————— Pre-test Yourself ———————

Group 1

1. sibilant
2. requiem
3. incredulous
4. digress
5. tepid
6. adjudge
7. voracity
8. chicanery

Group 2

1. categorical
2. immolation
3. acumen
4. ravage
5. transcendent
6. stricture
7. protagonist
8. disparage

Group 3

1. discern
2. chary
3. aphorism
4. redoubtable
5. stipulate
6. pique
7. verisimilitude
8. inadvertent

Group 4

1. dispassionate
2. respite
3. semantic
4. indigence
5. captious
6. vanguard
7. cogent
8. plebeian

——————— Quick Match ———————

Group 1

1. G
2. E
3. A
4. C
5. F
6. D
7. B
8. H

Group 2

1. F
2. G
3. A
4. E
5. H
6. C
7. B
8. D

Group 3

1. B
2. E
3. G
4. C
5. A
6. D
7. F
8. H

Group 4

1. C
2. F
3. A
4. D
5. H
6. E
7. B
8. G

Unit 19

Pre-test Yourself

Group 1

expatiate	kowtow	animosity	façade
pinnacle	cognizant	sedentary	dismantle

---

1. She hid her grief behind a _____ of levity.

2. Mount Everest's _____ was first reached in the 1950s.

3. His _____ came across in his derisive and acerbic comments.

4. The professor will _____ on the difficult process so that the students can understand.

5. When he failed to secure investors for his invention, the inventor decided to _____ the prototype.

6. Her awareness became acute when she became _____ of the causes of the disease.

7. Sycophants _____ to people they want to impress.

8. Weight problems often accompany _____ lifestyles.

Group 2

haughty	feasible	zest	explicate
incarcerate	pillory	caricature	onerous

---

1. He was so bad at what he did that he was a _____ of what should be done.

2. The police officer may _____ the dog owner if she does not keep her pet on a leash.

3. Backpacking soon became an _____ task for the expedition's porters.

4. She was _____ and supercilious when challenged.

5. The nasty editorial should _____ the unpopular politician.

6. Despite her advanced age, she skied, played basketball and tennis, and generally had a _____ for life.

7. The concert promoter decided that it would not be economically or logistically _____ to reschedule the cancelled event.

8. The film was so bad that not even the director could fully _____ the plot.

Unit 19 *(cont.)*

Pre-test Yourself *(cont.)*

Group 3

beguile	corroborate	aberration	moot
quaff	putrescent	resuscitate	discord

1. Crows can eat _____ road kill without getting sick.

2. She was so charming that she could _____ everyone she encountered.

3. If witnesses _____ his story, he will be exonerated.

4. The Adirondack ice storm of 1998 was, we hope, an _____.

5. Medical technicians can often _____ an unconscious victim.

6. A person can _____ too much water and become ill.

7. The answer became _____ when the question no longer mattered.

8. _____ on the issue split the town into partisan factions.

Group 4

ersatz	totemic	conjure	repartee
diffuse	soppy	assimilate	palliate

1. Constant immersion made his clothes _____.

2. Great cities _____ immigrants quickly.

3. Nurses _____ pain.

4. The flag was flown at all times as a _____ statement.

5. Witches _____ ghosts on Halloween.

6. They threw the wooden shack together and made it an _____ home.

7. He told a joke, in the hope that he might _____ the tense situation.

8. Their badinage and bantering provided pointed _____.

Unit 19 (cont.)

Words and Definitions

Group 1

expatiate (ex PAY shee ate): to explain fully; to elaborate
   Part of Speech: verb
   Example: Einstein would often *expatiate* for hours upon how light works.
   Other Form(s): expatiation (noun); expatiatory (adjective)

kowtow (kow TOW): to grovel; to genuflect
   Part of Speech: verb
   Example: Courtiers *kowtowed* to the ruling monarch.

animosity (an i MOS i tee): hatred; loathing
   Part of Speech: noun
   Example: The speaker's *animosity* was obvious from his tone of voice.

façade (fuh SOD): front; pretense
   Part of Speech: noun
   Example: In the face of tragedy, the protagonist put up a solid *facade*.

pinnacle (PIN uh kul): summit; peak
   Part of Speech: noun
   Example: When he became manager of the firm, he reached his long-sought *pinnacle*.

cognizant (KOG ni zunt): aware; conscious
   Part of Speech: adjective
   Example: Citizens became *cognizant* of the tax levy only after newspapers alerted them.
   Other Form(s): cognizance (noun)

sedentary (SED en tare ee): stationary; immobile
   Part of Speech: adjective
   Example: A *sedentary* lifestyle led to his obesity.

dismantle (dis MAN tul): to take apart; to strip
   Part of Speech: verb
   Example: Workers *dismantled* the aging ship.

Words and Definitions *(cont.)*

───────────── **Group 2** ─────────────

haughty (HAW tee): proud; arrogant
> **Part of Speech:** adjective
> **Example:** His *haughty* and supercilious attitudes angered many.

feasible (FEE zuh bul): able to be accomplished; possible
> **Part of Speech:** adjective
> **Example:** The company decided that it would not be financially *feasible* to move its headquarters.
> **Other Form(s):** feasibility (noun)

zest (ZEST): liveliness; spirit
> **Part of Speech:** noun
> **Example:** Her *zest* for life was sometimes misinterpreted by critics.

explicate (EX pli kate): to elucidate; to explain
> **Part of Speech:** verb
> **Example:** The teacher *explicated* the text for the students.

incarcerate (in KAR sur ate): to imprison; to confine
> **Part of Speech:** verb
> **Example:** The judge thought it was unnecessary to *incarcerate* the petty thief.
> **Other Form(s):** incarceration (noun)

pillory (PIL uh ree): to expose to ridicule; to abuse
> **Part of Speech:** verb
> **Example:** Art experts *pilloried* the painter and told people to avoid his work.

caricature (KARE i kuh chur): to parody; to satirize
> **Part of Speech:** verb
> **Example:** Cartoonists *caricatured* the man easily because he had large ears.
> **Other Form(s):** caricature (noun); caricatural (adjective); caricaturist (noun)

onerous (ON er us): burdensome; irksome
> **Part of Speech:** adjective
> **Example:** *Onerous* tasks are the least welcome.

Words and Definitions *(cont.)*

─────────── Group 3 ───────────

beguile (be GYLE): to charm; to delight
  Part of Speech: verb
  Example: Her winning ways *beguiled* even the most skeptical of her observers.
  Other Form(s): beguilement (noun)

quaff (KWOF): to drink; to imbibe
  Part of Speech: verb
  Example: He *quaffed* great tankards of ale and became queasy.

corroborate (ko ROB ur ate): to verify; to confirm
  Part of Speech: verb
  Example: Witnesses *corroborated* his story, and the judge acquitted him.
  Other Form(s): corroboration (noun); corroborator (noun)

putrescent (pyoo TRES ent): rotting; fetid
  Part of Speech: adjective
  Example: The food became *putrescent* after sitting in the sun for several days.
  Other Form(s): putrescence (noun)

aberration (ab uh RAY shun): deviation from the norm; anomaly
  Part of Speech: noun
  Example: Doctors have difficulty explaining medical *aberrations*.

resuscitate (re SUS i tate): to restore life; to restore vigor
  Part of Speech: verb
  Example: An infusion of money *resuscitated* the failing company.
  Other Form(s): resuscitation (noun)

moot (MOOT): debatable; arguable
  Part of Speech: adjective
  Example: They quibbled over the *moot* point of which tenor was better.

discord (DIS kord): disharmony; disunity
  Part of Speech: noun
  Example: General *discord* followed the Supreme Court decision.
  Other Form(s): discordant (adjective)

Words and Definitions *(cont.)*

─────────────── **Group 4** ───────────────

ersatz (ER sats): replacement; artificial
    Part of Speech: adjective
    Example: Without the proper ingredients, she had to make an *ersatz* tuna casserole.

totemic (to TEM ik): symbolic; emblematic
    Part of Speech: adjective
    Example: Certain village artifacts were *totemic* in nature and impractical for use.

conjure (KON jur): to summon by magic; to evoke
    Part of Speech: verb
    Example: The poem's images *conjured* memories of the game for the retired ballplayer.
    Other Form(s): conjurer (noun); conjuration (noun)

repartee (reh par TEE): witty reply; banter
    Part of Speech: noun
    Example: Oscar Wilde was known for his acerbic wit and scintillating *repartee*.

diffuse (dih FYOOS): to disperse; to dissipate
    Part of Speech: verb
    Example: Westerly winds *diffused* the smoke from the fire.

soppy (SOP ee): soggy; soaked
    Part of Speech: adjective
    Example: His socks and shoes were *soppy* from his walking in the rain.

assimilate (uh SIM i late): to absorb; to take in
    Part of Speech: adjective
    Example: Great cities *assimilate* immigrants better than rural areas do.
    Other Form(s): assimilation (noun)

palliate (PAL ee ate): to mitigate; to alleviate
    Part of Speech: verb
    Example: The analgesic balm *palliated* the pain and made it bearable.
    Other Form(s): palliative (adjective, noun)

Unit 19 (cont.)

Quick Match

Group 1

A. hatred	C. strip	E. immobile	G. fawn
B. summit	D. aware	F. elaborate	H. pretense

_____ 1. expatiate

_____ 2. kowtow

_____ 3. animosity

_____ 4. façade

_____ 5. pinnacle

_____ 6. cognizant

_____ 7. sedentary

_____ 8. dismantle

Group 2

A. parody	C. abuse	E. explain	G. possible
B. confine	D. spirit	F. burdensome	H. arrogant

_____ 1. haughty

_____ 2. feasible

_____ 3. zest

_____ 4. explicate

_____ 5. incarcerate

_____ 6. pillory

_____ 7. caricature

_____ 8. onerous

Group 3

A. anomaly	C. restore to life	E. disunity	G. fetid
B. confirm	D. delight	F. imbibe	H. arguable

_____ 1. beguile

_____ 2. quaff

_____ 3. corroborate

_____ 4. putrescent

_____ 5. aberration

_____ 6. resuscitate

_____ 7. moot

_____ 8. discord

Group 4

A. soaked	C. replacement	E. absorb	G. mitigate
B. dissipate	D. evoke	F. symbolic	H. witty reply

_____ 1. ersatz

_____ 2. totemic

_____ 3. conjure

_____ 4. repartee

_____ 5. diffuse

_____ 6. soppy

_____ 7. assimilate

_____ 8. palliate

Unit 19 *(cont.)*

Answer Key

──────────── **Pre-test Yourself** ────────────

Group 1
1. façade
2. pinnacle
3. animosity
4. expatiate
5. dismantle
6. cognizant
7. kowtow
8. sedentary

Group 2
1. caricature
2. incarcerate
3. onerous
4. haughty
5. pillory
6. zest
7. feasible
8. explicate

Group 3
1. putrescent
2. beguile
3. corroborate
4. aberration
5. resuscitate
6. quaff
7. moot
8. discord

Group 4
1. soppy
2. assimilate
3. palliate
4. totemic
5. conjure
6. ersatz
7. diffuse
8. repartee

──────────── **Quick Match** ────────────

Group 1
1. F
2. G
3. A
4. H
5. B
6. D
7. E
8. C

Group 2
1. H
2. G
3. D
4. E
5. B
6. C
7. A
8. F

Group 3
1. D
2. F
3. B
4. G
5. A
6. C
7. H
8. E

Group 4
1. C
2. F
3. D
4. H
5. B
6. A
7. E
8. G

Unit 20

Pre-test Yourself

Group 1

prolific	detritus	abrade	truculence
carnal	reprimand	emeritus	smirch

---

1. He was an intractable student who showed _____ toward his instructors.

2. Dissonant music will usually _____ the orthodox sensibility.

3. The general may _____ the soldier in front of the other troops.

4. His _____ needs led him into compromising situations.

5. Tabloids _____ and traduce the reputations of famous people.

6. At the time of his retirement, Babe Ruth was the most _____ home-run hitter in the history of professional baseball.

7. When he retired, he was offered the position of professor _____.

8. _____ from the manufacturing plant entered the river and polluted it.

Group 2

abeyance	proliferate	diabolic	tyro
catalyst	rapacious	encumber	slake

---

1. Marothoners _____ their thirst many times during a race.

2. Until plans were complete, the project was held in _____.

3. The soldiers' _____ invasion of the town left little of it standing.

4. Instigators are the _____ needed in revolutionary movements.

5. He was not a seasoned actor, and, as a _____, he made a lot of mistakes.

6. The football player did not let his broken finger _____ his ability to catch the ball.

7. Dandelions _____ during the spring.

8. His plans were cunning, _____, and insidious.

Unit 20 *(cont.)*

Pre-test Yourself *(cont.)*

Group 3

scotch	effigy	temerity	collude
ratiocinate	diametrical	procrastinate	abject

---

1. All great thinkers _____ before putting forth their ideas.

2. People who _____ are putting off the inevitable.

3. The director will _____ our plans for improvising on the script because he is a purist.

4. He had the _____ to call himself an orphan after killing his parents.

5. When companies _____ to fix prices, consumers pay the price.

6. Nihilism and religion are in more or less _____ opposition to each other.

7. An _____ of the unpopular mayor was burned in the village square.

8. Indigence such as theirs could only be described as _____ poverty.

Group 4

diffidence	capitulate	adduce	ephemeral
shibboleth	taciturn	prevaricate	rationale

---

1. Her _____ prevented her from being promoted.

2. When you _____ on the witness stand, you commit perjury.

3. Since their ammunition ran out, the soldiers will _____.

4. Her wishes for glory were _____ and insubstantial.

5. Diffident people tend to be _____ people.

6. He mitigated the pain of his failure with a _____ that was really a rationalization.

7. As a _____, people referred to the glib group "motor-mouths."

8. Please don't _____ something that is really no more than your opinion.

Unit 20 *(cont.)*

Words and Definitions

───────────── Group 1 ─────────────

prolific (pro LIF ik): abundant; copious
   Part of Speech: adjective
   Example: Joyce Carol Oates is a *prolific* writer, having many books to her credit.

detritus (di TRY tus): debris; rubbish
   Part of Speech: noun
   Example: Society treated the sociopath like *detritus* and moved to incarcerate him.

abrade (uh BRADE): to wear down; to chafe
   Part of Speech: verb
   Example: Her mordant remarks *abraded* her associates, and they eschewed her.
   Other Form(s): abrasive (adjective); abrasion (noun)

truculence (TRUK yoo lents): savagery; fierceness
   Part of Speech: noun
   Example: His aggressiveness and *truculence* frightened possible allies.
   Other Form(s): truculent (adjective); truculency (noun)

carnal (KAR nul): sensuous; voluptuous
   Part of Speech: adjective
   Example: Caligula had *carnal* interests that shocked his subjects.
   Other Form(s): carnality (noun)

reprimand (REP ri mand): to chastise; to admonish
   Part of Speech: verb
   Example: The principal *reprimanded* those students who behaved poorly.

emeritus (eh MER ih tus): honorary; titular
   Part of Speech: adjective
   Example: His position as dean *emeritus* kept him on the campus.

smirch (SMURCH): to dishonor; to defame
   Part of Speech: verb
   Example: Tabloids *smirch* famous people's names to titillate the popular consciousness.

Words and Definitions *(cont.)*

──────────────── **Group 2** ────────────────

abeyance (uh BAY ents): suspension; intermission
   Part of Speech: noun
   Example: She was not ready to proceed, so all plans were held in *abeyance*.
   Other Form(s): abeyant (adjective)

proliferate (pro LIF ur ate): to spread; to reproduce
   Part of Speech: verb
   Example: Dandelions *proliferate* so quickly, I have given up on eliminating them.
   Other Form(s): proliferation (noun); proliferative (adjective); proliferator (noun)

diabolic (di uh BOL ik): devilish; wicked
   Part of Speech: adjective
   Example: Hitler dealt in *diabolic* ways with his political problems.

tyro (TY ro): beginner; novice
   Part of Speech: noun
   Example: It is risky business to place a *tyro* in a leading role.

catalyst (KAT uh list): agent that causes change
   Part of Speech: noun
   Example: The small rebellion acted as a *catalyst* for the revolution.

rapacious (ra PAY shus): predatory; ravenous
   Part of Speech: adjective
   Example: The invading troops became a *rapacious* marauding hoard.

encumber (en KUM bur): to burden; to impede
   Part of Speech: verb
   Example: Climbing the mountain was difficult because her overstuffed pack *encumbered* her.

slake (SLAYK): to satisfy; to assuage
   Part of Speech: verb
   Example: The disgruntled employee *slaked* his desire for revenge by sabotaging his boss's presentation.

Words and Definitions *(cont.)*

—————————————————— **Group 3** ——————————————————

scotch (SKOTCH): to thwart; to frustrate
> **Part of Speech:** verb
> **Example:** An injury to their best player *scotched* their hopes of winning the championship.

effigy (EF i jee): image; likeness
> **Part of Speech:** noun
> **Example:** If a politician is disliked, he or she is likely to be burned in *effigy*.

temerity (teh MER i tee): rashness; audacity
> **Part of Speech:** noun
> **Example:** The multi-millionaire athlete showed *temerity* when he whined publicly about being underpaid.

collude (kuh LUDE): to conspire; to plot
> **Part of Speech:** verb
> **Example:** The judge found that the men *colluded* to commit the crime.
> **Other Form(s):** collusion (noun)

ratiocinate (ra she AHS ih nayt): to reason; to use logic
> **Part of Speech:** verb
> **Example:** The famous detective was known for his ability to *ratiocinate* and, eventually, solve any mystery.
> **Other Form(s):** ratiocination (noun); ratiocinative (adjective); ratiocinator (noun)

diametrical (di uh MET ri kul): contrary; antithetical
> **Part of Speech:** adjective
> **Example:** Their views are *diametrical*, and it is unlikely that they will ever concur.

procrastinate (pro KRAS ti nate): to delay; to put off
> **Part of Speech:** verb
> **Example:** He felt that he did his best work when he *procrastinated* and was forced to meet a tight deadline.
> **Other Form(s):** procrastination (noun); procrastinator (noun); prcrastinatory (adjective)

abject (AB jekt): degraded; wretched
> **Part of Speech:** adjective
> **Example:** *Abject* living conditions overtly affected the indigent aborigines.

───────────────────────────── **Group 4** ─────────────────────────────

diffidence (DIF i dents): shyness; apprehension
   Part of Speech: noun
   Example: Sometimes *diffidence* is a virtue; other times, it is a character defect.
   Other Form(s): diffident (adjective)

shibboleth (SHIB eh leth): group peculiarity; distinguishing phrase, custom, etc.
   Part of Speech: noun
   Example: "Gnarly" was a *shibboleth* of surfers in the '70s and '80s.

capitulate (kuh PIT choo late): to surrender; to yield
   Part of Speech: verb
   Example: The losing army *capitulated* to the overwhelming enemy forces.
   Other Form(s): capitulation (noun); capitulator (noun); capitulatory (adjective)

taciturn (TAS i turn): reserved; uncommunicative
   Part of Speech: adjective
   Example: Diffident people are often *taciturn* and laconic.
   Other Form(s): taciturnity (noun)

adduce (a DOOS): to cite as evidence; to offer as proof
   Part of Speech: verb
   Example: The prosecution *adduced* the DNA match to persuade the jury of the defendant's guilt.

prevaricate (pre VAIR i kate): to lie; to misrepresent
   Part of Speech: verb
   Example: When you *prevaricate* under oath, you commit perjury.
   Other Form(s): prevarication (noun); prevaricator (noun)

ephemeral (e FEM ur ul): transitory; temporary
   Part of Speech: adjective
   Example: Perhaps because he knew the joyous feeling would be *ephemeral*, he relished it all the more.

rationale (ra shu NAL): basis; fundamental reason
   Part of Speech: noun
   Example: The fans questioned the team's *rationale* for signing the aging athlete to a lucrative, long-term contract.

Unit 20 *(cont.)*

Quick Match

Group 1

A. honorary	C. sensuous	E. abundant	G. defame
B. admonish	D. debris	F. chafe	H. fierceness

_____ 1. prolific

_____ 2. detritus

_____ 3. abrade

_____ 4. truculence

_____ 5. carnal

_____ 6. reprimand

_____ 7. emeritus

_____ 8. smirch

Group 2

A. beginner	C. agent that causes change	E. spread	G. suspension
B. satisfy	D. ravenous	F. burden	H. devilish

_____ 1. abeyance

_____ 2. proliferate

_____ 3. diabolic

_____ 4. tyro

_____ 5. catalyst

_____ 6. rapacious

_____ 7. encumber

_____ 8. slake

Group 3

A. plot	C. delay	E. wretched	G. reason
B. thwart	D. antithetical	F. rashness	H. image

_____ 1. scotch

_____ 2. effigy

_____ 3. temerity

_____ 4. collude

_____ 5. ratiocinate

_____ 6. diametrical

_____ 7. procrastinate

_____ 8. abject

Group 4

A. cite as evidence	C. basis	E. group peculiarity	G. temporary
B. yield	D. reserved	F. lie	H. apprehension

_____ 1. diffidence

_____ 2. shibboleth

_____ 3. capitulate

_____ 4. taciturn

_____ 5. adduce

_____ 6. prevaricate

_____ 7. ephemeral

_____ 8. rationale

Unit 20 *(cont.)*

Answer Key

─────────── **Pre-test Yourself** ───────────

Group 1
1. truculence
2. abrade
3. reprimand
4. carnal
5. smirch
6. prolific
7. emeritus
8. detritus

Group 2
1. slake
2. abeyance
3. rapacious
4. catalyst
5. tyro
6. encumber
7. proliferate
8. diabolic

Group 3
1. ratiocinate
2. procrastinate
3. scotch
4. temerity
5. collude
6. diametrical
7. effigy
8. abject

Group 4
1. diffidence
2. prevaricate
3. capitulate
4. ephemeral
5. taciturn
6. rationale
7. shibboleth
8. adduce

─────────── **Quick Match** ───────────

Group 1
1. E
2. D
3. F
4. H
5. C
6. B
7. A
8. G

Group 2
1. G
2. E
3. H
4. A
5. C
6. D
7. F
8. B

Group 3
1. B
2. H
3. F
4. A
5. G
6. D
7. C
8. E

Group 4
1. H
2. E
3. B
4. D
5. A
6. F
7. G
8. C

Unit 21

Pre-test Yourself

Group 1

propensity	colloquial	accrete	sallow
epilogue	discourse	rationalize	tableau

---

1. His _____ for lying left him with no trusting friends.

2. Intelligent _____ requires knowledge.

3. Metal shaving _____ to magnets.

4. Humans _____ catastrophes so that they can live with them.

5. _____ speech is the casual speech of the people.

6. Her clever last testament was an _____ to her witty life.

7. The senior class presented the photographer with a pretty _____.

8. Malnutrition caused her skin to become _____.

Group 2

precursor	access	sedate	emblematic
coterie	thespian	dapper	reciprocal

---

1. _____ to the laboratory was available only through a security post.

2. The movie star's _____ followed a respectable distance behind her.

3. Some states have _____ agreements on extradition.

4. He was a wild young man, but as he grew older he became more _____.

5. Her father wouldn't let her become a _____ because he thought theater a base calling.

6. Corruption at the lowest levels of the government was _____ of what went on at the top.

7. Believe it or not, the abacus was a _____ to the modern computer.

8. A white tie, a carnation in his lapel, and an ivory-headed cane made him a _____ man.

Pre-test Yourself *(cont.)*

Group 3

| trammel | recant | alacrity | edification |
| preempt | cosmic | seclude | decadence |

---

1. Children act with _____ when candy is available.

2. A natural disaster will almost always _____ regularly-scheduled programming on TV.

3. The prosecution might _____ their star witness, as they fear for his safety.

4. On the eve of the election, the columnist may _____ her earlier prediction that the governor would never be elected president.

5. He thought on a large and _____ scale.

6. _____ at the top levels of any government will eventually bring it down.

7. Science teachers perform experiments for their students' _____.

8. Police _____ those who they arrest.

Group 4

| shackle | dearth | corona | precipitate |
| arboreal | turbid | emanate | recoup |

---

1. Many felt that the arrest of the uprising's leader would _____ a widespread rebellion.

2. The _____ around the moon was an optical illusion caused by humid air.

3. Frank Lloyd Wright created an _____ house that suited its sylvan setting.

4. Paddle-wheel boats created _____ water along their routes.

5. Guards _____ dangerous prisoners when they transfer them.

6. Nearby residents often complain about the noxious fumes that _____ from the city dump.

7. The dethroned king could _____ his throne.

8. A _____ of food led to widespread starvation.

Words and Definitions

--- **Group 1** ---

propensity (pro PEN si tee): inclination; predilection
Part of Speech: noun
Example: His *propensity* for imbibing large quantities of alcohol damaged his liver.

colloquial (kuh LOW kwee ul): informal; ordinary
Part of Speech: adjective
Example: *Colloquial* words are acceptable for everyday conversation.
Other Form(s): colloquialism (noun)

accrete (uh KREET): to increase; to grow together
Part of Speech: verb
Example: Silt *accreted* at the harbor mouth and created a delta.
Other Form(s): accretion (noun)

sallow (SAL oh): sickly yellow; pale brown
Part of Speech: adjective
Example: Lack of sunlight gave the prisoner a *sallow* look.

epilogue (EP i log): postscript; conclusion
Part of Speech: noun
Example: Authors sometimes use *epilogues* to sum up their books.

discourse (DIS kors): to address; to lecture
Part of Speech: verb
Example: The head doctor *discoursed* on the merits of a particular procedure.

rationalize (RA shun uh lize): to explain away; to make excuses for
Part of Speech: verb
Example: When he failed at something, he couldn't face the truth; instead, he would *rationalize* his failure.
Other Form(s): rationalization (noun)

tableau (TAB low): striking scene; vivid description
Part of Speech: noun
Example: Students created a living *tableau* for the photographer.

Unit 21 *(cont.)*

Words and Definitions *(cont.)*

─────────── **Group 2** ───────────

precursor (pre KUR sor): predecessor; forerunner
    Part of Speech: noun
    Example: Julius Erving was the *precursor* to Michael Jordan.

access (AK sess): to gain entry; to approach
    Part of Speech: verb
    Example: She could *access* the classified documents with the proper password.
    Other Form(s): access (noun); accessible (adjective)

sedate (seh DATE): calm; quiet
    Part of Speech: adjective
    Example: The *sedate* couple rarely went out.
    Other Form(s): sedated (adjective); sedative (noun); sedate (verb)

emblematic (em bluh MA tik): symbolic; suggestive
    Part of Speech: adjective
    Example: The latest setback was *emblematic* of the failure of the project.

coterie (CO tur ee): clique; society
    Part of Speech: noun
    Example: The well known author always traveled with her *coterie* of sycophants.

thespian (THES pee un): theatrical; dramatic
    Part of Speech: adjective
    Example: Her *thespian* talents earned her the lead role in the play.

dapper (DAP ur): neat; sprightly
    Part of Speech: adjective
    Example: Everyone agreed that the young man looked *dapper* in the tuxedo.

reciprocal (re SIP ruh kul): mutual; in return
    Part of Speech: adjective
    Example: Two states had *reciprocal* extradition agreements that simplified transfers.
    Other Form(s): reciprocate (verb); reciprocation (noun)

Words and Definitions *(cont.)*

─────────────── **Group 3** ───────────────

trammel (TRAM ul): to restrict; to restrain
    Part of Speech: verb
    Example: Authoritarian governments *trammel* the civil rights of ordinary citizens.

recant (re KANT): to withdraw; to renounce
    Part of Speech: verb
    Example: The witness *recanted* his testimony, and there was an uproar in the courtroom.

alacrity (a LAK ri tee): eagerness; cheerful readiness
    Part of Speech: noun
    Example: The waiter served the diners with great *alacrity*, and so they left him a large tip.

edification (ed i fi KAY shun): enlightenment; instruction
    Part of Speech: noun
    Example: He read Shakespeare's sonnets to them for their *edification*.
    Other Form(s): edify (verb); edifying (adjective)

preempt (pre EMPT): to forestall; to take possession
    Part of Speech: verb
    Example: The Pope's unexpected appearance *preempted* news being broadcast about anyone else.

cosmic (COS mik): of the universe; vast
    Part of Speech: adjective
    Example: Einstein's work changed our understanding of the *cosmic* landscape.

seclude (suh KLOOD): to isolate; to keep apart
    Part of Speech: verb
    Example: Scholars may *seclude* themselves when doing research.
    Other Form(s): seclusion (noun); secluded (adjective)

decadence (DEK uh dents): decay; self-indulgence
    Part of Speech: noun
    Example: The castle was a monument to *decadence*.
    Other Form(s): decadent (adjective)

Words and Definitions *(cont.)*

Group 4
---

shackle (SHA kul): to handcuff; to restrict
   Part of Speech: verb
   Example: Orders from his superiors *shackled* him, and he felt powerless.

dearth (DURTH): scarcity; lack
   Part of Speech: noun
   Example: Floods resulting from the hurricane caused a *dearth* of food in some areas.

corona (kuh RO nuh): halo; a circle of light
   Part of Speech: noun
   Example: The sun's *corona* becomes visible during a total solar eclipse.

precipitate (pre SIP i tate): to accelerate; to hasten
   Part of Speech: verb
   Example: Bad loans *precipitated* his financial fall and eventual bankruptcy.

arboreal (ar BORE ee ul): of trees; like a tree
   Part of Speech: adjective
   Example: His *arboreal* interests led to his taking a job as a park ranger.

turbid (TUR bid): clouded; unclear
   Part of Speech: adjective
   Example: The ship's propeller created *turbid* water.
   Other Form(s): turbidity (noun); turbidness

emanate (EM uh nate): issue; originate
   Part of Speech: verb
   Example: Clouds of dust *emanated* from the field where the wild horses played.

recoup (re COOP): to reclaim; to get back
   Part of Speech: verb
   Example: The bank *recouped* money lost on bad loans by raising service fees.

Unit 21 *(cont.)*

Quick Match

Group 1

A. striking scene	C. make excuses	E. inclination	G. postscript
B. sickly yellow	D. lecture	F. increase	H. informal

_____ 1. propensity

_____ 2. colloquial

_____ 3. accrete

_____ 4. sallow

_____ 5. epilogue

_____ 6. discourse

_____ 7. rationalize

_____ 8. tableau

Group 2

A. symbolic	C. neat	E. theatrical	G. gain entry
B. calm	D. forerunner	F. mutual	H. clique

_____ 1. precursor

_____ 2. access

_____ 3. sedate

_____ 4. emblematic

_____ 5. coterie

_____ 6. thespian

_____ 7. dapper

_____ 8. reciprocal

Group 3

A. renounce	C. forestall	E. restrain	G. self-indulgence
B. vast	D. isolate	F. eagerness	H. enlightenment

_____ 1. trammel

_____ 2. recant

_____ 3. alacrity

_____ 4. edification

_____ 5. preempt

_____ 6. cosmic

_____ 7. seclude

_____ 8. decadence

Group 4

A. halo	C. issue	E. reclaim	G. clouded
B. of trees	D. lack	F. handcuff	H. hasten

_____ 1. shackle

_____ 2. dearth

_____ 3. corona

_____ 4. precipitate

_____ 5. arboreal

_____ 6. turbid

_____ 7. emanate

_____ 8. recoup

Unit 21 *(cont.)*

Answer Key

Group 1
1. propensity
2. discourse
3. accrete
4. rationalize
5. colloquial
6. epilogue
7. tableau
8. sallow

Group 2
1. access
2. coterie
3. reciprocal
4. sedate
5. thespian
6. emblematic
7. precursor
8. dapper

Group 3
1. alacrity
2. preempt
3. seclude
4. recant
5. cosmic
6. decadence
7. edification
8. trammel

Group 4
1. precipitate
2. corona
3. arboreal
4. turbid
5. shackle
6. emanate
7. recoup
8. dearth

Quick Match

Group 1
1. E
2. H
3. F
4. B
5. G
6. D
7. C
8. A

Group 2
1. D
2. G
3. B
4. A
5. H
6. E
7. C
8. F

Group 3
1. E
2. A
3. F
4. H
5. C
6. B
7. D
8. G

Group 4
1. F
2. D
3. A
4. H
5. B
6. G
7. C
8. E

Unit 22

Pre-test Yourself

Group 1

allude	deference	traverse	permeate
critique	sear	effusive	rebut

1. Wetsuits are made of a material that water will not _____.

2. He made a bad gaffe and was _____ in his apologies.

3. When she would _____ to the defendant's past transgressions, his lawyer immediately objected.

4. Students let the professor through the crowd in _____ to her position.

5. His _____ of the work was incomplete, and he had to study the work some more.

6. Branding irons _____ an owner's sign on his cattle.

7. During his seven months abroad, he will _____ much of Europe.

8. He can _____ the prosecution's case by introducing new and contradictory evidence.

Group 2

enervate	throes	abstruse	saturnine
cogitate	pretext	discredit	fickle

1. Cosmologists speak in _____ terms.

2. Defeat after defeat gave the general a _____ look.

3. It is the small and not the large problems in life that _____ some people.

4. The statements he made while in the _____ of agony could not be taken seriously.

5. He loved the place and would visit it on any _____.

6. The child's tastes were so _____ that her parents often cooked three entrees, hoping she'd find at least one of them satisfactory .

7. He will set aside the weekend and _____ over the abstruse conundrum.

8. The defense lawyer could not _____ the damaging testimony of the "expert" witness.

Unit 22 (cont.)

Pre-test Yourself (cont.)

Group 3

| deify | rebuff | effete | surmise |
| acrimony | penultimate | catharsis | trenchant |

1. December 30 is the _____ day of the year.

2. The _____ society was completely enervated by political squabbles.

3. _____ filled the air as the two opponents went at one another.

4. Tragedy, according to Aristotle, should bring _____ and self-understanding.

5. Fearing that she would _____ him, he never summoned the courage to ask her on a date.

6. Young people often _____ professional athletes and use them as role models.

7. Based on her reaction towards him, he could _____ that she would not be interested in a second date.

8. Her _____ remarks cut right to the quick.

Group 4

| serrate | elucidate | recur | daunt |
| turpitude | arrant | penury | countenance |

1. Did Einstein truly _____ the workings of light and gravity for generations of people?

2. Profligate spenders often become insolvent and live in _____.

3. She will _____ the edge of the fabric to make it look unfinished.

4. His _____ was widely known, and he was considered a pariah of the community.

5. If you _____ disobedience, you encourage it in the future.

6. That he was guilty of _____ criminal behavior was beyond all doubt.

7. A dream that she'd had often as a child would _____ once she reached middle age.

8. Difficult challenges did not _____ her.

Unit 22 (cont.)

Words and Definitions

— Group 1 —

allude (uh LOOD): to refer to; to mention
    Part of Speech: verb
    Example: She was not happy when the critic *alluded* to her poor acting.
    Other Form(s): allusion (noun)

deference (DEF ur ence): respect; regard
    Part of Speech: noun
    Example: Citizens showed their *deference* by kneeling before the king.
    Other Form(s): deferential (adjective)

traverse (tra VURS): to travel over; to pass over
    Part of Speech: verb
    Example: The adventurous boys *traversed* the lake in order to explore the land on the other side.

permeate (PUR mee ate): to penetrate; to pass through
    Part of Speech: verb
    Example: Primer paint *permeates* unpainted surfaces and seals them.
    Other Form(s): permeation (noun)

critique (kri TEEK): analysis; review
    Part of Speech: noun
    Example: I finally understood the poem when a professor gave a *critique* of it.
    Other Form(s): critique (verb)

sear (SEAR): to char; to singe
    Part of Speech: verb
    Example: The recipe called for the chef to *sear* the meat when broiling it.

effusive (eh FYOO siv): exuberant; gushing
    Part of Speech: adjective
    Example: She was an *effusive* woman who enjoyed just about everything.
    Other Form(s): effuse (verb); effusion (noun); effusiveness (noun)

rebut (ree BUT): to refute; to turn back
    Part of Speech: verb
    Example: He could not *rebut* the argument, and so he conceded that his friend might be right.
    Other Form(s): rebuttal (noun); rebutment (noun); rebuttable (adjective)

Words and Definitions *(cont.)*

─────────────── **Group 2** ───────────────

enervate (en ur VATE): to weaken; to deprive of vigor
    Part of Speech: verb
    Example: A lengthy journey *enervated* the aging man.
    Other Form(s): enervating (adjective); enervation (noun)

throes (THROWS): violent pangs; anguish
    Part of Speech: noun
    Example: Her sister's death cast her into *throes* of remorse.

abstruse (ab STROOS): profound; hard to understand
    Part of Speech: adjective
    Example: The well-known intellectual spoke in *abstruse* terms that no one understood.

saturnine (SA tur nine): gloomy; brooding
    Part of Speech: adjective
    Example: The little lost boy had a *saturnine* and wistful look on his face.

cogitate (CODJ i tate): to think; to contemplate
    Part of Speech: verb
    Example: Problems made him *cogitate* for a long time.
    Other Form(s): cogitation (noun); cogitative (adjective); cogitator (noun)

pretext (PRE text): pretense; ostensible reason
    Part of Speech: noun
    Example: The woman enlisted the services of the handsome neighbor on the *pretext* of helping her lift a heavy box.

discredit (dis KRED it): harm the reputation of; cause to be disbelieved
    Part of Speech: verb
    Example: He feared that his brother's penchant for lying would *discredit* his family's reputation for honesty.

fickle (FIK ul): erratically changeable; inconstant
    Part of Speech: adjective
    Example: After leaving three different grooms at the altar in five years, the woman began to get a reputation for being *fickle*.

Words and Definitions *(cont.)*

--- **Group 3** ---

deify (DEE i fy): to make a god of; to worship
Part of Speech: verb
Example: Americans often *deify* celebrities.
Other Form(s): deification (noun)

rebuff (ree BUF): to reject; to snub
Part of Speech: verb
Example: She *rebuffed* all his advances and finally married someone else.

effete (i FEET): feeble; exhausted
Part of Speech: adjective
Example: Nations become *effete* when their rulers become decadent.
Other Form(s): effeteness (noun)

surmise (sur MIZE): conjecture; to suspect
Part of Speech: verb
Example: Based on their first few practices, the coach could *surmise* that their chances of capturing the championship title were slim.

acrimony (AK ri mo nee): bitterness; ill feeling
Part of Speech: noun
Example: There was quite a bit of *acrimony* in his criticism.
Other Form(s): acrimonious (adjective)

penultimate (pe NUL ti met): next to last
Part of Speech: adjective
Example: He was always the *penultimate* player picked for sports teams, and his little brother was always picked last.

catharsis (kuh THAR sis): purging; cleansing
Part of Speech: noun
Example: Some authors write because the process affords them a *catharsis*.
Other Form(s): cathartic (adjective)

trenchant (TREN chent): incisive; caustic
Part of Speech: adjective
Example: His acrimonious remarks proved *trenchant* enough to cause a riot.

Words and Definitions *(cont.)*

——————— **Group 4** ———————

serrate (SER ate): provide with a saw-like edge; to notch
    Part of Speech: verb
    Example: The knife's *serrated* edge made it especially dangerous.
    Other Form(s): serrated (adjective); serration (noun)

elucidate (e LOO si date): to make clear; to explain
    Part of Speech: verb
    Example: Teachers *elucidate* abstruse points for their students.
    Other Form(s): elucidation (noun); elucidator (noun); elucidatory (adjective)

recur (ree KUR): to occur again; to persist
    Part of Speech: verb
    Example: Certain themes, such as man versus nature, *recurred* throughout the author's works.
    Other Form(s): recurring (adjective); recurrant (adjective)

daunt (DAWNT): to intimidate; to unnerve
    Part of Speech: verb
    Example: Sheer ice cliffs *daunt* even the most experienced climbers.
    Other Form(s): daunting (adjective)

turpitude (TUR pih tood): depravity; corruption
    Part of Speech: noun
    Example: His *turpitude* was obvious, and the disgusted voters turned him out of office.

arrant (AR ent): utter; downright
    Part of Speech: adjective
    Example: His *arrant* lack of motivation led his mother to seek counseling for him.

penury (PEN yuh ree): poverty; indigence
    Part of Speech: noun
    Example: Welfare is supposed to ease *penury*, not stuff the pockets of the wealthy.
    Other Form(s): penurious (adjective)

countenance (KOWN tuh nence): to permit; to allow
    Part of Speech: verb
    Example: If a teacher *countenances* poor behavior, the teacher is teaching a bad lesson.

Unit 22 *(cont.)*

Quick Match

Group 1

A. travel over	C. exuberant	E. refute	G. refer to
B. analysis	D. respect	F. penetrate	H. singe

_____ 1. allude

_____ 2. deference

_____ 3. traverse

_____ 4. permeate

_____ 5. critique

_____ 6. sear

_____ 7. effusive

_____ 8. rebut

Group 2

A. contemplate	C. pretense	E. profound	G. inconstant
B. gloomy	D. anguish	F. weaken	H. cause to be disbelieved

_____ 1. enervate

_____ 2. throes

_____ 3. abstruse

_____ 4. saturnine

_____ 5. cogitate

_____ 6. pretext

_____ 7. discredit

_____ 8. fickle

Group 3

A. feeble	C. next to last	E. reject	G. worship
B. bitterness	D. cleansing	F. incisive	H. conjecture

_____ 1. deify

_____ 2. rebuff

_____ 3. effete

_____ 4. surmise

_____ 5. acrimony

_____ 6. penultimate

_____ 7. catharsis

_____ 8. trenchant

Group 4

A. persist	C. utter	E. poverty	G. allow
B. corruption	D. explain	F. intimidate	H. give a saw-like edge

_____ 1. serrate

_____ 2. elucidate

_____ 3. recur

_____ 4. daunt

_____ 5. turpitude

_____ 6. arrant

_____ 7. penury

_____ 8. countenance

Unit 22 *(cont.)*

Answer Key

Group 1	Group 2	Group 3	Group 4
1. permeate	1. abstruse	1. penultimate	1. elucidate
2. effusive	2. saturnine	2. effete	2. penury
3. allude	3. enervate	3. acrimony	3. serrate
4. deference	4. throes	4. catharsis	4. turpitude
5. critique	5. pretext	5. rebuff	5. countenance
6. sear	6. fickle	6. deify	6. arrant
7. traverse	7. cogitate	7. surmise	7. recur
8. rebut	8. discredit	8. trenchant	8. daunt

Quick Match

Group 1	Group 2	Group 3	Group 4
1. G	1. F	1. G	1. H
2. D	2. D	2. E	2. D
3. A	3. E	3. A	3. A
4. F	4. B	4. H	4. F
5. B	5. A	5. B	5. B
6. H	6. C	6. C	6. C
7. C	7. H	7. D	7. E
8. E	8. G	8. F	8. G

Unit 23

Pre-test Yourself

Group 1			
abstemious	promontory	discrepancy	tendentious
enfranchise	rattle	strident	conducive

1. Susan B. Anthony's example may _____ all women of the world.

2. A _____ in the account books caused alarm.

3. Monks live _____ lives.

4. A healthy diet is _____ to good health.

5. His short story was _____ and clearly had an agenda other than simply telling a story.

6. The baby's wails reverberated through the auditorium and began to _____ the actors on stage.

7. The spy signaled to the submarine from a _____ on the eastern shore.

8. He had a _____ voice that rattled a lot of the players.

Group 2			
shiftless	espouse	reconcile	cosmopolitan
pylon	dilettante	avuncular	transmute

1. What appears to be _____ tenderness may be nothing more than covert patriarchy.

2. If the player with the football touches the _____ that marks the end zone, he is credited with a touchdown.

3. Malingerers create a _____ society.

4. His status as a _____ is unlikely to change, since he never works at his craft.

5. Her _____ cachet made it easy for her to move in high society.

6. Winning the lottery will _____ the financial status of most anyone.

7. Mediators _____ the differences between the opposing parties.

8. Through his weekly column, the editorialist can _____ his ideas about alternative energy sources.

Pre-test Yourself *(cont.)*

Group 3

shirk	excoriate	copious	avaricious
pusillanimous	tractable	desultory	recourse

---

1. The boy would repeatedly _____ his responsibilities, and his parents found it necessary to discipline him.

2. Each time he visited Las Vegas, he lost _____ amounts of money on the slot machines.

3. His _____ nature was at odds with his meager salary.

4. Good literary critics _____ poorly written books.

5. He became daunted and _____ in the face of danger.

6. Domestic animals are _____ and docile animals.

7. When faced with the hard facts, he had no other _____ than to admit to them.

8. If you have _____ study habits, you will probably get mediocre marks.

Group 4

conduit	sere	daub	argot
progeny	toady	regress	elixir

---

1. Anyone can _____, but not everyone can really paint.

2. Those who seek the easiest way to climb the corporate ladder will _____ to their superiors.

3. The infomercial claimed that the secret formula in the _____ would make anyone who drank it feel 20 years younger.

4. Their _____ was difficult to understand because of its many idioms.

5. He figured toadying was the perfect _____ for his promotion.

6. The _____ ground could not support plant growth.

7. Bequeathing an estate to the oldest _____ has been traditional.

8. Another act of terrorism, and the peace talks will _____.

Unit 23 (cont.)

Words and Definitions

─────────────────── Group 1 ───────────────────

abstemious (ab STI mee us): moderate; temperate
  Part of Speech: adjective
  Example: Religious persons are supposed to lead *abstemious* lives.

promontory (PROM un tor ee): cliff; headland
  Part of Speech: noun
  Example: Lighthouses are usually situated on *promontories*.

discrepancy (dis KREP en see): variance; inconsistency
  Part of Speech: noun
  Example: There was a *discrepancy* in her accounts, and she had to find the error.

tendentious (ten DEN shus): promoting a particular cause, etc. ; biased
  Part of Speech: adjective
  Example: *Tendentious* talk showed him to be an arbitrary and unreasonable man.

enfranchise (en FRAN chize): to authorize; to sanction
  Part of Speech: verb
  Example: The 19th Amendment to the United States Constitution *enfranchised* women.

rattle (RAT ul): to unnerve; to perturb
  Part of Speech: verb
  Example: Constant yelling *rattled* him, and he missed the basket.

strident (STRY dent): harsh; loud
  Part of Speech: adjective
  Example: Her children would not obey her until her tone of voice became *strident*.

conducive (kun DOO siv): contributing; helping
  Part of Speech: adjective
  Example: Abstemious living is *conducive* to salubrious existence.

Words and Definitions *(cont.)*

─────────────────── **Group 2** ───────────────────

shiftless (SHIFT less): lazy; lacking ambition
    Part of Speech: adjective
    Example: The *shiftless* man refused to peruse the employment ads.

espouse (e SPOWZ): to adopt; to support
    Part of Speech: verb
    Example: Susan B. Anthony *espoused* the cause of enfranchisement for women.

reconcile (REK un sile): to resolve differences; to settle
    Part of Speech: verb
    Example: When the opposing parties *reconciled* their differences, peace reigned.
    Other Form(s): reconciliation (noun); reconciliatory (adjective); reconcilable (adjective); reconcilability (noun); reconcilement (noun); reconciler (noun)

cosmopolitan (kahz muh PAHL i ten): cultivated; of, from, or knowing many parts of the world
    Part of Speech: adjective
    Example: Travel in Europe is supposed to give a person a *cosmopolitan* cachet.

pylon (PY lon): a vertical marker
    Part of Speech: noun
    Example: The plane had difficulty landing because the lights on several of the runway *pylons* were out.

dilettante (dil eh TAUNT): dabbler; amateur
    Part of Speech: noun
    Example: Rarely did the *dilettante* take anything seriously.

avuncular (uh VUNG kyoo lur): like an uncle; kindly
    Part of Speech: adjective
    Example: The emperor's attitude was *avuncular*, and his people loved him for it.

transmute (tranz MYOOT): to transform; to convert
    Part of Speech: verb
    Example: College *transmuted* the student into a serious adult.
    Other Form(s): transmutation (noun); transmutable (adjective)

Unit 23 *(cont.)*

Words and Definitions *(cont.)*

shirk (SHURK): to avoid; to evade
   Part of Speech: verb
   Example: Deadbeat dads *shirk* responsibility for their children.

excoriate (ex KORE ee ate): to strip or peel off (skin); censure severely
   Part of Speech: verb
   Example: The book critic *excoriated* the novel, calling it a second-rate ripoff.

copious (CO pee us): plentiful; bounteous
   Part of Speech: adjective
   Example: Tears were *copious* at the hero's internment.
   Other Form(s): copiousness (noun)

avaricious (av uh RI shus): greedy; covetous
   Part of Speech: adjective
   Example: His *avaricious* ways aggrandized his personal fortune.
   Other Form(s): avarice (noun); avariciousness (noun)

pusillanimous (pyoo si LAN i mus): timid; cowardly
   Part of Speech: adjective
   Example: One cannot afford to be *pusillanimous* in the face of imminent danger.
   Other Form(s): pusillanimity (noun)

tractable (TRAK tuh bul): manageable; docile
   Part of Speech: adjective
   Example: The teacher noticed that her first-year students were *tractable*, while her upper-grade students were less so.
   Other Form(s): tractability (noun)

desultory (DES ul to ree): disconnected; aimless
   Part of Speech: adjective
   Example: His *desultory* work habits convinced his boss that he should be let go.

recourse (RE course): resort; access
   Part of Speech: noun
   Example: He felt trapped because he had no *recourse* left.

Unit 23 (cont.)

Words and Definitions (cont.)

— **Group 4** —

conduit (KAHN doo it): channel; duct
Part of Speech: noun
Example: Workmen damaged the electrical *conduit*, and the entire town went dark.

sere (SIR): withered; desiccated
Part of Speech: adjective
Example: Many old people have sere skin.

daub (DAWB): to smear; to smudge
Part of Speech: verb
Example: Vandals *daubed* paint all over the public library's walls.

argot (AR got): slang; dialect
Part of Speech: noun
Example: The foreigners spoke in an *argot* I couldn't understand.

progeny (PRAHJ uh nee): offspring; descendants
Part of Speech: noun
Example: All of the money was bequeathed to her *progeny*.

toady (TOE dee): to fawn; to flatter
Part of Speech: verb
Example: Court figures constantly *toadied* to the king.
Other Form(s): toady (noun); toadyism (noun)

regress (ree GRESS): to revert; to fall back to a former state
Part of Speech: verb
Example: Therapy didn't help, and his behavior *regressed*.
Other Form(s): regression (noun); regressive (adjective)

elixir (e LIX ir): wonder drug; rejuvenator
Part of Speech: noun
Example: Vasco de Gama searched for an *elixir* that would make him immortal.

Unit 23 *(cont.)*

Quick Match

Group 1

A. inconsistency	C. perturb	E. harsh	G. contributing
B. sanction	D. moderate	F. cliff	H. biased

_____ 1. abstemious

_____ 2. promontory

_____ 3. discrepancy

_____ 4. tendentious

_____ 5. enfranchise

_____ 6. rattle

_____ 7. strident

_____ 8. conducive

Group 2

A. vertical marker	C. kindly	E. make compatible	G. adopt
B. lazy	D. dabbler	F. transform	H. cultivated

_____ 1. shiftless

_____ 2. espouse

_____ 3. reconcile

_____ 4. cosmopolitan

_____ 5. pylon

_____ 6. dilettante

_____ 7. avuncular

_____ 8. transmute

Group 3

A. plentiful	C. avoid	E. censure	G. greedy
B. timid	D. manageable	F. resort	H. aimless

_____ 1. shirk

_____ 2. excoriate

_____ 3. copious

_____ 4. avaricious

_____ 5. pusillanimous

_____ 6. tractable

_____ 7. desultory

_____ 8. recourse

Group 4

A. smudge	C. offspring	E. duct	G. desiccated
B. slang	D. revert	F. rejuvenator	H. flatter

_____ 1. conduit

_____ 2. sere

_____ 3. daub

_____ 4. argot

_____ 5. progeny

_____ 6. toady

_____ 7. regress

_____ 8. elixir

Unit 23 *(cont.)*

Answer Key

Pre-test Yourself

Group 1	Group 2	Group 3	Group 4
1. enfranchise	1. avuncular	1. shirk	1. daub
2. discrepancy	2. pylon	2. copious	2. toady
3. abstemious	3. shiftless	3. avaricious	3. elixir
4. conducive	4. dilettante	4. excoriate	4. argot
5. tendentious	5. cosmopolitan	5. pusillanimous	5. conduit
6. rattle	6. transmute	6. tractable	6. sere
7. promontory	7. reconcile	7. recourse	7. progeny
8. strident	8. espouse	8. desultory	8. regress

Quick Match

Group 1	Group 2	Group 3	Group 4
1. D	1. B	1. C	1. E
2. F	2. G	2. E	2. G
3. A	3. E	3. A	3. A
4. H	4. H	4. G	4. B
5. B	5. A	5. B	5. C
6. C	6. D	6. D	6. H
7. E	7. C	7. H	7. D
8. G	8. F	8. F	8. F

Unit 24

Pre-test Yourself

Group 1

ineluctable	apoplexy	profligate	caustic
torpor	endemic	raze	delete

---

1. _____ individuals are often spendthrifts.

2. When he saw the hospital bill, he suffered from _____.

3. It has been said that death and taxes are the two _____ truths of life.

4. The publishers asked if author would _____ the controversial passage from the manuscript.

5. His burns from the _____ solution took a long time to heal.

6. If the city council does _____ the historic landmark, it will be an awful mistake.

7. Constant _____ led him to be late very often.

8. Sluggishness was _____ to the team, and it lost most of its games.

Group 2

pithy	delineate	titular	complicity
relinquish	adjure	emporium	sepulcher

---

1. He had poor sense of direction and could not _____ the quickest route to the treasure.

2. His position was only _____, and no one paid any attention to him.

3. He was a man of few words whose _____ statements were always pertinent.

4. The dean will _____ the students to cut the rally short.

5. _____ in a crime carries penalties under the laws of conspiracy.

6. He was of the mind that men should always _____ their seats to women on crowded public conveyances.

7. His _____ in the mall sold computer software at discount prices.

8. Their family name is inscribed on a _____ in that cemetery.

Group 3			
alimentary	tipple	protean	senility
crass	reminisce	euphemism	deprecate

1. No one could understand why the old man would _____ everyone he met.

2. He would often _____ until he didn't know where he was.

3. Fruits and vegetables are considered _____ foods.

4. "Pleasantly plump" is a _____ for "fat."

5. Whenever the alumni got together, they would _____ and indulge in nostalgia.

6. _____ overtook him in his 90th year.

7. As a result of her _____ personality, he never knew if their relationship would last.

8. His speech in favor of one store over the other was nothing more than _____ commercialism.

Group 4			
adamant	plumb	demur	timorous
credulous	seminal	remnant	eschew

1. Dishonest telemarketers seek out _____ people and defraud them.

2. It is said that a _____ heart will never win a fair lady.

3. When the health department releases a negative report on a restaurant, many customers will _____ it.

4. Nothing could shake the man from his _____ views on the matter.

5. Cosmologists _____ the depths of the universe.

6. Timorous people will generally _____ when given the opportunity to speak in front of a crowd.

7. New inventions resulted from her _____ studies in magnetism.

8. Not a _____ of the razed building could be found.

Unit 24 *(cont.)*

Words and Definitions

─────── **Group 1** ───────

ineluctable (in i LUK tuh bul): inescapable; unavoidable
  Part of Speech: adjective
  Example: For most people, making egregious errors in judgement is an *ineluctable* part of growing up.
  Other Form(s): ineluctability (noun)

apoplexy (AP o plek see): stroke; extreme emotion
  Part of Speech: noun
  Example: A sudden drop in his blood pressure resulted in *apoplexy*.
  Other Form(s): apoplectic (adjective)

profligate (PROF li gate): dissolute; dissipated
  Part of Speech: adjective
  Example: Spendthrifts who lead *profligate* lives often become insolvent very quickly.

delete (duh LEET): to cross out; to erase
  Part of Speech: verb
  Example: The editors *deleted* unnecessary verbiage.
  Other Form(s): deletion (noun)

torpor (TOR pur): inactivity; stagnation
  Part of Speech: noun
  Example: A general *torpor* affected the team, and it lost by a record margin.

endemic (en DEM ik): native; peculiar to one area
  Part of Speech: adjective
  Example: A superior attitude seemed *endemic* and widespread in the little town.

raze (RAYZ): to demolish; to tear down
  Part of Speech: verb
  Example: Engineers *razed* the old dam after they had built a new one.

caustic (KAWS tik): bitter; burning
  Part of Speech: adjective
  Example: His closing remarks were *caustic* and full of animosity.
  Other Form(s): causticity (noun)

Unit 24 *(cont.)*

Words and Definitions *(cont.)*

──────────────── **Group 2** ────────────────

pithy (PIH thee): concise; substantiative
    Part of Speech: adjective
    Example: The American cowboy is often pictured as a *pithy* individualist.
    Other Form(s): pithiness (noun)

delineate (de LIN ee ate): to sketch; to describe
    Part of Speech: verb
    Example: As a preliminary model, the artist *delineated* what she wanted to draw.
    Other Form(s): delineation (noun); delineator (noun)

titular (TIT choo lur): relating to title; in name only
    Part of Speech: adjective
    Example: He had little influence and was director only in a *titular* way.

complicity (kum PLIS i tee): collusion; involvement
    Part of Speech: noun
    Example: They were found guilty of *complicity* in the crime and sentenced as conspirators.

relinquish (reh LING kwish): to surrender; to cede
    Part of Speech: verb
    Example: The beaten nation *relinquished* all of its rights to the land.

adjure (ad JUR): to command; to oblige
    Part of Speech: verb
    Example: Deans *adjure* the students to obey the rules.

emporium (em PORE ee um): market; store
    Part of Speech: noun
    Example: She opened an *emporium* with a Small Business Administration loan.

sepulcher (SEP ul kur): burial vault; tomb
    Part of Speech: noun
    Example: The widow left a single rose at her beloved's *sepulcher* every year on their anniversary.

Words and Definitions *(cont.)*

─────────────────── **Group 3** ───────────────────

alimentary (al i MEN tuh ree): nourishing; nutritious
    Part of Speech: adjective
    Example: School cafeterias are supposed to serve *alimentary* lunches.

tipple (TIP ul): to drink alcohol
    Part of Speech: verb
    Example: He led a profligate life and *tippled* quite a bit.

euphemism (YOO fuh mizm): a mild expression
    Part of Speech: noun
    Example: She was a kind woman who resorted to *euphemisms* to avoid hurting anyone's feelings.
    Other Form(s): euphemistic (adjective); euphemist (noun); euphemize (verb)

senility (se NIL i tee): of old age; deterioration related to old age
    Part of Speech: noun
    Example: In his *senility*, he was always forgetting where he parked his car.
    Other Form(s): senile (adjective)

crass (KRASS): crude; vulgar
    Part of Speech: adjective
    Example: The writer described the mammoth Las Vegas casino as meretricious and *crass*.

reminisce (reh mi NISS): to recall; to think back
    Part of Speech: verb
    Example: Older people often *reminisce* about "the good old days."
    Other Form(s): reminiscence (noun); reminiscent (adjective)

protean (PRO tee un): changeable; mutable
    Part of Speech: adjective
    Example: Picasso was known for his *protean* personality.

deprecate (DEP ruh kate): to censure; to impeach
    Part of Speech: adjective
    Example: You may reveal a lot about yourself when you *deprecate* someone else.
    Other Form(s): deprecating (adjective); deprecation (noun); deprecatory (adjective)

─────────────── **Group 4** ───────────────

adamant (AD uh mant): resolute; resistant to persuasion
    Part of Speech: adjective
    Example: She was *adamant* about a woman's right to vote.

plumb (PLUM): to examine; to fathom
    Part of Speech: verb
    Example: Archaeologists *plumb* the sites of old cities to find artifacts.

demur (deh MUR): to object; to disapprove
    Part of Speech: verb
    Example: He asked her to leave, but she *demurred*.

timorous (TI mur us): apprehensive; timid
    Part of Speech: adjective
    Example: His pusillanimous nature was obvious from his *timorous* actions.

credulous (KRED yoo lus): trusting; gullible
    Part of Speech: adjective
    Example: Crooks are always seeking out *credulous* people so they can bilk them.
    Other Form(s): credulity (noun); credulousness (noun)

seminal (SEM i nul): as the basis; of the beginning
    Part of Speech: adjective
    Example: Observers call her art *seminal* because it started a revolution in approach.

remnant (REM nant): reminder; leftover
    Part of Speech: noun
    Example: Engineers left no *remnant* of the old dam when they razed it.

eschew (eh SHOO): to avoid; to shun
    Part of Speech: verb
    Example: He *eschewed* fatty food because it exacerbated his cholesterol level.
    Other Form(s): eschewal (noun)

Unit 24 *(cont.)*

Quick Match

Group 1

A. demolish	C. erase	E. bitter	G. native
B. stagnation	D. stroke	F. unavoidable	H. dissipated

_____ 1. ineluctable

_____ 2. apoplexy

_____ 3. profligate

_____ 4. delete

_____ 5. torpor

_____ 6. endemic

_____ 7. raze

_____ 8. caustic

Group 2

A. collusion	C. surrender	E. in name only	G. tomb
B. concise	D. command	F. market	H. describe

_____ 1. pithy

_____ 2. delineate

_____ 3. titular

_____ 4. complicity

_____ 5. relinquish

_____ 6. adjure

_____ 7. emporium

_____ 8. sepulcher

Group 3

A. mild expression	C. recall	E. censure	G. drink alcohol
B. of old age	D. nutritious	F. mutable	H. vulgar

_____ 1. alimentary

_____ 2. tipple

_____ 3. euphemism

_____ 4. senility

_____ 5. crass

_____ 6. reminisce

_____ 7. protean

_____ 8. deprecate

Group 4

A. examine	C. resolute	E. object	G. gullible
B. timid	D. as the basis	F. remainder	H. avoid

_____ 1. adamant

_____ 2. plumb

_____ 3. demur

_____ 4. timorous

_____ 5. credulous

_____ 6. seminal

_____ 7. remnant

_____ 8. eschew

Unit 24 *(cont.)*

Answer Key

Group 1

1. profligate
2. apoplexy
3. ineluctable
4. delete
5. caustic
6. raze
7. torpor
8. endemic

Group 2

1. delineate
2. titular
3. pithy
4. adjure
5. complicity
6. relinquish
7. emporium
8. sepulcher

Group 3

1. deprecate
2. tipple
3. alimentary
4. euphemism
5. reminisce
6. senility
7. protean
8. crass

Group 4

1. credulous
2. timorous
3. eschew
4. adamant
5. plumb
6. demur
7. seminal
8. remnant

Quick Match

Group 1

1. F
2. D
3. H
4. C
5. B
6. G
7. A
8. E

Group 2

1. B
2. H
3. E
4. A
5. C
6. D
7. F
8. G

Group 3

1. D
2. G
3. A
4. B
5. H
6. C
7. F
8. E

Group 4

1. C
2. A
3. E
4. B
5. G
6. D
7. F
8. H

Unit 25

Pre-test Yourself

Group 1

permutation	asymmetrical	relish	connoisseur
tantamount	deign	similitude	erudite

1. He felt that, being royalty, he shouldn't _____ to speak to commoners.

2. He was transformed by his love for the child, and the _____ was for the good.

3. Her slightly _____ face gave her a unique beauty.

4. Countenancing bad behavior is _____ to encouraging it.

5. He was known worldwide as a _____ of fine art.

6. Teams usually _____ the idea of beating the teams that have embarrassed them in the past.

7. Zygotic twins share an astounding _____.

8. The lecturer was _____ in the field of quantum physics.

Group 2

simulate	defile	temporize	countermand
remiss	eulogize	pastoral	assuage

1. The video game can _____ the feeling of flying a jet fighter.

2. When they _____, the opportunity may pass them by.

3. Alpine meadows present a _____ tableau.

4. Vandals _____ both public and private property.

5. He felt guilty about being _____ in his duties.

6. The jazz greats will probably _____ the musician at his requiem.

7. A superior officer can _____ the orders of a lower officer.

8. Time will often _____ even the greatest pain.

Unit 25 *(cont.)*

Pre-test Yourself *(cont.)*

Group 3

shrew	diminutive	talisman	convivial
pungent	auspicious	epitaph	regimen

---

1. The superstitious man carried a _____ to ward off evil.

2. Three straight victories amounted to an _____ start of the season.

3. Despite his _____ size, he was able to dunk a basketball.

4. All of the revelers were _____ and gregarious.

5. All of his friends thought his wife was a _____ and couldn't understood why he stayed married to her.

6. If she did not follow the same _____ every morning, her entire day was confused.

7. Chinese table settings often contain sweet and _____ sauces.

8. The sepulcher bore his _____ in Cyrillic script.

Group 4

impecunious	nostrum	halcyon	patrician
frenetic	gambit	reprisal	verbatim

---

1. As a _____, he rarely deigned to attend town meetings.

2. After invaders had decimated the town, a resistance group carried out a _____ on them.

3. Spendthrift ways lead to a _____ old age.

4. He quoted the article _____ for the audience.

5. The Three Stooges were _____ comedians.

6. The Surgeon General advised that the supposed wonder drug was only a _____.

7. His _____ was brilliant, and his opponent could not counter it.

8. Old age is supposed to be a _____ time.

Unit 25 *(cont.)*

Words and Definitions

permutation (pur myoo TAY shun): alteration; transformation
   Part of Speech: noun
   Example: Most viewed his *permutation* from convict to philanthropist with incredulity.

asymmetrical (ay si MEH tri kul): unbalanced; uneven
   Part of Speech: adjective
   Example: The painting was purposely *asymmetrical* just to draw the eye to one side.
   Other Form(s): asymmetry (noun)

similitude (si MIL i tood): resemblance; likeness
   Part of Speech: noun
   Example: The Adirondack Mountains bear a *similitude* to the Alps.

erudite (AIR yoo dite): learned; scholarly
   Part of Speech: adjective
   Example: Professors are supposed to be *erudite* people.
   Other Form(s): erudition (noun)

tantamount (TAN tuh mount): equivalent; equal to
   Part of Speech: adjective
   Example: Saying no was *tantamount* to treason in this case.

deign (DANE): to condescend; to stoop
   Part of Speech: verb
   Example: The king *deigned* to see his subjects only on certain occasions.

relish (REL ish): to enjoy; to take pleasure
   Part of Speech: verb
   Example: Great athletes *relish* championship competition.

connoisseur (con o SEWR): authority; specialist
   Part of Speech: noun
   Example: She was a *connoisseur* of aboriginal art.

Words and Definitions *(cont.)*

─────────────── **Group 2** ───────────────

simulate (SIM yoo late): to pretend; to feign
    Part of Speech: verb
    Example: Actors *simulate* the emotions of the characters they play.
    Other Form(s): simulation (noun); simulated (adjective); simulator (noun)

defile (de FILE): to pollute; to taint
    Part of Speech: verb
    Example: When vandals daubed paint on the library walls, they *defiled* a place of learning.
    Other Form(s): defiled (adjective)

temporize (TEM po rize): to procrastinate; to delay
    Part of Speech: verb
    Example: If you *temporize*, you may miss the opportunity.

countermand (COWN tur mand): to revoke; to cancel
    Part of Speech: verb
    Example: The lieutenant gave an order, but the major *countermanded* it.

remiss (re MISS): negligent; careless
    Part of Speech: adjective
    Example: If you are *remiss* in your studies, you will not do well.

eulogize (YOO luh gize): to praise; to promote
    Part of Speech: verb
    Example: Many notables *eulogized* the dead writer.
    Other Form(s): eulogy (noun); eulogist (noun); eulogistic (adjective)

pastoral (PAS tour ul): bucolic; idyllic
    Part of Speech: adjective
    Example: Many city people yearn for *pastoral* scenes when they go on vacation.

assuage (uh SWAYJ): to ease; to lessen severity
    Part of Speech: verb
    Example: She *assuaged* the child's grief by singing soft songs.

Words and Definitions *(cont.)*

--- **Group 3** ---

shrew (SHROO): scold; nag
    Part of Speech: noun
    Example: He viewed his mother-in-law as a *shrew* who made family gatherings miserable for everyone.

diminutive (di MIN yoo tiv): small; little
    Part of Speech: adjective
    Example: His *diminutive* stature precluded his playing basketball.

talisman (TAL is man): amulet; lucky piece
    Part of Speech: noun
    Example: She carried a *talisman* at all times to ward off evil spirits.

convivial (kun VIV ee ul): jovial; jolly
    Part of Speech: adjective
    Example: Everyone enjoyed the *convivial* party.
    Other Form(s): conviviality (noun)

pungent (PUN jent): sharp; biting
    Part of Speech: adjective
    Example: Good ale is often *pungent*.
    Other Form(s): pungency (noun)

auspicious (aw SPISH us): prosperous; favorable
    Part of Speech: adjective
    Example: Her victory in the first set was an *auspicious* sign.

epitaph (EP i taf): tombstone inscription; tombstone marking
    Part of Speech: noun
    Example: Many people have witty *epitaphs* put on their sepulchers.

regimen (REJ i men): method; system
    Part of Speech: noun
    Example: Special forces soldiers undergo a very difficult training *regimen*.
    Other Form(s): regimented (adjective)

Unit 25 *(cont.)*

Words and Definitions *(cont.)*

──────────── **Group 4** ────────────

impecunious (im pe KYOO nee us): insolvent; bankrupt
    Part of Speech: adjective
    Example: Profligacy led to his *impecunious* position.

nostrum (NOS trum): quack medicine; magic solution
    Part of Speech: noun
    Example: Itinerant medical impersonators used to sell *nostrums* to the unsuspecting.

halcyon (HAL see un): tranquil; peaceful
    Part of Speech: adjective
    Example: The mountain lake was a *halcyon* setting.

patrician (puh TRISH un): aristocrat; nobleman
    Part of Speech: noun
    Example: Only *patricians* were allowed at the royal court.
    Other Form(s): patrician (adjective)

frenetic (freh NEH tik): frenzied; frantic
    Part of Speech: adjective
    Example: Some clowns get their laughs by acting in a *frenetic* way.

gambit (GAM bit): stratagem; device
    Part of Speech: noun
    Example: He was known for a chess *gambit* that thoroughly misled his opponent.

reprisal (re PRY zul): revenge; counterattack
    Part of Speech: noun
    Example: Insurgent soldiers promised *reprisals* if their leader was not released.

verbatim (vur BAY tim): literal; word-for-word
    Part of Speech: adjective
    Example: Quotations in scholarly journals should be *verbatim* quotations.

Unit 25 (cont.)

Quick Match

Group 1

A. enjoy
B. learned
C. equivalent
D. uneven
E. resemblance
F. transformation
G. authority
H. condescend

_____ 1. permutation
_____ 2. asymmetrical
_____ 3. similitude
_____ 4. erudite

_____ 5. tantamount
_____ 6. deign
_____ 7. relish
_____ 8. connoisseur

Group 2

A. cancel
B. delay
C. careless
D. feign
E. idyllic
F. ease
G. taint
H. praise

_____ 1. simulate
_____ 2. defile
_____ 3. temporize
_____ 4. countermand

_____ 5. remiss
_____ 6. eulogize
_____ 7. pastoral
_____ 8. assuage

Group 3

A. tomb's inscription
B. nag
C. favorable
D. amulet
E. small
F. sharp
G. jovial
H. system

_____ 1. shrew
_____ 2. diminutive
_____ 3. talisman
_____ 4. convivial

_____ 5. pungent
_____ 6. auspicious
_____ 7. epitaph
_____ 8. regimen

Group 4

A. peaceful
B. aristocrat
C. bankrupt
D. revenge
E. magic solution
F. literal
G. frenzied
H. stratagem

_____ 1. impecunious
_____ 2. nostrum
_____ 3. halcyon
_____ 4. patrician

_____ 5. frenetic
_____ 6. gambit
_____ 7. reprisal
_____ 8. verbatim

Unit 25 *(cont.)*

Answer Key

---------- **Pre-test Yourself** ----------

Group 1	**Group 2**	**Group 3**	**Group 4**
1. deign	1. simulate	1. talisman	1. patrician
2. permutation	2. temporize	2. auspicious	2. reprisal
3. asymmetrical	3. pastoral	3. diminutive	3. impecunious
4. tantamount	4. defile	4. convivial	4. verbatim
5. connoisseur	5. remiss	5. shrew	5. frenetic
6. relish	6. eulogize	6. regimen	6. nostrum
7. similitude	7. countermand	7. pungent	7. gambit
8. erudite	8. assuage	8. epitaph	8. halcyon

---------- **Quick Match** ----------

Group 1	**Group 2**	**Group 3**	**Group 4**
1. F	1. D	1. B	1. C
2. D	2. G	2. E	2. E
3. E	3. B	3. D	3. A
4. B	4. A	4. G	4. B
5. C	5. C	5. F	5. G
6. H	6. H	6. C	6. H
7. A	7. E	7. A	7. D
8. G	8. F	8. H	8. F

Unit 26

Pre-test Yourself

Group 1

augment	silhouette	etymology	convex
taxonomy	pundit	rejuvenate	diaphanous

---

1. The car's _____ rearview mirror allowed the driver to see a wide area behind him.

2. The department head may _____ his staff in order to handle the additional workload.

3. Some sort of grouping had to be made, so she constructed a _____ for the group.

4. Knowing word roots, prefixes, and suffixes helps in studying _____.

5. Time after time, the Washington _____ had the wrong predictions about the elections.

6. An elixir he sought might never _____ men who took it.

7. The fabric was so fine it was almost _____.

8. Firing ranges have full frontal view targets and _____ targets.

Group 2

somber	dilate	purgative	ascetic
traduce	conscription	reparations	ethereal

---

1. If he wished, the tabloid columnist could _____ the celebrity and give the public the wrong impression of events that had occurred.

2. Wartime survivors of the Holocaust wanted _____ from Germany for their suffering.

3. In order to induce the patient to vomit out the poisen, the doctor administered a _____.

4. Many people protested _____ for the war by burning their draft cards

5. The fog gave the forest an _____ look.

6. Requiems are usually _____ affairs.

7. Your pupils _____ when you enter a dark room.

8. She gave up the life of a jetsetter and became _____ in her ways.

Unit 26 (cont.)

Pre-test Yourself (cont.)

Group 3

contentious	tumescent	artifice	prattle
sojourn	epitome	renounce	deft

1. They returned to work after a _____ in Florence.

2. The columnist wrote that the quarterback was an avaricious thug and was the _____ of what was wrong with the modern athlete.

3. Whining and _____ behavior were his trademarks.

4. The balloon became _____ as he blew air into it.

5. The con man's _____ kept him wealthy for a long time.

6. The casino dealer was _____ at shuffling cards.

7. The monks would all _____ their wordly possessions before entering the monastery.

8. Children _____ on with their imaginary friends.

Group 4

propitiate	dispensation	oligarchy	temporal
continence	renegade	exacerbate	arrogate

1. Monks in that religious order practice _____ and poverty.

2. After the Civil War, _____ soldiers from the Confederate army ransacked the Southwest.

3. The team can _____ the quarterback's displeasure with the game plan by letting him call some of his own plays.

4. Many argued that the country was not really a democracy but an _____.

5. Dictators usually _____ power by first gaining control of the military.

6. While he did not make the team as a player, he was in charge of the _____ of water and sports drinks to the athletes.

7. Whether you place more importance on the _____ or the spiritual depends on your philosophy of life.

8. If you throw water on an electrical fire, you will only _____ the problem.

Unit 26 (cont.)

Words and Definitions

---------------------------- Group 1 ----------------------------

augment (awg MENT): to increase; to add to
  Part of Speech: verb
  Example: City Hall *augmented* the budget to cover new projects.
  Other Form(s): augmented (adjective); augmentation (noun)

silhouette (sil oh WET): outline; profile
  Part of Speech: noun
  Example: The tree stood in *silhouette* against the setting sun.

etymology (et i MOLL uh jee): word study; language study
  Part of Speech: noun
  Example: Teachers of English as a Second Language have to study *etymology*.
  Other Form(s): etymological (adjective)

convex (KON vex): curved outward; rounded
  Part of Speech: adjective
  Example: The red, *convex* bumps on his legs were evidence that him mosquito netting had not worked.

taxonomy (tak SAHN uh mee): classification; categorization
  Part of Speech: noun
  Example: *Taxonomy* is used in most every field of specialization.
  Other Form(s): taxonomical (adjective)

pundit (PUN dit): expert; learned person
  Part of Speech: noun
  Example: The political *pundits* had it all wrong, and the man was re-elected.

rejuvenate (ree JOO veh nate): to revitalize; to renew
  Part of Speech: verb
  Example: The aging athlete hoped that changing teams would *rejuvenate* his career.
  Other Form(s): rejuvenating (adjective); rejuvenation (noun)

diaphanous (dy AF uh nus): sheer; transparent
  Part of Speech: adjective
  Example: Her veil was *diaphanous*, so her facial features were discernible.

─────────────────── **Group 2** ───────────────────

somber (SAHM bur): gloomy; solemn
　　Part of Speech: adjective
　　Example: Sable is a color often worn on *somber* occasions.

dilate (dy LATE): to widen; to expand
　　Part of Speech: verb
　　Example: A women's cervix will *dilate* just prior to her giving birth.
　　Other Form(s): dilated (adjective); dilation (noun)

purgative (PUR guh tiv): cleanser; cathartic
　　Part of Speech: noun
　　Example: The nurse administered a *purgative* to get the patient detoxified.

ascetic (eh SET ik): abstemious; disciplined
　　Part of Speech: adjective
　　Example: Monastic life is supposed to be an *ascetic* life.
　　Other Form(s): ascetic (noun); ascetism (noun)

traduce (truh DOOS): to defame; to dishonor
　　Part of Speech: verb
　　Example: Scandal sheets *traduced* his name, and he sued for libel.

conscription (kun SKRIP shun): draft (into the military); enrollment
　　Part of Speech: noun
　　Example: Upon turning 18 years of age, all males in the U.S. must register for *conscription*.
　　Other Form(s): conscript (verb); conscripted (adjective)

reparations (rep eh RAY shuns): compensation; amends
　　Part of Speech: noun
　　Example: Some *reparations* were paid to the people who had been abused during the war.

ethereal (e THEER ee ul): heavenly; celestial
　　Part of Speech: adjective
　　Example: The diaphanous veil gave the woman's face an *ethereal* look.

Words and Definitions *(cont.)*

———————————— Group 3 ————————————

contentious (kun TEN shus): quarrelsome; combative
    Part of Speech: adjective
    Example: *Contentious* people are unwelcome at celebrations.
    Other Form(s): contentiousness (noun)

tumescent (too MES ent): swollen; swelling
    Part of Speech: adjective
    Example: The malignancy's *tumescent* shape alarmed the doctors.
    Other Form(s): tumescence (noun); tumesce (verb)

artifice (AR ti fis): cunning; skill
    Part of Speech: noun
    Example: Spies use *artifice* to get information.

prattle (PRAT ul): to chatter; to babble
    Part of Speech: verb
    Example: The child *prattled* on and on, and her mother ignored the nonsense.

sojourn (SO jurn): stopover; visit
    Part of Speech: noun
    Example: Part of her itinerary was a brief *sojourn* in Rome.

epitome (eh PIT uh mee): perfect example; paradigm
    Part of Speech: noun
    Example: The straight A student was the *epitome* of an assiduous student.
    Other Form(s): epitomize (verb)

renounce (ree NOWNTS): to forego; to give up
    Part of Speech: verb
    Example: Martin Luther *renounced* his ties with the Roman Catholic Church.
    Other Form(s): renunciation (noun)

deft (DEFT): adroit; dexterous
    Part of Speech: adjective
    Example: With a single, *deft* move, the magician drew balloons from his pocket.

Group 4

propitiate (pro PISH ee ate): to appease; to placate
   Part of Speech: verb
   Example: International peacekeepers *propitiated* the warring parties, and an armistice resulted.
   Other Form(s): propitiating (adjective); propitiation (noun); propitiatory (adjective)

dispensation (dis pen SAY shun): management; allotment
   Part of Speech: noun
   Example: Red Cross volunteers were in charge of the *dispensation* of food and water.
   Other Form(s): dispense (verb); dispensational (adjective)

oligarchy (OHL i gar kee): government by a few; elite rule
   Part of Speech: noun
   Example: Some critics argue that the United States will become an *oligarchy* in the near future.
   Other Form(s): oligarchic (adjective); oligarchal (adjective)

temporal (TEM puh rul): worldly; secular
   Part of Speech: adjective
   Example: His interests were not spiritual; his interests were *temporal*.

continence (KON ti nence): self-restraint; self-discipline
   Part of Speech: noun
   Example: Many religious orders demand *continence* of their priests or ministers.
   Other Form(s): continent (adjective)

renegade (REN eh gade): rebel; outlaw
   Part of Speech: noun
   Example: Vigilante groups harbored *renegades* when the West was young.
   Other Form(s): renegade (adjective)

exacerbate (eg ZASS ur bate): to aggravate; to worsen
   Part of Speech: verb
   Example: Sent to propitiate the groups, he instead *exacerbated* the problems between them.
   Other Form(s): exacerbated (adjective); exacerbation (noun)

arrogate (EHR oh gate): to confiscate; to claim without justification
   Part of Speech: verb
   Example: Each candidate tried to *arrogate* the election while the true result was still in question.
   Other Form(s): arrogation (noun)

Unit 26 *(cont.)*

Quick Match

Group 1

A. rounded	C. expert	E. renew	G. transparent
B. add to	D. outline	F. word study	H. classification

_____ 1. augment

_____ 2. silhouette

_____ 3. etymology

_____ 4. convex

_____ 5. taxonomy

_____ 6. pundit

_____ 7. rejuvenate

_____ 8. diaphanous

Group 2

A. expand	C. heavenly	E. gloomy	G. cathartic
B. defame	D. draft	F. compensation	H. abstemious

_____ 1. somber

_____ 2. dilate

_____ 3. purgative

_____ 4. ascetic

_____ 5. traduce

_____ 6. conscription

_____ 7. reparations

_____ 8. ethereal

Group 3

A. babble	C. stopover	E. give up	G. dexterous
B. cunning	D. perfect example	F. combative	H. swollen

_____ 1. contentious

_____ 2. tumescent

_____ 3. artifice

_____ 4. prattle

_____ 5. sojourn

_____ 6. epitome

_____ 7. renounce

_____ 8. deft

Group 4

A. allotment	C. worsen	E. appease	G. claim without justification
B. mundane	D. self-discipline	F. elite rule	H. rebel

_____ 1. propitiate

_____ 2. dispensation

_____ 3. oligarchy

_____ 4. temporal

_____ 5. continence

_____ 6. renegade

_____ 7. exacerbate

_____ 8. arrogate

Unit 26 (cont.)

Answer Key

Pre-test Yourself

Group 1	Group 2	Group 3	Group 4
1. convex	1. traduce	1. sojourn	1. continence
2. augment	2. reparations	2. epitome	2. renegade
3. taxonomy	3. purgative	3. contentious	3. propitiate
4. etymology	4. conscription	4. tumescent	4. oligarchy
5. pundit	5. ethereal	5. artifice	5. arrogate
6. rejuvenate	6. somber	6. deft	6. dispensation
7. diaphanous	7. dilate	7. renounce	7. temporal
8. silhouette	8. ascetic	8. prattle	8. exacerbate

Quick Match

Group 1	Group 2	Group 3	Group 4
1. B	1. E	1. F	1. E
2. D	2. A	2. H	2. A
3. F	3. G	3. B	3. F
4. A	4. H	4. A	4. B
5. H	5. B	5. C	5. D
6. C	6. D	6. D	6. H
7. E	7. F	7. E	7. C
8. G	8. C	8. G	8. G

Unit 27

Pre-test Yourself

Group 1

skittish	debonair	tenable	cavalier
archaic	rendezvous	euphoria	paradox

1. His _____ manners and old ways made the young people nervous.

2. When victory was finally theirs, a _____ came over them.

3. The _____ lay in the fact that the more he did the more he was asked to do.

4. When faced with the truth, the children became _____ and evasive.

5. The plan was that they would _____ at the meeting place at precisely 2:35.

6. What bothered the teacher the most was the student's _____ and careless attitude.

7. Cosmopolites are sophisticated and _____.

8. His position was _____, and he propounded it well.

Group 2

apropos	propound	epicurean	terminus
sinew	cauterize	debilitate	render

1. When the trolley reached its _____, it entered a turnabout and turned around.

2. He demanded the best because his tastes were _____.

3. Severe illnesses will _____ even the strongest among us.

4. Do not try to eat the tough _____ in turkey.

5. Her clever remarks were _____ as usual.

6. The motivational speaker will _____ her services for a large fee.

7. Before the development of antibiotics, doctors would _____ wounds to kill bacteria.

8. Philosophers _____ systems of thought that they believe elucidate one type of truth or another.

Pre-test Yourself (cont.)

Group 3

apathy	proverbial	defray	thicket
coalesce	repellent	equable	snivel

1. After the many plans _____, the program can be put into action.

2. His constant antics made him the _____ class clown.

3. The hunchback of Notre Dame had a warm heart but a _____ appearance.

4. A spoiled child will _____ and whine when he does not get his way.

5. The man suffered from _____ and was unable to motivate himself.

6. The students will wash cars and _____ the cost of the trip.

7. The dense _____ obscured his view of the highway.

8. Her demeanor was always that of a calm, sedate, and _____ woman.

Group 4

equivocal	repose	apogee	putative
cognitive	smug	debauchery	therapeutic

1. The car salesman gave _____ answers to all of the customer's questions.

2. I didn't mind that he won so much as I resented his _____ attitude after winning.

3. Sojourns in Lake Placid were _____ for tubercular patients.

4. The king had only _____ power; the real power lay with his lord chamberlain.

5. His tales of his famous brother's life of _____ always made interesting party conversation.

6. The missile's _____ was at 100,000 feet, and then it headed back toward earth.

7. Sweet _____ lay at the end of the long journey.

8. Her _____ abilities were, according to her teachers, unsurpassed.

Unit 27 (cont.)

Words and Definitions

―――――――――― Group 1 ――――――――――

skittish (SKIT ish): restless; jumpy
Part of Speech: adjective
Example: Animals become *skittish* when they feel a big storm coming in.

debonair (deb oh NAIR): suave; cosmopolitan
Part of Speech: adjective
Example: His travels and experiences made him quite *debonair*.

tenable (TEN uh bul): defendable; maintainable
Part of Speech: adjective
Example: His thinking was *tenable*, and a lot of people agreed with him.

cavalier (kah vuh LEER): haughty; blasé
Part of Speech: adjective
Example: The *cavalier* young man estranged everyone he met.

archaic (ar KAY ik): out-of-date; antequated
Part of Speech: adjective
Example: *Archaic* words are identified as such in dictionaries.
Other Form(s): archaism (noun); archaistic (adjective)

rendezvous (RON day voo): to meet; to assemble
Part of Speech: verb
Example: The planes *rendezvoused* over the target.

euphoria (yoo FOR ee uh): elation; joy
Part of Speech: noun
Example: The victory by the home team created a *euphoria* in the town.
Other Form(s): euphoric (adjective)

paradox (PARE uh dox): seeming contradiction; riddle
Part of Speech: noun
Example: "The more things change, the more they stay the same" is both a maxim and a *paradox*.
Other Form(s): paradoxical (adjective)

Words and Definitions *(cont.)*

———————————— **Group 2** ————————————

apropos (ap ruh PO): appropriate; pertinent
   Part of Speech: adjective
   Example: She had a knack of doing things that were *apropos* of certain situations.

propound (pro POWND): offer for consideration; propose
   Part of Speech: verb
   Example: Missionaries *propound* their church's doctrine.

epicurean (ep ih kyur EE un): devoted to enjoyment; hedonistic
   Part of Speech: adjective
   Example: His *epicurean* needs created many problems for him.

terminus (TUR mih nus): end; final point
   Part of Speech: noun
   Example: When the train reached its *terminus*, it turned around for the return trip.

sinew (SIH noo): tendon; ligament
   Part of Speech: noun
   Example: Steak can be tough if the *sinews* are left in the meat.
   Other Form(s): sinewy (adjective)

cauterize (KAW tur ize): burn; sear
   Part of Speech: verb
   Example: The veterinarian *cauterized* the animal's wound to close it.
   Other Form(s): cauterization (noun)

debilitate (de BIL i tate): to make feeble; to weaken
   Part of Speech: verb
   Example: After many illnesses had *debilitated* him, and he finally gave up his goal to run a marathon.
   Other Form(s): debilitation (noun); debilitating (adjective)

render (REN dur): cause to be or become; give
   Part of Speech: verb
   Example: Teachers *render* services to young people.

Words and Definitions *(cont.)*

─────────────── **Group 3** ───────────────

apathy (AH puh thee): indifference; lack of emotion
    Part of Speech: noun
    Example: Feelings of powerlessness often lead to *apathy*.
    Other Form(s): apathetic (adjective)

proverbial (pruh VUR bee ul): renowned; of a proverb
    Part of Speech: adjective
    Example: The *proverbial* third time turned out to be the charm as he hit the jackpot on his third pull of the slot machine's lever.

defray (de FRAY): to pay for; to bear the cost
    Part of Speech: verb
    Example: Schools *defrayed* the costs of trips by holding various money raising events.

thicket (THICK et): a tangle of shrubs or trees; underbrush
    Part of Speech: noun
    Example: He sliced his drive, and his golf ball became lost in a *thicket*.

coalesce (ko uh LES): to come together; to unite
    Part of Speech: verb
    Example: Disparate ideas *coalesced* and the project began to take shape.

repellent (re PEL ent): revolting; offensive
    Part of Speech: adjective
    Example: People eschewed him because he had a *repellent* demeanor.
    Other Form(s): repel (verb)

equable (EK wuh bul): uniform; fair
    Part of Speech: adjective
    Example: She was *equable* with her policies, and every one admired her.

snivel (SNIV ul): to sniffle; to whine
    Part of Speech: verb
    Example: Cowards often *snivel* when faced with imminent danger.

Unit 27 *(cont.)*

Words and Definitions *(cont.)*

──────────── **Group 4** ────────────

equivocal (ee KWIV uh kul): intentionally ambiguous; deliberately misleading
    Part of Speech: adjective
    Example: No one knew what the *equivocal* politician believed in.
    Other Form(s): equivocate (verb); equivocation (noun)

repose (ruh POZE): rest; sleep
    Part of Speech: noun
    Example: Her *repose* came during a sojourn in Rome.

apogee (AH po jee): apex; most distant point
    Part of Speech: noun
    Example: Her career reached an *apogee* when she was made CEO.

putative (PYOO tuh tiv): supposed; reputed
    Part of Speech: adjective
    Example: His *putative* powers proved to be all talk and no action.

cognitive (KOG ni tiv): intellectual; perceptive
    Part of Speech: adjective
    Example: Man's *cognitive* powers separate him from other animals.
    Other Form(s): cognition (noun)

smug (SMUG): self-satisfied; complacent
    Part of Speech: adjective
    Example: When a civilization becomes *smug* about its power, it is in danger of losing it.

debauchery (de BOT chur ee): self-indulgence; immoderation
    Part of Speech: noun
    Example: Widespread *debauchery* was the cause for the government's decline.
    Other Form(s): debauch (verb); debaucher (noun); debauchee (noun)

therapeutic (ther uh PYOO tik): curative; medicinal
    Part of Speech: adjective
    Example: Music is often used as a *therapeutic* agent in cases of autism.

Unit 27 (cont.)

Quick Match

Group 1

A. maintainable   C. jumpy   E. elation   G. seeming contradiction
B. haughty   D. meet   F. cosmopolitan   H. out-of-date

_____ 1. skittish

_____ 2. debonair

_____ 3. tenable

_____ 4. cavalier

_____ 5. archaic

_____ 6. rendezvous

_____ 7. euphoria

_____ 8. paradox

Group 2

A. hedonistic   C. give   E. burn   G. propose
B. pertinent   D. tendon   F. weaken   H. end

_____ 1. apropos

_____ 2. propound

_____ 3. epicurean

_____ 4. terminus

_____ 5. sinew

_____ 6. cauterize

_____ 7. debilitate

_____ 8. render

Group 3

A. tangle of brush   C. fair   E. indifference   G. renowned
B. whine   D. revolting   F. pay for   H. unite

_____ 1. apathy

_____ 2. proverbial

_____ 3. defray

_____ 4. thicket

_____ 5. coalesce

_____ 6. repellent

_____ 7. equable

_____ 8. snivel

Group 4

A. perceptive   C. rest   E. reputed   G. self-satisfied
B. immoderation   D. apex   F. intentionally ambiguous   H. curative

_____ 1. equivocal

_____ 2. repose

_____ 3. apogee

_____ 4. putative

_____ 5. cognitive

_____ 6. smug

_____ 7. debauchery

_____ 8. therapeutic

Unit 27 _(cont.)_

Answer Key

─────── **Pre-test Yourself** ───────

Group 1	Group 2	Group 3	Group 4
1. archaic	1. terminus	1. coalesce	1. equivocal
2. euphoria	2. epicurean	2. proverbial	2. smug
3. paradox	3. debilitate	3. repellent	3. therapeutic
4. skittish	4. sinew	4. snivel	4. putative
5. rendezvous	5. apropos	5. apathy	5. debauchery
6. cavalier	6. render	6. defray	6. apogee
7. debonair	7. cauterize	7. thicket	7. repose
8. tenable	8. propound	8. equable	8. cognitive

─────── **Quick Match** ───────

Group 1	Group 2	Group 3	Group 4
1. C	1. B	1. E	1. F
2. F	2. G	2. G	2. C
3. A	3. A	3. F	3. D
4. B	4. H	4. A	4. E
5. H	5. D	5. H	5. A
6. D	6. E	6. D	6. G
7. E	7. F	7. C	7. B
8. G	8. C	8. B	8. H

Unit 28

Pre-test Yourself

1. Etiquette was her forte, and her _____ behavior impressed everyone.

2. His _____ actions were punished very quickly.

3. The _____ spray protected the children from bacteria.

4. In westerns, cowpokes often _____ their horses to posts in front of saloons.

5. He went from not making his high school basketball team to an _____ of a professional basketball player in just five years.

6. Engineers opened the dam's _____ to relieve pressure on its walls.

7. His fame turned out to be _____ , and he was soon back to being anonymous.

8. There was a rift in the political party, and one group formed a _____ .

1. The governor may _____ a prisoner's sentence when he feels there is mitigating evidence.

2. Pompous and righteous demagogues _____ in their speeches.

3. She lost all her _____ when the audience started to throw food at her.

4. The commandos will _____ the guards so they will not make noise.

5. The play turned into a _____ when the scenery collapsed on top of the actors.

6. Native Americans are _____ to North America.

7. The workers sat down for a small _____ before resuming their activities.

8. With his lousy study habits and miserable grades, he was the _____ of what a star student should be.

Unit 28 *(cont.)*

Pre-test Yourself *(cont.)*

Group 3			
nuance	esoteric	ogle	quantum
vie	largess	illusory	usury

1. Super Bowl teams _____ for the Vince Lombardi trophy.

2. His _____ ideas did not garner a good reception from the longshoremen.

3. Her rendition of the song contained a _____ that had never before been heard.

4. The philanthropist's _____ kept the museum open for another year.

5. It used to be that 20% interest was considered _____, but now it's par for the course.

6. Many feel that permanence and immutability are _____ in this world.

7. She would _____ her professor each time he lectured the class.

8. He asked for the _____ of food guaranteed on his ration ticket.

Group 4			
bumptious	imposition	limpid	vindictive
orotund	epiphany	nondescript	plutocracy

1. The package was _____, and it blended in with the other packages.

2. As a _____ person, he was known for his need to revenge imagined insults.

3. Arrogant people display _____ behavior.

4. Rich men formed a _____ to run the country.

5. He experienced an _____ when he discovered his special talent.

6. She considered a guest's staying for a year as an unforgivable _____.

7. His _____ way of speaking did little to inspire the graduating class.

8. When I fished along the Maine coast, I saw right to the bottom of the _____ water.

Unit 28 (cont.)

Words and Definitions

Group 1

prophylactic (pro fi LAK tik): preventive; protective
  Part of Speech: adjective
  Example: Gloves provided *prophylactic* protection from deadly bacteria.
  Other Form(s): prophylactic (noun)

decorous (DEK ur us): proper; tasteful
  Part of Speech: adjective
  Example: She was a staid and *decorous* woman who never acted out of role.
  Other Form(s): decorousness (noun)

tether (TEH thur): to tie up; to secure
  Part of Speech: verb
  Example: He made sure to *tether* the boat to the dock.
  Other Form(s): tether (noun)

sluice (SLOOS): release gate for water; channel
  Part of Speech: noun
  Example: The dam's *sluices* were opened to prevent upland flooding.

evanescent (ev uh NES ent): ephemeral; transient
  Part of Speech: adjective
  Example: The mist was *evanescent* and floated off on various zephyrs.
  Other Form(s): evanescence (noun); evanesce (verb)

caucus (KAW kus): meeting; council
  Part of Speech: noun
  Example: The small faction held a *caucus* and agreed to vote against an issue.

reprehensible (rep re HEN si bul): blameworthy; deserving rebuke
  Part of Speech: adjective
  Example: His *reprehensible* behavior shocked many decorous people.
  Other Form(s): reprehensibility (noun); reprehend (verb); reprehensive (adjective)

apotheosis (uh poth ee O sis): deification; glorification
  Part of Speech: noun
  Example: Many a pop star is an *apotheosis* one minute and virtually forgotten the next.

Words and Definitions *(cont.)*

─────────── **Group 2** ───────────

pontificate (pon TIF i kate): to preach; to pretend to be infallible
    Part of Speech: verb
    Example: Reformers *pontificate* about how bad things are.
    Other Form(s): pontification (noun)

throttle (THRAW tul): to choke; to strangle
    Part of Speech: verb
    Example: The older sister made a gesture that let her younger sibling know that she would *throttle* him if he wasn't quiet.

repast (re PAST): meal; food
    Part of Speech: noun
    Example: They rested for a while, had a brief *repast*, and then continued the journey.

antithesis (an TITH e sis): exact opposite; complete contrast
    Part of Speech: noun
    Example: Infinity is the *antithesis* of zero.
    Other Form(s): antithetical (adjective)

indigenous (in DIJ uh nus): native; occurring naturally to an area
    Part of Speech: adjective
    Example: The animals *indigenous* to the area were known to be unafraid of humans.

debacle (de BAW kul): collapse; disaster
    Part of Speech: noun
    Example: The score was lopsided, and sportswriters called the game a *debacle*.

commute (kuh MYOOT): to exchange; to change for something lesser
    Part of Speech: verb
    Example: In light of the new evidence, the governor decided to *commute* the prisoner's sentence.
    Other Form(s): commutable (adjective); commutability (noun)

equanimity (eh kwuh NIM i tee): calmness; serenity
    Part of Speech: noun
    Example: Her *equanimity* made her the perfect choice for mediator.
    Other Form(s): equanimous (adjective)

Words and Definitions *(cont.)*

─────────────── **Group 3** ───────────────

nuance (NOO ahnts): subtlety; shade of meaning
  Part of Speech: noun
  Example: There are *nuances* in his writing that only the most astute reader can comprehend.
  Other Form(s): nuanced (adjective); nuance (verb)

esoteric (es o TAIR iK): recondite; understandable to only a few
  Part of Speech: adjective
  Example: The world of quantum physics is an *esoteric* one, since its realities are different than our everyday ones.
  Other Form(s): esotericism (noun); esotericist (noun)

illusory (i LOO suh ree): deceptive; unreal
  Part of Speech: adjective
  Example: Buddha said that reality itself is *illusory*.

quantum (KWON tum): amount; portion
  Part of Speech: noun
  Example: Scientists carefully inspected the *quantum* of uranium to assess its size and scope.

vie (VY): to contend; to struggle
  Part of Speech: verb
  Example: Competitors *vie* for the right to perform in the Olympics.

largess (lar JESS): money or gifts freely given; philanthropy
  Part of Speech: noun
  Example: She was known for her kindness and *largess* to the poor.

ogle (O gul): to leer; to stare at
  Part of Speech: verb
  Example: The lascivious and lecherous man *ogled* the pretty maiden.
  Other Form(s): ogler (noun)

usury (YOO zhuh ree): extortion; lending money with interest (especially with a high rate)
  Part of Speech: noun
  Example: Loan sharks deal in *usury*.
  Other Form(s): usurious (adjective); usurer (noun)

Words and Definitions *(cont.)*

–––––––––––––––––––––––––––––––– **Group 4** ––––––––––––––––––––––––––––––––

bumptious (BUMP shus): conceited; offensively self-assertive

  Part of Speech: adjective

  Example: The whole team's *bumptious* attitude made it a target for other teams.

  Other Form(s): bumptiousness (noun)

imposition (im puh ZISH un): burden; onus

  Part of Speech: noun

  Example: Some people consider being asked for a loan an unforgiveable *imposition*.

  Other Form(s): impose (verb)

nondescript (non de SKRIPT): dull; unremarkable

  Part of Speech: adjective

  Example: The music critic irked the pop star when he described her music as *nondescript*.

vindictive (vin DIK tiv): spiteful; vengeful

  Part of Speech: adjective

  Example: The *vindictive* attack was full of animosity.

orotund (OR uh tund): bombastic; sonorous

  Part of Speech: adjective

  Example: The demagogue spoke in an *orotund* manner.

epiphany (uh PIF uh nee): revelation; enlightenment

  Part of Speech: noun

  Example: The seminal filmmaker's use of shadows was an *epiphany* for many of his successors.

  Other Form(s): epiphanic (adjective)

limpid (LIM pid): clear; transparent

  Part of Speech: adjective

  Example: The sculpture was made of *limpid* materials, and so the light in the room was part of it.

plutocracy (ploo TOK ruh see): government by the wealthy

  Part of Speech: noun

  Example: When millionaires run a government, you have a *plutocracy*.

  Other Form(s): plutocratic (adjective)

Unit 28 (cont.)

Quick Match

Group 1

A. blameworthy	C. protective	E. secure	G. tasteful
B. transient	D. meeting	F. deification	H. channel

_____ 1. prophylactic   _____ 5. evanescent

_____ 2. decorous   _____ 6. caucus

_____ 3. tether   _____ 7. reprehensible

_____ 4. sluice   _____ 8. apotheosis

Group 2

A. strangle	C. serenity	E. native	G. opposite
B. preach	D. disaster	F. exchange	H. meal

_____ 1. pontificate   _____ 5. repast

_____ 2. throttle   _____ 6. debacle

_____ 3. indigenous   _____ 7. commute

_____ 4. antithesis   _____ 8. equanimity

Group 3

A. deceptive	C. recondite	E. generosity	G. extortion
B. contend	D. leer	F. amount	H. subtlety

_____ 1. nuance   _____ 5. vie

_____ 2. esoteric   _____ 6. largess

_____ 3. illusory   _____ 7. ogle

_____ 4. quantum   _____ 8. usury

Group 4

A. dull	C. government by wealthy	E. revelation	G. vengeful
B. pompous	D. burden	F. conceited	H. clear

_____ 1. bumptious   _____ 5. orotund

_____ 2. imposition   _____ 6. epiphany

_____ 3. nondescript   _____ 7. limpid

_____ 4. vindictive   _____ 8. plutocracy

Unit 28 *(cont.)*

Answer Key

Group 1	Group 2	Group 3	Group 4
1. decorous	1. commute	1. vie	1. nondescript
2. reprehensible	2. pontificate	2. esoteric	2. vindictive
3. prophylactic	3. equanimity	3. nuance	3. bumptious
4. tether	4. throttle	4. largess	4. plutocracy
5. apotheosis	5. debacle	5. usury	5. epiphany
6. sluice	6. indigenous	6. illusory	6. imposition
7. evanescent	7. repast	7. ogle	7. orotund
8. caucus	8. antithesis	8. quantum	8. limpid

Quick Match

Group 1	Group 2	Group 3	Group 4
1. C	1. B	1. H	1. F
2. G	2. A	2. C	2. D
3. E	3. E	3. A	3. A
4. H	4. G	4. F	4. G
5. B	5. H	5. B	5. B
6. D	6. D	6. E	6. E
7. A	7. F	7. D	7. H
8. F	8. C	8. G	8. C

Unit 29

Pre-test Yourself

Group 1

nascent	retract	utile	omnipotent
waive	premonition	munificent	hermetic

1. His magnanimity and largess showed him to be a _____ philanthropist.

2. The plans were _____, and more preparation was necessary before they started.

3. New evidence forced him to say that he would _____ his statement.

4. A defendant can _____ his right to a trial by pleading guilty.

5. Her uncanny _____ alerted the sentries to possible incursions.

6. The _____ seal prevented air from getting into the life-saving bubble.

7. The tribe viewed the deity as both omniscient and _____.

8. He was interested in practical and _____ tools.

Group 2

finicky	nether	referendum	vacuous
heterogeneous	genealogy	preamble	loath

1. The issue was put to a _____ so that everyone could vote on it.

2. He wrote a _____ that introduced the main concepts in the book.

3. Fastidious and meticulous people are often _____ individuals.

4. According to many mythologies and religions, evil sinners are sent to the _____ regions when they die.

5. His _____ traced the family back to the eleventh century.

6. When the ball struck him, he was stunned and had a _____ look on his face.

7. She couldn't decide which ring she wanted but was _____ to let either one go.

8. When _____ grouping is used, students of varied abilities are placed in one class.

Unit 29 (cont.)

Pre-test Yourself (cont.)

Group 3

warp	facet	hoary	formative
progenitor	vantage	respiration	junta

1. Every _____ of the diamond gave off scintillating beams.

2. The old man shook his grizzled and _____ head.

3. In football circles, the coach is revered as the _____ of the style of offense that most teams now employ.

4. A strong shock to the heart brought his _____ back.

5. Terror gripped the entire nation when the _____ deposed the president.

6. From her _____, everything she saw was pleasing.

7. A wooden deck will _____ from exposure to water if it is not treated.

8. The psychologist concluded that the recidivist's lifestyle could be traced back to his lack of guidance in his _____ years.

Group 4

verbiage	gestate	mundane	prig
fulsome	obtuse	usurp	ribald

1. The young of the mammal typically would _____ in the womb for several months before being born.

2. Ribald jokes upset the _____.

3. Excess _____ spoiled his oral presentation.

4. The ribald jokes were _____ to the prig.

5. The sexual connotations in his _____ jokes upset a lot of people.

6. Her main motivation for marrying the aged tycoon was to eventually _____ his finances.

7. Most people find being struck in traffic almost insufferably _____.

8. His answers were _____ and weren't really answers.

Words and Definitions

--- **Group 1** ---

nascent (NAY sint): beginning; young
   Part of Speech: adjective
   Example: His *nascent* basketball skills attracted scouts from major colleges.
   Other Form(s): nascence (noun); nascency (noun)

retract (ree TRAKT): to withdraw; to recant
   Part of Speech: verb
   Example: Part of the libel suit demanded that the paper *retract* its scurrilous remarks.
   Other Form(s): retraction (noun); retractable (verb)

utile (YOO tul): useful; practical
   Part of Speech: adjective
   Example: His methods were *utile* even though they were unorthodox.

omnipotent (om NI po tent): all-powerful; all-dominant
   Part of Speech: adjective
   Example: As strong as Superman is, he is not *omnipotent*.
   Other Form(s): omnipotence (noun)

waive (WAVE): to pass up; to surrender
   Part of Speech: verb
   Example: Some defendants *waived* their right to a jury trial and let a judge do the deciding.

premonition (preh mo NISH un): forewarning; a presentiment
   Part of Speech: noun
   Example: Some animals give *premonitions* of severe weather changes.

munificent (myoo NI fi sent): magnanimous; bountiful
   Part of Speech: adjective
   Example: Philanthropists are *munificent* persons.
   Other Form(s): munificence (noun)

hermetic (her MET ik): with an airtight closure; protected from outside forces
   Part of Speech: adjective
   Example: If submarines are not *hermetic*, they sink.
   Other Form(s): hermeticism (noun); hermetical (adjective)

Words and Definitions *(cont.)*

─────────────────── **Group 2** ───────────────────

finicky (FIN ik ee): fastidious; not easily pleased
   Part of Speech: adjective
   Example: He obsessed over which meal to prepare for his date because he knew she was a *finicky* eater.
   Other Form(s): finickiness (noun)

nether (NEH thur): lower; of the depths
   Part of Speech: adjective
   Example: In Greek mythology, Orpheus sought Eurydice in the *nether* regions.

referendum (ref ur EN dum): a popular vote; a vote of all citizens
   Part of Speech: noun
   Example: Critics of the mayor lobbied for a *referendum* on the ballpark financing issue.

vacuous (VAK yoo us): empty; stupid
   Part of Speech: adjective
   Example: Most of the students had *vacuous* looks on their faces, and the professor realized that the material was too recondite for their present sensibilities.
   Other Form(s): vacuity (noun); vacuousness (noun)

heterogeneous (het ur oh JEE nee us): diverse; varied
   Part of Speech: adjective
   Example: Some school administrators believe in the *heterogenous* grouping of students.
   Other Form(s): heterogeneity (noun); heterogeneousness (noun)

genealogy (jee nee OL o jee): pedigree; family origins
   Part of Speech: noun
   Example: A search into her *genealogy* showed she was a direct descendant of Betsy Ross.
   Other Form(s): genealogical (adjective)

preamble (PRE am bul): opening; beginning
   Part of Speech: noun
   Example: Some books have both a *preamble* and an epilogue.

loath (LOWTH): reluctant; unwilling
   Part of Speech: adjective
   Example: His finicky nature made him *loath* to choose a roommate.

Words and Definitions *(cont.)*

———————————— **Group 3** ————————————

warp (WORP): to twist; to turn
   Part of Speech: verb
   Example: Carpenters purposely *warp* wood to make staves for barrels.

facet (FAS et): aspect; detail
   Part of Speech: noun
   Example: Scientists scrutinized every *facet* of the experimental drug.
   Other Form(s): faceted (adjective)

hoary (HOR ee): gray- or white-haired; aged
   Part of Speech: adjective
   Example: The dating service set the widow up with a man who was a bit too *hoary* for her taste.

formative (FOR muh tiv): pertaining to development; pertaining to growth
   Part of Speech: adjective
   Example: His good looks and dynamic personality brought attention to the nascent sport during its *formative* years.

progenitor (pro JEN ih tur): ancestor; predecessor
   Part of Speech: noun
   Example: The authors of our Constitution are our political *progenitors*.
   Other Form(s): progenitorial (adjective); progenitorship (noun); progenitive (adjective)

vantage (VAN tij): a place affording a good view; viewpoint
   Part of Speech: noun
   Example: From Cassius's *vantage*, it appeared that Brutus's army was surrounded.

respiration (reh spi RAY shun): breathing; gasping
   Part of Speech: noun
   Example: The ventilator aided his *respiration*.

junta (HOON tuh): cabal; self-appointed committee
   Part of Speech: noun
   Example: A revolution resulted in a *junta* getting control of the country.

Group 4

verbiage (VUR bee idj): wordiness; prolixity
Part of Speech: noun
Example: The professor insisted that his students re-read their essays and eliminate any excess *verbiage*.

gestate (jess TATE): to incubate; to develop
Part of Speech: verb
Example: Creative thinkers often *gestate* their ideas before sharing them.
Other Form(s): gestation (noun)

mundane (mun DANE): banal; hackneyed
Part of Speech: adjective
Example: Most critics agreed that the film's plot was *mundane* despite the presence of several highly respected actors.
Other Form(s): mundanity (noun)

prig (PRIG): moralistic person; self-righteous person
Part of Speech: noun
Example: The radio personality labelled his nemesis as a *prig* who had no concept of comedy.

fulsome (FUL sum): disgusting by excess of flattery; cloying
Part of Speech: adjective
Example: His *fulsome* innuendo caused several members of the sorority to boycott functions that involved him.
Other Form(s): fulsomeness (noun)

obtuse (ob TOOS): dull; blunt
Part of Speech: adjective
Example: He was considered a dolt because he offered *obtuse* solutions to complex problems.
Other Form(s): obtuseness (noun); obtusity (noun)

usurp (yoo SURP): seize or assume wrongfully; encroach
Part of Speech: verb
Example: A junta *usurped* management of the government.
Other Form(s): usurper (noun); usurpation (noun)

ribald (RIH buld): bawdy; scurrilous
Part of Speech: adjective
Example: Stand-up comedians often resort to *ribald* jokes for a laugh.
Other Form(s): ribaldry (noun)

Unit 29 *(cont.)*

Quick Match

Group 1

A. all-powerful	C. airtight	E. bountiful	G. beginning
B. surrender	D. withdraw	F. forewarning	H. practical

_____ 1. nascent

_____ 2. retract

_____ 3. utile

_____ 4. omnipotent

_____ 5. waive

_____ 6. premonition

_____ 7. munificent

_____ 8. hermetic

Group 2

A. lower	C. diverse	E. reluctant	G. pedigree
B. empty	D. fastidious	F. opening	H. popular vote

_____ 1. finicky

_____ 2. nether

_____ 3. referendum

_____ 4. vacuous

_____ 5. heterogeneous

_____ 6. genealogy

_____ 7. preamble

_____ 8. loath

Group 3

A. aspect	C. viewpoint	E. breathing	G. gray- or white-haired
B. pertaining to growth	D. ancestor	F. twist	H. cabal

_____ 1. warp

_____ 2. facet

_____ 3. hoary

_____ 4. formative

_____ 5. progenitor

_____ 6. vantage

_____ 7. respiration

_____ 8. junta

Group 4

A. moralistic person	C. prolixity	E. develop	G. bawdy
B. banal	D. dull	F. seize unjustly	H. cloying

_____ 1. verbiage

_____ 2. gestate

_____ 3. mundane

_____ 4. prig

_____ 5. fulsome

_____ 6. obtuse

_____ 7. usurp

_____ 8. ribald

Unit 29 *(cont.)*

Answer Key

Pre-test Yourself

Group 1
1. munificent
2. nascent
3. retract
4. waive
5. premonition
6. hermetic
7. omnipotent
8. utile

Group 2
1. referendum
2. preamble
3. finicky
4. nether
5. genealogy
6. vacuous
7. loath
8. heterogeneous

Group 3
1. facet
2. hoary
3. progenitor
4. respiration
5. junta
6. vantage
7. warp
8. formative

Group 4
1. gestate
2. prig
3. verbiage
4. fulsome
5. ribald
6. usurp
7. mundane
8. obtuse

Quick Match

Group 1
1. G
2. D
3. H
4. A
5. B
6. F
7. E
8. C

Group 2
1. D
2. A
3. H
4. B
5. C
6. G
7. F
8. E

Group 3
1. F
2. A
3. G
4. B
5. D
6. C
7. E
8. H

Group 4
1. C
2. E
3. B
4. A
5. H
6. D
7. F
8. G

Unit 30

Pre-test Yourself

Group 1

fawn	poignancy	riparian	huckster
validate	maverick	obloquy	idyll

1. It was a moment that was full of _____ when the two sisters reunited after many years apart.

2. The Corps of Engineers restricted the _____ rights of the steamboat company.

3. _____ followed the evil man everywhere he went.

4. Toadies _____ over their superiors.

5. If he offers to sell you the Brooklyn Bridge, he's a _____.

6. Assessment evaluators _____ tests and test results.

7. The paramours shared an _____ when they reached the rendezvous.

8. As a _____, he had great difficulty following the rules.

Group 2

waft	prototype	encroach	morose
impervious	quantitative	fallow	opprobrium

1. The new school building was to be a _____ for all subsequent school-building projects.

2. Students who do not allow learning into their lives have _____ minds.

3. From his bedroom window he could see the smoke from the factory _____ over the lake.

4. His devious ways were met with _____ and general disapproval.

5. You could tell she was unhappy from the _____ look on her face.

6. If you _____ on someone else's property, you may be found guilty of trespassing.

7. Since there was not a large _____ difference between the size of the two pieces, he let his girlfriend choose which piece of pie she wanted.

8. Her strong moral character was _____ to temptation.

Unit 30 *(cont.)*

Pre-test Yourself *(cont.)*

Group 3

| vilify | retort | furtive | myriad |
| encomium | preen | gaudy | quorum |

---

1. In a negative electoral ad campaign, the candidates will generally _____ one another.

2. The shore was composed of _____ grains of sand.

3. He gave a quick _____ to the criticism leveled at him.

4. He received an _____ from the CEO at his retirement party.

5. The thief stole a _____ glance at his neighbor's locker combination.

6. The actress enjoyed the spotlight so much that she would _____ in front of the paparazzi.

7. When a _____ was reached, the committee started to vote on issues.

8. The meretricious woman tended to favor _____ jewelry.

Group 4

| fey | wary | prorate | retrogress |
| matrix | veer | homily | ornithology |

---

1. Aerospace engineers study _____ for valuable information.

2. He was an eccentric, and his _____ ways amused his family.

3. A company will _____ its products in order to make them more affordable.

4. The minister delivered a _____ for all the parishioners.

5. Civil rights causes may _____ as a result of the new leader's regime.

6. A prototype is a _____.

7. When a front tire blows, the car will _____ dangerously.

8. Recent losses on the stock market made him _____ of investing any more money.

Unit 30 (cont.)

Words and Definitions

—— Group 1 ——

fawn (FAWN): to kowtow; to behave servilely
    Part of Speech: verb
    Example: The courtiers *fawned* over their gracious queen.

poignancy (POYN yan see): painful sharpness to emotions or senses
    Part of Speech: noun
    Example: In the play, the tragic hero's death was full of *poignancy*.
    Other Form(s): poignant (adjective); poignance (noun)

riparian (ri PAIR ee un): having to do with a river bank
    Part of Speech: adjective
    Example: Levees are *riparian* fortifications intended to enclose a river.

huckster (HUK stur): peddler; salesman
    Part of Speech: noun
    Example: *Hucksters* traveled the countryside selling basic items to isolated farmwives.

validate (VAL i date): to verify; to prove
    Part of Speech: verb
    Example: The students' marks *validated* his teaching methods.
    Other Form(s): validation (noun); validity (noun)

maverick (MAV ur ik): unorthodox person; independent-minded person
    Part of Speech: noun
    Example: Andy Warhol was a *maverick* in the art community.
    Other Form(s): maverick (adjective)

obloquy (OB luh kwee): disrepute; disfavor
    Part of Speech: noun
    Example: After he committed heinous acts, *obloquy* followed him for the rest of his life.

idyll (IH dil): something blissful and peaceful; a short description of such a scene
    Part of Speech: noun
    Example: Her brief sojourn in Rome became an *idyll* that she always remembered.
    Other Form(s): idyllic (adjective); idyllize (verb); idyllist (noun)

Words and Definitions (cont.)

--- Group 2 ---

waft (WAFT): to float; to drift
  Part of Speech: verb
  Example: Smoke *wafted* over the ruins for several days.

prototype (PRO toe type): original; pattern
  Part of Speech: noun
  Example: Sikorsky developed the working helicopter's *prototype* and is considered its inventor.
  Other Form(s): prototypical (adjective)

encroach (en KROACH): to intrude; to trespass
  Part of Speech: verb
  Example: Neighbors *encroached* on my property, and I had to tell them to go away.
  Other Form(s): encroachment (noun)

morose (muh ROHS): sullen; saturnine
  Part of Speech: adjective
  Example: The sad and somber man always had a *morose* look about him.

impervious (im PUR vee us): impenetrable; impassable
  Part of Speech: adjective
  Example: He had been in so many political campaigns that he was *impervious* to jeers.
  Other Form(s): imperviousness (noun)

quantitative (KWAN ti tay tiv): pertaining to quantity; regarding measurement
  Part of Speech: adjective
  Example: *Quantitative* words tell us about size or number.

fallow (FA loh): inactive; uncultivated
  Part of Speech: adjective
  Example: He let the fields lie *fallow* for a year.

opprobrium (o PRO bree um): disgrace; shame
  Part of Speech: noun
  Example: People felt obloquy and *opprobrium* for the evil man.
  Other Form(s): oppobrious (adjective)

Words and Definitions *(cont.)*

———————————— **Group 3** ————————————

vilify (VIL i fy): to defame; to denigrate
    Part of Speech: verb
    Example: Newspapers and magazines *vilified* the hypocritical reformer.
    Other Form(s): vilification (noun); vilifier (noun)

retort (ree TORT): an answer; a reply
    Part of Speech: noun
    Example: She answered his calumny with a quick *retort*.
    Other Form(s): retort (verb)

furtive (FUR tiv): clandestine; covert
    Part of Speech: adjective
    Example: He knew he wasn't supposed to be looking, so he stole a *furtive* glance.

myriad (MEER ee ad): innumerable; countless
    Part of Speech: adjective
    Example: Soldiers appeared in *myriad* phalanxes across the field.
    Other Form(s): myriad (noun)

encomium (en KOE mee um): tribute; praise
    Part of Speech: noun
    Example: Many *encomiums* came her way when she retired.
    Other Form(s): encomiastic (ajdective)

preen (PREEN): admire oneself; pride oneself
    Part of Speech: verb
    Example: The woman *preened* in front of a mirror before she went downstairs.
    Other Form(s): preener (noun)

gaudy (GAWD ee): garish; flashy
    Part of Speech: adjective
    Example: Pink trousers, a yellow shirt, and a green hat make for a *gaudy* outfit.

quorum (KWOR um): required group; minimum number
    Part of Speech: noun
    Example: An important vote could not be taken because a *quorum* was not present.

—————————————————— **Group 4** ——————————————————

fey (FAY): strange; otherwordly
Part of Speech: adjective
Example: Senility encroached upon his mind, and he answered questions in a *fey* manner.
Other Form(s): feyness (noun)

prorate (pro RATE): to assess separately; to distribute evenly
Part of Speech: verb
Example: The health club *prorated* its fees because not everyone used the same facilities.
Other Form(s): prorated (adjective)

homily (HOM i lee): sermon; lecture
Part of Speech: noun
Example: The preacher's *homily* concerned charity and its blessings.

retrogress (REH tro gress): to revert; to go back
Part of Speech: verb
Example: His therapy had been going well, when all of a sudden he *retrogressed*.
Other Form(s): retrogression (noun); retrogressive (adjective)

matrix (MAY trix): mold; environment in which a thing is created
Part of Speech: noun
Example: Since the *matrix* for the intricate statues had been lost, no more exact replicas could be made.

wary (WARE ee): cautious; circumspect
Part of Speech: adjective
Example: Fruitless love affairs had made her *wary* of all relationships.
Other Form(s): wariness (noun)

veer (VEER): to swerve; to deviate
Part of Speech: verb
Example: The wave hit the ship broadside, and the ship *veered* sharply.

ornithology (or ni THAWL uh jee): study of birds
Part of Speech: noun
Example: His *ornithology* led to the establishment of aviaries all over the world.
Other Form(s): ornithological (adjective)

Unit 30 *(cont.)*

Quick Match

Group 1

A. of a river bank   C. painful sharpness   E. disfavor   G. kowtow

B. salesman   D. unorthodox person   F. something blissful and peaceful   H. prove

_____ 1. fawn

_____ 2. poignancy

_____ 3. riparian

_____ 4. huckster

_____ 5. validate

_____ 6. maverick

_____ 7. obloquy

_____ 8. idyll

Group 2

A. float   C. impenetrable   E. saturnine   G. pattern

B. trespass   D. regarding measurement   F. disgrace   H. uncultivated

_____ 1. waft

_____ 2. prototype

_____ 3. encroach

_____ 4. morose

_____ 5. impervious

_____ 6. quantitative

_____ 7. fallow

_____ 8. opprobrium

Group 3

A. covert   C. denigrate   E. admire oneself   G. reply

B. praise   D. garish   F. minimum number   H. countless

_____ 1. vilify

_____ 2. retort

_____ 3. furtive

_____ 4. myriad

_____ 5. encomium

_____ 6. preen

_____ 7. gaudy

_____ 8. quorum

Group 4

A. mold   C. swerve   E. study of birds   G. cautious

B. sermon   D. strange   F. distribute evenly   H. revert

_____ 1. fey

_____ 2. prorate

_____ 3. homily

_____ 4. retrogress

_____ 5. matrix

_____ 6. wary

_____ 7. veer

_____ 8. ornithology

Unit 30 (cont.)

Answer Key

Pre-test Yourself

Group 1

1. poignancy
2. riparian
3. obloquy
4. fawn
5. huckster
6. validate
7. idyll
8. maverick

Group 2

1. prototype
2. fallow
3. waft
4. opprobrium
5. morose
6. encroach
7. quantitative
8. impervious

Group 3

1. vilify
2. myriad
3. retort
4. encomium
5. furtive
6. preen
7. quorum
8. gaudy

Group 4

1. ornithology
2. fey
3. prorate
4. homily
5. retrogress
6. matrix
7. veer
8. wary

Quick Match

Group 1

1. G
2. C
3. A
4. B
5. H
6. D
7. E
8. F

Group 2

1. A
2. G
3. B
4. E
5. C
6. D
7. H
8. F

Group 3

1. C
2. G
3. A
4. H
5. B
6. E
7. D
8. F

Group 4

1. D
2. F
3. B
4. H
5. A
6. G
7. C
8. E

Unit 31

Pre-test Yourself

Group 1

epigram	posthumous	wax	natal
viscous	quizzical	oblique	zephyr

1. Severe cold made the oil too _____ for proper use.

2. His mother and father celebrated his _____ day by throwing a big party.

3. The clever playwrite was known to always have an _____ at the ready.

4. His rantings and ravings drew _____ looks from the assemblage.

5. _____ thinking leads nowhere.

6. The wife of the dead policeman accepted his _____ award from the mayor.

7. The moon will both _____ and wane during the month.

8. A slight _____ moved the daisies on the windowsill.

Group 2

officious	impeccable	quirk	welter
notional	stalwart	unsung	philander

1. He was a _____ fan and never missed a game.

2. Hypothetical ideas are _____ ideas.

3. Those who are faithful to their spouses never _____.

4. Many an anonymous hero lies _____ in the grave.

5. Bad manners indicated his _____ nature.

6. The government's policies were nothing more than a _____ of stop-gap solutions.

7. The dandy's clothing was always _____.

8. He had the _____ of being virtually unable to remember anyone's name.

Pre-test Yourself *(cont.)*

Group 3

vagrant	tortuous	patois	fetter
lozenge	xenophobia	improvident	rhetorical

1. As a result of his _____, the man visited the same places each day and shied away from new experiences.

2. The route into the cave was _____ and harrowing.

3. Insolvency can sometimes be traced to _____ investments.

4. He had difficulty concentrating, and _____ thoughts went through his mind.

5. His dialect and idiom formed a _____ I couldn't understand.

6. She never expected an answer to her _____ question.

7. She could not take medicine as a _____, and usually purchased it in liquid form.

8. Her busy work schedule might _____ her social life.

Group 4

quack	impromptu	fulminate	motif
phlegmatic	voluble	staccato	deposition

1. The drill sergeant's _____ orders were clear to the soldiers.

2. Their lassitude and _____ manner disturbed the coach.

3. An _____ appearance by the movie star delighted the surprised teens.

4. He got away with the pretense of being a doctor until someone found out he was a _____.

5. Reformers _____ against the evils of an existing administration.

6. The student's assignment for the weekend was to write an essay on the story's primary _____.

7. The witness had signed the _____ that was offered in court.

8. Reformers who fulminate against administrations usually do so in a _____ manner.

Unit 31 (cont.)

Words and Definitions

─────────────── **Group 1** ───────────────

epigram (EP i gram): witticism; sharp jest
   Part of Speech: noun
   Example: His retort took the form of an ascerbic *epigram*.
   Other Form(s): epigrammatical (adjective); epigrammatist (noun)

posthumous (PAWST yoo mus): after death; postmortem
   Part of Speech: adjective
   Example: Sainthood is always a *posthumous* honor

wax (WAX): grow larger; to become more intense
   Part of Speech: verb
   Example: The wave *waxed* as it approached the shore.

natal (NAY tul): of birth; of genesis
   Part of Speech: adjective
   Example: Washington's *natal* day is a national holiday.

viscous (VIS kus): thick; sticky
   Part of Speech: adjective
   Example: The oil in his car became *viscous* on very cold days.
   Other Form(s): viscosity (noun)

quizzical (KWIZ i kul): with mild or amused perplexity; peculiar
   Part of Speech: adjective
   Example: The student's answer was so vacuous that the professor gave him a *quizzical* look.
   Other Form(s): quizzicalness (noun); quizzicality (noun)

oblique (o BLEEK): roundabout; indirect
   Part of Speech: adjective
   Example: The spy gave *oblique* answers when questioned by the enemy.
   Other Form(s): obliqueness (noun); obliquity (noun)

zephyr (ZEF ur): gentle breeze; west wind
   Part of Speech: noun
   Example: A *zephyr* moved the flowers in the field into a delicate dance.

Unit 31 (cont.)

Words and Definitions (cont.)

———————— Group 2 ————————

officious (o FISH us): meddling; domineering
> **Part of Speech:** adjective
> **Example:** Civil servants have long had a reputation for being *officious* and condescending.

impeccable (im PEK uh bul): faultless; exemplary
> **Part of Speech:** adjective
> **Example:** His record was *impeccable*, and the people voted him into office.
> **Other Form(s):** impeccability (noun)

quirk (KWIRK): idiosyncrasy; peculiarity
> **Part of Speech:** noun
> **Example:** It seems that genius is often accompanied by personal *quirks* of a large order.

welter (WEL tur): confusion; jumble
> **Part of Speech:** noun
> **Example:** When she read the tax instructions, they seemed a *welter* of regulations.

notional (NO shuh nul): speculative; hypothetical
> **Part of Speech:** adjective
> **Example:** His *notional* ideas led to vast improvements in the vehicle's braking system
> **Other Form(s):** notion (noun)

stalwart (STAL wurt): robust; resolute
> **Part of Speech:** adjective
> **Example:** The doctor told the healthy man he had a *stalwart* constitution.

unsung (un SUNG): unnoticed; uncelebrated
> **Part of Speech:** adjective
> **Example:** Some heroes get medals and parades while others go *unsung*.

philander (fih LAN dur): to flirt; to womanize
> **Part of Speech:** verb
> **Example:** His wife finally left him because he *philandered* once too often.
> **Other Form(s):** philanderer (noun)

Words and Definitions *(cont.)*

─────────────────── **Group 3** ───────────────────

vagrant (VAY grint): unrestrained; wayward
  Part of Speech: adjective
  Example: *Vagrant* thoughts entered his head and he tried to control them.
  Other Form(s): vagrancy (noun)

tortuous (TOR choo us): twisting; winding
  Part of Speech: adjective
  Example: Some ski trails have *tortuous* paths.

patois (PA twauh): dialect; idiom
  Part of Speech: noun
  Example: I had difficulty understanding him because he spoke in a *patois* I had never heard.

fetter (FEH tur): to restrain; to restrict
  Part of Speech: verb
  Example: Bureaucracies *fetter* creative thinking.

lozenge (LAH zenj): tablet; pill
  Part of Speech: noun
  Example: The medicine came in *lozenges* that seemed much too large to swallow.

xenophobia (zeen o FO bee uh): fear of strangers; contempt for strangers
  Part of Speech: noun
  Example: Historians indicate that *xenophobia* is often the cause of war.
  Other Form(s): xenophobic (adjective)

improvident (im PROV i dent): unwary; imprudent
  Part of Speech: adjective
  Example: Spendthrifts are profligate and *improvident* people.
  Other Form(s): improvidence (noun)

rhetorical (rih TOR i kul): for effect; artificial
  Part of Speech: adjective
  Example: The orator used every *rhetorical* device in his repertoire.
  Other Form(s): rhetoric (noun); rhetorician (noun)

Words and Definitions *(cont.)*

─────────── **Group 4** ───────────

quack (KWAK): pretender; impostor
   Part of Speech: noun
   Example: The hospital board of directors fired a *quack* who had passed himself off as a doctor.
   Other Form(s): quackish (adjective); quackery (noun)

impromptu (im PROMP too): unprepared; spontaneous
   Part of Speech: adjective
   Example: Saturday Night Live was originally praised for its *impromptu* atmosphere.

fulminate (FUL mi nate): to denounce forcibly; to explode violently
   Part of Speech: verb
   Example: Church elders *fulminated* against what they saw as widespread debauchery.
   Other Form(s): fulmination (noun); fulminatory (adjective)

motif (mo TEEF): theme; pattern
   Part of Speech: noun
   Example: His novel lacked a consistent *motif*, and everyone considered it a mess.

phlegmatic (fleg MAT ik): lethargic; unemotional
   Part of Speech: adjective
   Example: Her *phlegmatic* nature prevented her from being the star she could have been.

voluble (VOL yoo bul): garrulous; speaking or spoken incessantly, fluently, etc.
   Part of Speech: adjective
   Example: The old man was a *voluble* person, and a lot of people avoided him.

staccato (stuh KAW toe): detached or separated sound; disconnected
   Part of Speech: adjective
   Example: We knew the deer hunters were in the hills because of the *staccato* gunfire.

deposition (deh po ZISH un): sworn testimony; binding statement
   Part of Speech: adjective
   Example: The judge allowed *depositions* to be filed when witnesses couldn't appear.

Unit 31 *(cont.)*

Quick Match

Group 1

A. thick	C. postmortem	E. of birth	G. witticism
B. grow larger	D. peculiar	F. roundabout	H. west wind

_____ 1. epigram

_____ 2. posthumous

_____ 3. wax

_____ 4. natal

_____ 5. viscous

_____ 6. quizzical

_____ 7. oblique

_____ 8. zephyr

Group 2

A. confusion	C. flirt	E. faultless	G. peculiarity
B. meddling	D. speculative	F. unnoticed	H. robust

_____ 1. officious

_____ 2. impeccable

_____ 3. quirk

_____ 4. welter

_____ 5. notional

_____ 6. stalwart

_____ 7. unsung

_____ 8. philander

Group 3

A. dialect	C. fear of strangers	E. for effect	G. imprudent
B. restrict	D. wayward	F. winding	H. tablet

_____ 1. vagrant

_____ 2. tortuous

_____ 3. fetter

_____ 4. patois

_____ 5. lozenge

_____ 6. xenophobia

_____ 7. improvident

_____ 8. rhetorical

Group 4

A. denounce	C. theme	E. impostor	G. spontaneous
B. detached sound	D. garrulous	F. binding statement	H. lethargic

_____ 1. quack

_____ 2. impromptu

_____ 3. fulminate

_____ 4. motif

_____ 5. phlegmatic

_____ 6. voluble

_____ 7. staccato

_____ 8. deposition

Unit 31 *(cont.)*

Answer Key

Pre-test Yourself

Group 1
1. viscous
2. natal
3. epigram
4. quizzical
5. oblique
6. posthumous
7. wax
8. zephyr

Group 2
1. stalwart
2. notional
3. philander
4. unsung
5. officious
6. welter
7. impeccable
8. quirk

Group 3
1. xenophobia
2. tortuous
3. improvident
4. vagrant
5. patois
6. rhetorical
7. lozenge
8. fetter

Group 4
1. staccato
2. phlegmatic
3. impromptu
4. quack
5. fulminate
6. motif
7. deposition
8. voluble

Quick Match

Group 1
1. G
2. C
3. B
4. E
5. A
6. D
7. F
8. H

Group 2
1. B
2. E
3. G
4. A
5. D
6. H
7. F
8. C

Group 3
1. D
2. F
3. B
4. A
5. H
6. C
7. G
8. E

Group 4
1. E
2. G
3. A
4. C
5. H
6. D
7. B
8. F

Unit 32

Pre-test Yourself

Group 1

vitreous	undulate	nausea	gerrymander
obdurate	quench	lampoon	palpable

---

1. The coach advised the players to drink water, not soda, so they could _____ their thirst.

2. The pain was severe enough to cause _____ and vomiting.

3. Many fake diamonds have a _____ look that real diamonds do not have.

4. Politicians sometimes _____ districts so that they can get more votes.

5. The school's principal did not appreciate the students' _____ of him.

6. The rows of wheat _____ in the zephyrs.

7. At the sight of the tarantula, the woman's fear was nearly _____.

8. She had an _____ will that few cared to test.

Group 2

quail	odium	heinous	squalor
impassive	winsome	pettifog	flaccid

---

1. Opprobrium and _____ followed the cruel leader wherever he went.

2. Indigence and _____ plagued the depressed nation.

3. Her _____ ways and blithe spirit won her many friends.

4. Cowards _____ when danger appears.

5. Stoic and _____ people are not necessarily fatalists.

6. Judges may censure attorneys who _____.

7. There was an odium attached to his _____ actions that he couldn't avoid.

8. The pennant was _____, indicating a lack of wind.

Unit 32 *(cont.)*

Pre-test Yourself *(cont.)*

Group 3

irksome	plagiarism	facetious	vehement
haggard	quotidian	gauche	comely

---

1. After missing sleep for several days, he had a _____ and enervated look about him.

2. _____ cost the professor his job.

3. There is a touch of haughtiness in people who are _____.

4. It is the small problems that prove most _____ to some people.

5. She vilified her opponent in the most _____ terms.

6. The invitation called for black tie, but he was _____ and wore a regular suit.

7. People were attracted to her because she was _____, winsome, and blithe.

8. Brushing one's teeth is but one of the many _____ matters most of us deal with without a second thought.

Group 4

histrionic	bucolic	qualm	icon
pander	fiats	wrest	geriatric

---

1. The murderer had no _____ about having killed his ex-wife and her friend.

2. The old artist was an _____ to up-and-coming artists.

3. The citizens were forced to follow the _____ issued by the dictator.

4. Age and feebleness are the main concerns of a _____ nurse.

5. The thespian's role called for him to act in a _____ ways.

6. Fawners and toadies _____ to their superior's every wish.

7. The junta may _____ power from the civilian government.

8. Landscape artists of the Hudson School painted _____ settings.

Words and Definitions

---------- Group 1 ----------

vitreous (VIT ree us): glass-like; crystalline
Part of Speech: adjective
Example: A *vitreous* film covers the human eye and gives it a mirrored look.
Other Form(s): vitreousness (noun)

undulate (UN dyoo late): to become wavy; to move in waves
Part of Speech: verb
Example: Wheat *undulated* in the zephyrs that blew steadily.
Other Form(s): undulating (adjective); undulation (noun)

nausea (NAW zhuh): a feeling of sickness with an inclination to vomit; revulsion
Part of Speech: noun
Example: When I see Holocaust pictures, I suffer from *nausea* and disbelief.
Other Form(s): nauseating (adjective); nauseous (adjective); nauseousness (noun); nauseate (verb)

gerrymander (JER ree man dur): to manipulate into unfair divisions; to give unfair advantage
Part of Speech: verb
Example: Politicians gerrymandered the district so that their party would win.
Other Form(s): *gerrymanderer* (noun)

obdurate (OB dur et): stubborn; adamant
Part of Speech: adjective
Example: Grandfather was *obdurate* when it came to his outdated fashion sense.
Other Form(s): obduracy (noun); obdurateness (noun)

quench (KWENCH): to satisfy; to slake
Part of Speech: verb
Example: The horses *quench* their thirst in the river.

lampoon (lam POON): to mock; to ridicule
Part of Speech: verb
Example: Some college publications *lampoon* pretentious occurrences on campus.
Other Form(s): lampoon (noun); lampooner (noun); lampoonery (noun); lampoonist (noun)

palpable (PAL puh bul): tangible; manifest
Part of Speech: adjective
Example: Poe made horror and dread *palpable* in his stories.

Words and Definitions *(cont.)*

——————————————— **Group 2** ———————————————

quail (KWAIL): to be apprehensive with fear; to recoil
Part of Speech: verb
Example: The young child *quailed* at the sight of the ogre.

odium (O dee um):ececration; loathing
Part of Speech: noun
Example: *Odium* followed him everywhere because of his evil acts.

heinous (HAY nus): wicked; atrocious
Part of Speech: adjective
Example: He committed *heinous* acts, and an odium followed him everywhere.
Other Form(s): heinousness (noun)

squalor (SKWAH lor): filth; great poverty
Part of Speech: noun
Example: Impoverished people often live in *squalor*.

impassive (im PAS iv): emotionless; expressionless
Part of Speech: adjective
Example: The defendant had an *impassive* look on his face when the verdict was read.
Other Form(s): impassivity (noun); impassiveness (noun)

winsome (WIN sum): charming; engaging
Part of Speech: adjective
Example: She got away with a lot of things because of her *winsome* ways.
Other Form(s): winsomeness (noun)

pettifog (PET i fog): to quibble; to nit-pick
Part of Speech: verb
Example: Some judges get very upset when lawyers before them *pettifog* and obfuscate.
Other Form(s): pettifogger (noun); pettifoggery (noun)

flaccid (FLAS id): flabby; limp
Part of Speech: adjective
Example: Muscles become *flaccid* if they aren't used.
Other Form(s): flaccidity (noun)

Words and Definitions *(cont.)*

──────────── **Group 3** ────────────

irksome (IRK sum): irritating; aggravating
  Part of Speech: adjective
  Example: He never got away with anything because he had *irksome* ways.

plagiarism (PLAY jur izm): literary piracy; literary theft
  Part of Speech: noun
  Example: *Plagiarism* is academic theft.
  Other Form(s): plagiarize (verb); plagiarist (noun)

facetious (fuh SEE shus): sarcastic; ironic
  Part of Speech: adjective
  Example: *Facetious* people are often condescending people.
  Other Form(s): facetiousness (noun)

vehement (VEE uh ment): ardent; passionate
  Part of Speech: adjective
  Example: The attack on the artist drew *vehement* comments from his supporters.
  Other Form(s): vehemence (noun)

haggard (HAG urd): exhausted looking; worn-out in appearance
  Part of Speech: adjective
  Example: Lack of sleep for three days gave the rescuer a *haggard* visage.
  Other Form(s): haggardness (noun)

quotidian (kwo TID ee un): daily; everyday
  Part of Speech: adjective
  Example: Genius often finds *quotidian* matters too mundane.

gauche (GOSHE): uncouth; socially awkward
  Part of Speech: adjective
  Example: His table manners at the banquet were *gauche* and provincial.
  Other Form(s): gaucheness (noun)

comely (KUM lee): pleasant to look at; attractive
  Part of Speech: adjective
  Example: The winsome maid had a *comely* appearance.
  Other Form(s): comeliness (noun)

Words and Definitions *(cont.)*

─────────── **Group 4** ───────────

histrionic (his tree AW nik): dramatic; affected
Part of Speech: adjective
Example: Clarence Darrow was known for his *histrionic* courtroom gambits.
Other Form(s): histrionics (noun)

bucolic (byoo KAWL ik): pastoral; rustic
Part of Speech: adjective
Example: Upper Maine provides the vacationer with *bucolic* scenes.

qualm (KWALM): doubt; compunction
Part of Speech: noun
Example: Amoral people have no *qualms* about their behavior.

icon (I kon): image; likeness
Part of Speech: noun
Example: When the Bolsheviks pillaged the churches, they destroyed *icons* of saints.
Other Form(s): iconic (adjective)

pander (PAN dur): indulge; play down to
Part of Speech: verb
Example: Mountebanks *pander* to those who would be rich.
Other Form(s): panderer (noun)

fiat (FEE ot): decree; ordinance
Part of Speech: noun
Example: Martinets promulgate *fiats* that the suppressed must follow.

wrest (REST): to take by force; to twist violently
Part of Speech: verb
Example: One country *wrested* disputed land from another.

geriatric (jeh ree AT rik): pertaining to old people; age-afflicted
Part of Speech: adjective
Example: *Geriatric* hospitals are sprouting up everywhere because people are living longer.
Other Form(s): geriatrics (noun); geriatrician (noun)

Unit 32 *(cont.)*

Quick Match

Group 1

A. move in waves	C. tangible	E. satisfy	G. revulsion
B. glass-like	D. stubborn	F. ridicule	H. manipulate unfairly

_____ 1. vitreous   _____ 5. obdurate

_____ 2. undulate   _____ 6. quench

_____ 3. nausea   _____ 7. lampoon

_____ 4. gerrymander   _____ 8. palpable

Group 2

A. emotionless	C. limp	E. charming	G. filth
B. recoil	D. wicked	F. loathing	H. quibble

_____ 1. quail   _____ 5. impassive

_____ 2. odium   _____ 6. winsome

_____ 3. heinous   _____ 7. pettifog

_____ 4. squalor   _____ 8. flaccid

Group 3

A. attractive	C. literary theft	E. uncouth	G. exhausted looking
B. ardent	D. daily	F. irritating	H. sarcastic

_____ 1. irksome   _____ 5. haggard

_____ 2. plagiarism   _____ 6. quotidian

_____ 3. facetious   _____ 7. gauche

_____ 4. vehement   _____ 8. comely

Group 4

A. doubt	C. indulge	E. of old people	G. take by force
B. decree	D. pastoral	F. image	H. dramatic

_____ 1. histrionic   _____ 5. pander

_____ 2. bucolic   _____ 6. fiat

_____ 3. qualm   _____ 7. wrest

_____ 4. icon   _____ 8. geriatric

Unit 32 *(cont.)*

Answer Key

Pre-test Yourself

Group 1	Group 2	Group 3	Group 4
1. quench	1. odium	1. haggard	1. qualm
2. nausea	2. squalor	2. plagiarism	2. icon
3. vitreous	3. winsome	3. facetious	3. fiat
4. gerrymander	4. quail	4. irksome	4. geriatric
5. lampoon	5. impassive	5. vehement	5. histrionic
6. undulate	6. pettifog	6. gauche	6. pander
7. palpable	7. heinous	7. comely	7. wrest
8. obdurate	8. flaccid	8. quotidian	8. bucolic

Quick Match

Group 1	Group 2	Group 3	Group 4
1. B	1. B	1. F	1. H
2. A	2. F	2. C	2. D
3. G	3. D	3. H	3. A
4. H	4. G	4. B	4. F
5. D	5. A	5. G	5. C
6. E	6. E	6. D	6. B
7. F	7. H	7. E	7. G
8. C	8. C	8. A	8. E

Unit 33

Pre-test Yourself

Group 1

opaque	untoward	piquant	veracity
nomenclature	repugnant	wraith	subjugate

---

1. Every specialty constructs its own _____.

2. He seemed to have an _____ mind that prevented the light of learning to enter.

3. Unseemly and _____ behavior should not be condoned under any circumstances.

4. Her unquestioned probity dissuaded anyone from questioning the _____ of what she was saying.

5. She was saucy and sassy with her _____ remarks.

6. A conquering army will _____ the once-free citizens.

7. The boy swore he had seen a _____ in the haunted house.

8. Untoward behavior was _____ to the strict teacher.

Group 2

quagmire	mélange	hierarchy	orient
umbrage	subpoena	punctilious	wan

---

1. His work was a _____ of several distinct genres.

2. He was a meticulous man who prided himself on being _____ for appointments.

3. The welter of ideas became a _____ from which he couldn't escape.

4. The judge will _____ several of the witnesses.

5. Teachers take _____ at unruly students.

6. His morose and _____ appearance indicated a profound unhappiness.

7. Her place in the _____ was limited by a glass ceiling.

8. Tour guides _____ visitors to museums.

Pre-test Yourself *(cont.)*

Group 3

unseemly	panache	whet	queue
nefarious	derange	omniscient	subservient

---

1. Subjugated citizens are forced to act in _____ ways.

2. Kitchen aromas _____ the appetite of the hungry.

3. Her brilliant piano playing exhibited her _____ in approaching difficult works.

4. Fans _____ for tickets to watch Phish.

5. Narrators in novels are sometimes _____ and can read characters' minds.

6. The state imprisoned him for his _____ acts.

7. Playing loud music at a funeral is _____ and out of place.

8. No one knows why certain events _____ some while leaving others seemingly uneffected.

Group 4

demarcation	egregious	vacillate	succulent
reputable	provincial	waylay	fatuous

---

1. No one questioned him because he came from a _____ family.

2. Xenophobia often accompanies _____ thinking.

3. In nineteenth-century England, highwaymen would _____ travelers.

4. The show was inane, _____, and vacuous.

5. The Rio Grande is part of the _____ between the United States and Mexico.

6. Irresolute people _____ on issues.

7. The pear is a _____ fruit.

8. His crimes were so _____ that, despite his young age, he was sent to a maximum-security prison.

Unit 33 (cont.)

Words and Definitions

Group 1

opaque (o PAKE): not transmitting light; impenetrable to sight
  Part of Speech: adjective
  Example: His arguments were so abstruse, one observer called them *opaque*.
  Other Form(s): opacity (noun); opaqueness (noun)

untoward (un TORD): refractory; awkward
  Part of Speech: adjective
  Example: Deans of discipline deal with *untoward* students.
  Other Form(s): untowardness

piquant (PEE kunt): sharp; pungent
  Part of Speech: adjective
  Example: The sauce had a *piquant* taste designed to wake up the tastebuds.
  Other Form(s): piquancy (noun)

veracity (veh RAS i tee): candor; truthfulness
  Part of Speech: noun
  Example: His *veracity* was questioned because he had prevaricated in the past.

nomenclature (NO men clay chur): terminology; taxonomy
  Part of Speech: noun
  Example: A new *nomenclature* has evolved with the birth of the Internet.

repugnant (ree PUG nunt): obnoxious; revolting
  Part of Speech: adjective
  Example: Gratuitous violence and sex in movies have made them *repugnant* to many people.
  Other Form(s): repugnance (noun)

wraith (RAYTH): ghost; apparition
  Part of Speech: noun
  Example: Gothic novels almost always contain *wraiths* that haunt the living.

subjugate (SUB juh gate): to subdue; to vanquish
  Part of Speech: verb
  Example: Superior forces *subjugated* the armed citadel.
  Other Form(s): subjugation (noun); subjugator (noun); subjugable (adjective)

Unit 33 *(cont.)*

Words and Definitions *(cont.)*

────────────── **Group 2** ──────────────

quagmire (KWAG mire): marsh; difficult predicament
Part of Speech: noun
Example: Details of the event became so tangled, they formed a *quagmire* for detectives.

mélange (muh LANJ): mixture; medley
Part of Speech: noun
Example: Eclectic writing consists of a *melange* of styles.

hierarchy (HY ur ar kee): ranking system; caste system
Part of Speech: noun
Example: Every society has a *hierarchy*.
Other Form(s): hierarchic (adjective); hierarchical (adjective); hierarchism (noun); hierarchize (verb)

orient (OR ee ent): to adjust to; accustom oneself
Part of Speech: verb
Example: Colleges hire guides who *orient* new students to the campus buildings.
Other Form(s): orientation (noun); orientate (verb)

umbrage (UM brij): offense; resentment
Part of Speech: noun
Example: Wicked criticism caused him to take *umbrage* at the critics.

subpoena (suh PEE nuh): to call in; to summon
Part of Speech: verb
Example: Judges *subpoena* reluctant witnesses.
Other Form(s): subpoena (noun)

punctilious (punk TIL ee us): decorous; precise in behavior
Part of Speech: adjective
Example: People of the "old school" were much more *punctilious* than people are today.
Other Form(s): punctiliousness (noun)

wan (WAUN): pale; worn or exhausted
Part of Speech: adjective
Example: Sleep deprivation made her skin look *wan* and ashen.
Other Form(s): wanness (noun)

Unit 33 (cont.)

Words and Definitions (cont.)

——————————— Group 3 ———————————

unseemly (un SEEM lee): indecorous; unbecoming
  Part of Speech: adjective
  Example: *Unseemly* behavior marked the fraternity party.
  Other Form(s): unseemliness (noun)

panache (puh NOSH): flamboyant confidence in style or manner; brilliance
  Part of Speech: noun
  Example: Her *panache* at the piano drew raves from audiences.

whet (WET): to sharpen; to stimulate
  Part of Speech: verb
  Example: Her course in film history *whet* her interest in the art form.

queue (KYOO): to line up; to wait in line
  Part of Speech: verb
  Example: Example: Patrons of the highly praised movie *queued* up in front of the theatre.
  Other Form(s): queue (noun)

nefarious (nuh FAR ee us): heinous; wicked
  Part of Speech: adjective
  Example: Caligula's *nefarious* acts frightened all around him.
  Other Form(s): nefariousness (noun)

derange (de RAYNJ): to disorganize; to make insane
  Part of Speech: verb
  Example: The quagmire of personal tragedies *deranged* him, and he was hospitalized.
  Other Form(s): deranged (adjective); derangement (noun)

omniscient (om NISH unt): all-knowing; all-cognizant
  Part of Speech: adjective
  Example: The Western concepts of God hold that He is *omniscient*.
  Other Form(s): omniscience (noun)

subservient (sub SUR vee unt): subordinate; inferior
  Part of Speech: adjective
  Example: Toadies are *subservient* by nature.
  Other Form(s): subservience (noun); subserviency (noun)

Words and Definitions (cont.)

─────────────── Group 4 ───────────────

demarcation (de mar KAY shun): border; boundary
    Part of Speech: noun
    Example: The U.N. provided the warring parties with a *demarcation* that pleased neither nation.
    Other Form(s): demarcated (adjective); demarcate (verb)

egregious (i GREE jus): flagrant; exceptionally bad
    Part of Speech: adjective
    Example: His behavior at the funeral was *egregious* and unforgivable.
    Other Form(s): egregiousness (noun)

vacillate (VAS i late): to waver; to fluctuate
    Part of Speech: verb
    Example: Voters *vacillated*, and no one could tell who was going to win.
    Other Form(s): vacillating (adjective); vacillation (noun); vacillator (noun)

succulent (SUK yoo lent): juicy; fleshy
    Part of Speech: adjective
    Example: Mangoes are considered a *succulent* fruit.
    Other Form(s): succulence (noun)

reputable (REH pyoo tuh bul): honest; legitimate
    Part of Speech: adjective
    Example: Her honor was never questioned because she came from a *reputable* background.

provincial (pro VIN chul): rural; limited in scope
    Part of Speech: adjective
    Example: *Provincial* thinking often leads to bias.
    Other Form(s): provincialism (noun); provincialist (noun); provincialize (verb)

waylay (WAY lay): to ambush; to lie in wait
    Part of Speech: verb
    Example: Highwaymen *waylay* travelers during 18th century England.
    Other Form(s): waylayer (noun)

fatuous (FAT choo us): silly; inane
    Part of Speech: adjective
    Example: Scientists ignored *fatuous* claims.
    Other Form(s): fatuousness (noun)

Unit 33 *(cont.)*

Quick Match

Group 1

A. sharp   C. overcome   E. impenetrable to sight   G. candor
B. taxonomy   D. refractory   F. revolting   H. ghost

_____ 1. opaque   _____ 5. piquant

_____ 2. nomenclature   _____ 6. wraith

_____ 3. untoward   _____ 7. veracity

_____ 4. repugnant   _____ 8. subjugate

Group 2

A. summon   C. mixture   E. ranking system   G. adjust
B. pale   D. offense   F. decorous   H. marsh

_____ 1. quagmire   _____ 5. hierarchy

_____ 2. umbrage   _____ 6. punctilious

_____ 3. mélange   _____ 7. orient

_____ 4. subpoena   _____ 8. wan

Group 3

A. confidence in style   C. indecorous   E. all-knowing   G. stimulate
B. disorganize   D. subordinate   F. wicked   H. line up

_____ 1. unseemly   _____ 5. whet

_____ 2. nefarious   _____ 6. omniscient

_____ 3. panache   _____ 7. queue

_____ 4. derange   _____ 8. subservient

Group 4

A. flagrant   C. juicy   E. rural   G. fluctuate
B. boundary   D. ambush   F. inane   H. legitimate

_____ 1. demarcation   _____ 5. vacillate

_____ 2. reputable   _____ 6. waylay

_____ 3. egregious   _____ 7. succulent

_____ 4. provincial   _____ 8. fatuous

Unit 33 _(cont.)_

Answer Key

Pre-test Yourself

Group 1

1. nomenclature
2. opaque
3. untoward
4. veracity
5. piquant
6. subjugate
7. wraith
8. repugnant

Group 2

1. mélange
2. punctilious
3. quagmire
4. subpoena
5. umbrage
6. wan
7. hierarchy
8. orient

Group 3

1. subservient
2. whet
3. panache
4. queue
5. omniscient
6. nefarious
7. unseemly
8. derange

Group 4

1. reputable
2. provincial
3. waylay
4. fatuous
5. demarcation
6. vacillate
7. succulent
8. egregious

Quick Match

Group 1

1. E
2. B
3. D
4. F
5. A
6. H
7. G
8. C

Group 2

1. H
2. D
3. C
4. A
5. E
6. F
7. G
8. B

Group 3

1. C
2. F
3. A
4. B
5. G
6. E
7. H
8. D

Group 4

1. B
2. H
3. A
4. E
5. G
6. D
7. C
8. F

Unit 34

Pre-test Yourself

Group 1

orifice	voluptuous	resilience	genre
static	brusque	petulant	winnow

---

1. His life seemed _____ to him, and he felt he was in a rut.

2. She wrote many detective novels and was highly respected by followers of that _____.

3. A pore is a tiny _____ in the skin.

4. Her _____ after so many failures helped her on the comeback road.

5. Heroines in romance novels are often _____ and have limpid eyes.

6. She had little patience with fools and spoke to them in a _____ manner.

7. The child was _____, whining, and generally irksome.

8. Personnel directors _____ out people who are unsuitable for their company.

Group 2

titillate	guise	repudiate	underwrite
ostentatious	morass	strew	panoply

---

1. Nude scenes in movies _____ prurient viewers.

2. The queen appeared in full and impressive _____ before her courtiers.

3. Witnesses often _____ the accounts of events given by the accused.

4. He wanted the whole world to know about him and was _____ in his ways.

5. The spy entered the country in the _____ of a farmer.

6. The man's financial records were a _____, and the auditor was dismayed.

7. Guests at the wedding reception will _____ roses on the main table.

8. Banks _____ stock offerings.

Pre-test Yourself *(cont.)*

Group 3

| yoke | querulous | stoicism | vociferous |
| overweening | fecund | paradigm | concomitant |

---

1. Poe had a _____ imagination and used it in his many stories.

2. _____ people are a pain in the neck.

3. His _____ arrogance proved to be quite irksome.

4. Prior to the advent of tractors, farmers would _____ plows to oxen.

5. He always hustled and put his team's success before his own, and his coach would often refer to him as the _____ of a team player.

6. Her skills were _____ with his, and so they worked well together.

7. Spectators on the home side of the arena were _____ in their rooting.

8. _____ in the face of terrible ordeals strengthens character.

Group 4

| vertiginous | glib | peruse | badinage |
| extemporaneous | unkempt | harangue | stereotype |

---

1. He felt _____ when he looked over the promontory's edge.

2. He appeared _____ at the interview and was asked to leave.

3. Politicians _____ each other during contentious debates.

4. The two comics engaged in witty _____.

5. If you _____ an entire people, you do them an injustice.

6. Good salespeople often have _____ tongues.

7. After breakfast, he would _____ the morning newspaper.

8. The defense attorney argued that his clients actions were _____ and not premeditated.

Words and Definitions

— Group 1 —

orifice (OR i fis): opening; hole
    Part of Speech: noun
    Example: Ears are sensitive *orifices*.

voluptuous (vuh LUP choo us): sensual; carnal
    Part of Speech: adjective
    Example: Judith Krantz's heroines are always *voluptuous*.
    Other Form(s): voluptuousness

resilience (reh ZIL yents): readily recovering; maintaining original shape
    Part of Speech: noun
    Example: Bones lose their *resilience* as the human body ages.
    Other Form(s): resilient (adjective); resiliency (noun)

genre (ZHON ruh): style; form
    Part of Speech: noun
    Example: Novel writing was the *genre* she chose.

static (STAT ik): motionless; unmoving
    Part of Speech: adjective
    Example: Scientific progress was *static* during the Dark Ages.

brusque (BRUSK): blunt; curt
    Part of Speech: adjective
    Example: He was a *brusque* man who had little time for small talk.
    Other Form(s): brusqueness (noun)

petulant (PET choo lent): peevish; testy
    Part of Speech: adjective
    Example: *Petulant* and irksome children harassed the wan-looking mother.
    Other Form(s): petulance (noun)

winnow (WIH no): to separate; to blow free
    Part of Speech: verb
    Example: Editors *winnow* out grammatical errors and the like.
    Other Form(s): winnower (noun)

Unit 34 _(cont.)_

Words and Definitions _(cont.)_

———————————— **Group 2** ————————————

morass (muh RASS): marsh; entanglement
   Part of Speech: noun
   Example: The witnesses' stories became a _morass_ to the jury and it asked for advice.

titillate (TIH tih late): to excite; to stimulate
   Part of Speech: verb
   Example: Tabloids _titillate_ the prurient tastes of a lot of readers.
   Other Form(s): titillating (adjective); titillation (noun)

repudiate (re PYOO dee ate): to reject; to renounce
   Part of Speech: verb
   Example: Students _repudiated_ the unjust article in the school newspaper.
   Other Form(s): repudiation (noun); repudiator (noun)

underwrite (UN dur rite): to ensure; to accept liability
   Part of Speech: verb
   Example: Brokerage houses _underwrite_ new stock issues.
   Other Form(s): underwriter (noun)

ostentatious (os ten TAY shus): pretentious; vulgarly showy
   Part of Speech: adjective
   Example: He had an _ostentatious_ style that set him apart from the common people.
   Other Form(s): ostentation (noun)

guise (GIZE): external appearance; semblance
   Part of Speech: noun
   Example: Spies gather information under the _guise_ of innocence.

strew (STREW): to scatter; to spread about
   Part of Speech: verb
   Example: Wedding guests _strewed_ the reception hall with rose petals.

panoply (PAN o plee): impressive display; a full suit of armor
   Part of Speech: noun
   Example: Masquerade parties in old New York required guests to wear _panoply_.

Words and Definitions *(cont.)*

―――――――――――――――――――――― Group 3 ――――――――――――――――――――――

yoke (YOKE): to harness; to link
  Part of Speech: verb
  Example: She *yoked* herself to her computer and worked 80-hour weeks.
  Other Form(s): yoke (noun)

querulous (KWER uh luss): complaining; peevish
  Part of Speech: adjective
  Example: Irksome people are often contentious and *querulous* people.
  Other Form(s): querulousness (noun)

stoicism (STOW i sizm): impassiveness; great self control
  Part of Speech: noun
  Example: Everyone admired her *stoicism* in the face of tragedy.
  Other Form(s): stoic (adjective); stoical (adjective)

vociferous (vo SIF ur us): loud; bellowing
  Part of Speech: adjective
  Example: The crowds became *vociferous* at the rally.
  Other Form(s): vociferousness (noun)

overweening (o vur WEEN ing): presumptuous; overconfident
  Part of Speech: adjective
  Example: Most members of the audience considered the man to be a bit *overweening* when he claimed that he was the most talented human being alive.
  Other Form(s): overweeningness (noun)

fecund (FEE kund): fertile; prolific
  Part of Speech: adjective
  Example: John Grisham has a *fecund* imagination.
  Other Form(s): fecundity (noun); fecundability (noun); fecundate (verb); fecundation (noun)

paradigm (PEHR uh dime): prototype; example
  Part of Speech: noun
  Example: Her perpetual decorousness made her a *paradigm* for polite society.
  Other Form(s): paradigmatic (adjective)

concomitant (kon KAH mi tant): accompanying; coexistent
  Part of Speech: adjective
  Example: *Concomitant* ideas mark the birth of all inventions.
  Other Form(s): concomitance (noun); concomitancy (noun)

—————————————— **Group 4** ——————————————

vertiginous (vur TIJ i nus): causing a whirling sensation; causing dizziness
    Part of Speech: adjective
    Example: Helicopter rides gave him a *vertiginous* sensation.
    Other Form(s): vertigo (noun)

glib (GLIB): fluent, but insincere; smooth
    Part of Speech: adjective
    Example: Snake oil salesmen in the Old West were *glib* and unctuous.
    Other Form(s): glibness (noun)

peruse (puh RUSE): to examine; to study
    Part of Speech: verb
    Example: Her father always *perused* the newspaper at the dinner table.
    Other Form(s): perusal (noun)

badinage (bad ih NAZH): banter; teasing word play
    Part of Speech: noun
    Example: The popular television series was known for the *badinage* between its two main characters.

extemporaneous (ek stem puh RAIN ee us): improvised; spontaneous
    Part of Speech: adjective
    Example: The candidate received an ovation for his *extemporaneous* speech about personal freedoms.
    Other Form(s): extemporization (noun); extemporaneousness (noun); extemporary (adjective); extempore (adjective); extemporize (verb)

unkempt (un KEMPT): messy; rumpled
    Part of Speech: adjective
    Example: Strong winds and rain gave him an *unkempt* appearance.

harangue (huh RANG): to speechify; to speak earnestly and at length
    Part of Speech: verb
    Example: The minister *harangued* churchgoers with a long sermon about sin and damnation.
    Other Form(s): harangue (noun); haranguer (noun)

stereotype (STER ee o type): overgeneralization; oversimplified idea
    Part of Speech: noun
    Example: He was treated like a *stereotype* and resented being classified.
    Other Form(s): stereotypical (adjective); stereotype (verb)

Unit 34 (cont.)

Quick Match

Group 1

A. readily recovering   C. motionless   E. style   G. carnal
B. peevish   D. opening   F. separate   H. curt

_____ 1. orifice

_____ 2. voluptuous

_____ 3. resilience

_____ 4. genre

_____ 5. static

_____ 6. brusque

_____ 7. petulant

_____ 8. winnow

Group 2

A. guarantee   C. excite   E. semblance   G. reject
B. pretentious   D. array   F. scatter   H. marsh

_____ 1. titillate

_____ 2. morass

_____ 3. repudiate

_____ 4. underwrite

_____ 5. ostentatious

_____ 6. guise

_____ 7. strew

_____ 8. panoply

Group 3

A. overconfident   C. coexistent   E. prototype   G. loud
B. impassiveness   D. harness   F. complaining   H. fertile

_____ 1. yoke

_____ 2. querulous

_____ 3. stoicism

_____ 4. vociferous

_____ 5. overweening

_____ 6. fecund

_____ 7. paradigm

_____ 8. concomitant

Group 4

A. study   C. spontaneous   E. overgeneralization   G. banter
B. messy   D. fluent, but insincere   F. causing a whirling sensation   H. speechify

_____ 1. vertiginous

_____ 2. glib

_____ 3. peruse

_____ 4. badinage

_____ 5. extemporaneous

_____ 6. unkempt

_____ 7. harangue

_____ 8. stereotype

Unit 34 *(cont.)*

Answer Key

Pre-test Yourself

Group 1	Group 2	Group 3	Group 4
1. static	1. titillate	1. fecund	1. vertiginous
2. genre	2. panoply	2. querulous	2. unkempt
3. orifice	3. repudiate	3. overweening	3. harangue
4. resilience	4. ostentatious	4. yoke	4. badinage
5. voluptuous	5. guise	5. paradigm	5. stereotype
6. brusque	6. morass	6. concomitant	6. glib
7. petulant	7. strew	7. vociferous	7. peruse
8. winnow	8. underwrite	8. stoicism	8. extemperaneous

Quick Match

Group 1	Group 2	Group 3	Group 4
1. D	1. C	1. D	1. F
2. G	2. H	2. F	2. D
3. A	3. G	3. B	3. A
4. E	4. A	4. G	4. G
5. C	5. B	5. A	5. C
6. H	6. E	6. H	6. B
7. B	7. F	7. E	7. H
8. F	8. D	8. C	8. E

Unit 35

Pre-test Yourself

Group 1			
verbose	factotum	pathology	buffet
reprove	lugubrious	germane	delude

1. Though most of his music was rather _____, the performer was generally a very happy and content person.

2. The general's aide was a _____ who saw to all minor things in the general's life.

3. The prognosis for the _____ was not encouraging.

4. Everything she said was relevant and _____ to the subject.

5. His stories would be more interesting if they weren't so _____.

6. He would often _____ himself into thinking he could pass the tests without studying.

7. It was an extremely heavy sea, and winds would _____ the foundering ship.

8. Those entrenched in the status quo often _____ those who try to bring about change.

Group 2			
quintessence	hapless	pernicious	indolence
feign	braggadocio	suave	vagary

1. Malingerers are guilty of _____.

2. He thought his _____ would get him through the dangerous situation.

3. She is the _____ of what it is to be a true lyric soprano.

4. A team that has a losing record 15 years in a row is a _____ team.

5. His influence on the children was insidious and _____.

6. To throw its predators off the track, the animal would _____ death.

7. As a cosmopolitan and an aesthete, he had a _____ cachet about him.

8. There seems to be a _____ about natural disasters.

Pre-test Yourself (cont.)

Group 3

bovine	revert	wreak	metaphysical
perspicacious	impetuous	stature	utopian

---

1. The biographer asserted that John Donne wrote _____ poetry that transcended the ordinary.

2. She soon realized that, although her new boyfriend was handsome, he had a _____ wit, and she quickly grew bored with him.

3. _____ preparations precluded any accidents.

4. The _____ ideal interested many philosophers in the nineteenth century.

5. Buffeting winds and strong seas can _____ havoc with a ship.

6. Recidivists _____ to the behavior that got them incarcerated in the first place.

7. Rave reviews of her plays brought her greater _____ in the art community.

8. Catastrophe resulted from his _____ actions.

Group 4

unequivocal	requite	belie	panacea
indemnify	wane	spearhead	lexicon

---

1. The musician realized that the popularity of his formulaic pop band would eventually _____, and he resisted the temptation to spend all of his earnings.

2. Refer to a _____ when you have an etymological problem.

3. Utopians believed that a _____ existed for the ills of the world.

4. No one doubted her devotion because it was always _____ and unrestrained.

5. Insurance companies _____ homeowners against natural disasters.

6. The boxer vowed that he would _____ his opponent for the kidney punch that had prematurely ended their previous bout.

7. The spy feigned disinterest so he could _____ his true intentions.

8. Volunteers would _____ the fund drive before professionals took over.

Unit 35 (cont.)
Words and Definitions

———————————————— Group 1 ————————————————

verbose (vur BOSE): wordy; prolix
Part of Speech: adjective
Example: The long harangue was quite *verbose*.
Other Form(s): verbosity (noun)

factotum (fak TOE tum): aide; errand runner
Part of Speech: noun
Example: One's valet is one's *factotum*.

pathology (puh THAW luh jee): symptomology; of a disorder
Part of Speech: noun
Example: Disease *pathology* was her field of study.
Other Form(s): pathological (adjective); pathologist (noun)

buffet (BUH fit): to hit; to beat
Part of Speech: verb
Example: Hurricane winds *buffeted* the small ship.

reprove (re PROOV): to scold; to rebuke
Part of Speech: verb
Example: Mothers *reprove* children who do thoughtless things.
Other Form(s): reprovable (adjective); reprover (noun)

lugubrious (luh GOO bree us): mournful; dismal
Part of Speech: adjective
Example: Requiems are *lugubrious* affairs.
Other Form(s): lugubriousness (noun)

germane (jur MANE): relevant; pertinent
Part of Speech: adjective
Example: She made cogent points because her observations were *germane*.
Other Form(s): germaneness (noun)

delude (de LOOD): to deceive; to mislead
Part of Speech: verb
Example: The embezzler was able to *delude* himself into thinking that his employers deserved to be stolen from.
Other Form(s): delusional (adjective); delusion (noun)

Words and Definitions *(cont.)*

────────────── **Group 2** ──────────────

quintessence (kwin TEH sunts): essential part; purest form
    Part of Speech: noun
    Example: Rose attar is the *quintessence* of the rose.
    Other Form(s): quintessential (adjective)

hapless (HAP less): unfortunate; inept
    Part of Speech: adjective
    Example: The team's record of 0-24 showed how *hapless* it was.
    Other Form(s): haplessness (noun)

pernicious (pur NIH shus): destructive; ruinous
    Part of Speech: adjective
    Example: Disease proved *pernicious* for the entire population.

indolence (IN duh lents): laziness; idleness
    Part of Speech: noun
    Example: Assiduous workers do not suffer from *indolence*.
    Other Form(s): indolent (adjective)

feign (FANE): to fake; to pretend
    Part of Speech: verb
    Example: Malingerers *feign* illness to avoid work.

braggadocio (brag uh DOE shee o): boasting; swaggering
    Part of Speech: noun
    Example: The Three Musketeers were full of *braggadocio*.

suave (SWAHV): sophisticated; urbane
    Part of Speech: adjective
    Example: Travel in Europe had made him a *suave* and cosmopolitan roue.
    Other Form(s): suaveness (noun); suavity (noun)

vagary (VAY guh ree): caprice; an eccentric act
    Part of Speech: noun
    Example: If you act on every *vagary*, you will invite disaster.
    Other Form(s): vagarious (adjective)

Words and Definitions *(cont.)*

—————————————— Group 3 ——————————————

bovine (BO vine): cow-like; dull or stupid
 Part of Speech: adjective
 Example: He had a *bovine* way about him that made people avoid him.

revert (ree VURT): to return; to retrogress
 Part of Speech: verb
 Example: Ex-convicts who *revert* to criminal behavior are recidivistic.
 Other Form(s): reverter (noun); revertible (adjective)

wreak (REEK): to inflict; to vent
 Part of Speech: verb
 Example: Mountainous seas *wreaked* great damage on the oil tanker.

metaphysical (met uh FIH zih kul): abstract; supernatural
 Part of Speech: adjective
 Example: In Islamic theology, Allah is a *metaphysical* being.
 Other Form(s): metaphysics (noun); metaphysician (noun); metaphysicality (noun)

perspicacious (pur spi KAY shus): discerning; astute
 Part of Speech: adjective
 Example: Good instructors are *perspicacious* people who are aware of learning differences.
 Other Form(s): perspicacity (noun); perspicaciousness (noun)

impetuous (im PEH choo us): impulsive; rash
 Part of Speech: adjective
 Example: He indulged his vagaries and was considered an *impetuous* fool.
 Other Form(s): impetuousness (noun); impetuousity (noun)

stature (STA chure): position; rank
 Part of Speech: noun
 Example: Her high *stature* in the community was earned by hard work.

utopian (yoo TOE pee en): ideal; perfect
 Part of Speech: adjective
 Example: Men and women of vision had *utopian* ideals in the eighteenth century.
 Other Form(s): utopia (noun)

Words and Definitions *(cont.)*

─────────── **Group 4** ───────────

unequivocal (un ih KWI vuh kul): unambiguous; unmistakable
   Part of Speech: adjective
   Example: He remained *unequivocal* about his desire to be the highest paid athlete in history.

requite (ree KWITE): to repay; to revenge
   Part of Speech: verb
   Example: Nothing *requited* her for the loss of her paramour.
   Other Form(s): requited (adjective); requital (noun)

belie (be LIE): to contradict; to misrepresent
   Part of Speech: verb
   Example: Bright and sparkling eyes *belied* the bovine mind of the student.

panacea (pan uh SEE uh): cure-all; magic elixir
   Part of Speech: noun
   Example: Utopians dreamed of *panaceas* for man's discontent.

indemnify (in DEM ni fy): to protect from loss; to secure against
   Part of Speech: verb
   Example: Lloyd's of London is famous for its willingness to *indemnify* celebrity body parts—legs, noses, etc.
   Other Form(s): indemnifying (adjective); indemnification (noun); indemnifier (noun)

wane (WANE): to decline; to diminish
   Part of Speech: verb
   Example: The force of the wind *waned*, and the ship was able to reach port.

spearhead (SPEAR head): to lead; to initiate
   Part of Speech: verb
   Example: In the old days, infantry troops *spearheaded* invasions.

lexicon (LEX i kon): dictionary; word book
   Part of Speech: noun
   Example: She referred to a *lexicon* for the proper spelling.
   Other Form(s): lexicography (noun); lexicographer (noun)

Unit 35 (cont.)

Quick Match

Group 1

A. symptomology   C. beat   E. mislead   G. prolix
B. mournful   D. aide   F. pertinent   H. rebuke

_____ 1. verbose
_____ 2. factotum
_____ 3. pathology
_____ 4. buffet

_____ 5. reprove
_____ 6. lugubrious
_____ 7. germane
_____ 8. delude

Group 2

A. swaggering   C. caprice   E. urbane   G. fake
B. idleness   D. purest form   F. unfortunate   H. ruinous

_____ 1. quintessence
_____ 2. hapless
_____ 3. pernicious
_____ 4. indolence

_____ 5. feign
_____ 6. braggadocio
_____ 7. suave
_____ 8. vagary

Group 3

A. rash   C. retrogress   E. supernatural   G. inflict
B. astute   D. ideal   F. rank   H. dull

_____ 1. bovine
_____ 2. revert
_____ 3. wreak
_____ 4. metaphysical

_____ 5. perspicacious
_____ 6. impetuous
_____ 7. stature
_____ 8. utopian

Group 4

A. cure-all   C. initiate   E. unambiguous   G. repay
B. secure against loss   D. dictionary   F. misrepresent   H. decline

_____ 1. unequivocal
_____ 2. requite
_____ 3. belie
_____ 4. panacea

_____ 5. indemnify
_____ 6. wane
_____ 7. spearhead
_____ 8. lexicon

Unit 35 *(cont.)*

Answer Key

——— Pre-test Yourself ———

Group 1
1. lugubrious
2. factotum
3. pathology
4. germane
5. verbose
6. delude
7. buffet
8. reprove

Group 2
1. indolence
2. braggadocio
3. quintessence
4. hapless
5. pernicious
6. feign
7. suave
8. vagary

Group 3
1. metaphysical
2. bovine
3. perspicacious
4. utopian
5. wreak
6. revert
7. stature
8. impetuous

Group 4
1. wane
2. lexicon
3. panacea
4. unequivocal
5. indemnify
6. requite
7. belie
8. spearhead

——— Quick Match ———

Group 1
1. G
2. D
3. A
4. C
5. H
6. B
7. F
8. E

Group 2
1. D
2. F
3. H
4. B
5. G
6. A
7. E
8. C

Group 3
1. H
2. C
3. G
4. E
5. B
6. A
7. F
8. D

Group 4
1. E
2. G
3. F
4. A
5. B
6. H
7. C
8. D

Unit 36

Pre-test Yourself

Group 1

hackneyed	qualitative	inception	pervade
zealous	urbane	masticate	complement

1. The differences were _____ rather than quantitative.

2. A lot of animals swallow their food whole and do not _____ it.

3. Excitement can _____ an arena when a rock 'n' roll band comes.

4. The plan nearly failed at its _____, but was saved by constant attention.

5. His phrases were _____ and worn out, so few purchased his book.

6. The Oakland Raiders seem to attract _____ and unrestrained fans.

7. His _____ manner impressed the ladies.

8. When it comes to formal dress, a cummerbund is considered a _____ to a tuxedo.

Group 2

desecrate	familial	resonant	junket
plangent	venerate	malapropism	gauntlet

1. The anarchists will vandalize and _____ the church if they can.

2. The air grew _____ with thunder as the storm approached.

3. _____ ties kept him close to his brothers.

4. Yogi Berra is considered the all-time king of the _____.

5. Freshmen are forced to run the _____ at military academies.

6. The mayor went on a _____ to Europe to study the trolley systems there.

7. Most boxers and boxing fans _____ Muhammad Ali.

8. The obese boy produced a _____ sound as he belly-flopped into the pool.

Pre-test Yourself *(cont.)*

Group 3

uxorious	oxymoron	thwart	impugn
perpetuate	veneer	stealthy	wistful

---

1. "Jumbo shrimp" is one widely used _____.

2. Her happy demeanor was only a _____; underneath it, she was quite sad.

3. _____ sensitivities required him to be home for dinner on time.

4. Our heavy fortifications will _____ the invading army.

5. Infiltrators use _____ methods so they won't be found out.

6. When the details of his extra-marital affairs became known, he could no longer _____ the public's notion of him as a faithful husband.

7. You may be sued for slandor or libel if you falsely _____ someone's character or actions.

8. The child's _____ look affected the mother deeply.

Group 4

voluminous	hyperbole	platitude	bereave
idiosyncrasy	query	nonplus	felicitous

---

1. _____ is often used by poets to emphasize something.

2. A dog's death will _____ a loving owner.

3. Aristocratic Southern women wore _____ skirts in antebellum times.

4. A student's _____ opened up new avenues of thought on the subject.

5. Winning the lottery was _____ and serendipitous for the whole family.

6. Surprises would always _____ her.

7. "Beauty is as beauty does" is an American _____.

8. She found his _____ of clucking his tongue when displeased quite unbearable.

Unit 36 *(cont.)*

Words and Definitions

─────────── **Group 1** ───────────

hackneyed (HAK need): overused; trite
    Part of Speech: adjective
    Example: His music was *hackneyed* because it was nothing but a pastiche of common styles.

qualitative (KWAH l i tay tiv): pertaining to quality
    Part of Speech: adjective
    Example: The *qualitative* nature of his life depressed him.

masticate (MAS ti kate): to chew; to munch
    Part of Speech: verb
    Example: Some animals *masticate* their food, while others swallow it whole.
    Other Form(s): mastication (noun); masticator (noun); masticatory (adjective)

pervade (pur VADE): to permeate; to saturate
    Part of Speech: verb
    Example: Fear *pervaded* the besieged town.
    Other Form(s): pervading (adjective); pervasion (noun)

zealous (ZEL us): earnest; eager
    Part of Speech: adjective
    Example: True believers are *zealous* people.
    Other Form(s): zeal (noun); zealot (noun); zealousness (noun)

urbane (ur BANE): sophisticated; elegant
    Part of Speech: adjective
    Example: His *urbane* manners made him welcome at society's major banquets.
    Other Form(s): urbaneness (noun); urbanity (noun)

inception (in SEP shun): beginning; start
    Part of Speech: noun
    Example: Bad ideas are often doomed from their *inception*.

complement (KOM ple ment): to complete; to naturally augment
    Part of Speech: verb
    Example: A violet scarf *complemented* her lilac dress.
    Other Form(s): complementary (adjective); complement (noun); complemental (adjective)

Unit 36 (cont.)

Words and Definitions (cont.)

──────────── Group 2 ────────────

desecrate (DES eh krate): to defile; to blaspheme
Part of Speech: verb
Example: Bolshevik zealots *desecrated* churches by destroying icons.
Other Form(s): desecration (noun); desecrator (noun)

venerate (VEN ur ate): to revere; to worship
Part of Speech: verb
Example: Roman Catholics *venerate* the Pope.
Other Form(s): veneration (noun); venerator (noun)

resonant (REH zuh nant): resounding; echoing
Part of Speech: adjective
Example: The orator's *resonant* tones could be heard outside the auditorium.
Other Form(s): resonance (noun)

junket (JUNG kit): excursion; trip
Part of Speech: noun
Example: The senator's publicly-funded vacation *junket* made for sensational news.

plangent (PLAN jent): loud and reverberating; (of a sound) plaintive
Part of Speech: adjective
Example: *Plangent* sounds came out of the well when the bucket was dropped into it.
Other Form(s): plangency

familial (fuh MEEL ee ul): hereditary; family-related
Part of Speech: adjective
Example: Her fair skin and yellow hair were *familial* traits.

malapropism (MAL uh prop izm): humorous misuse of a word; verbal inappropriateness
Part of Speech: noun
Example: Mrs. Malaprop used a *malapropism* in referring to "all together" as "alligator."

gauntlet (GAUNT let): ordeal; trial
Part of Speech: noun
Example: She survived the *gauntlet* and became a hero.

Words and Definitions (cont.)

─────────────── Group 3 ───────────────

uxorious (yook SOR ee us): devoted to one's wife; submissive to one's wife
Part of Speech: adjective
Example: Her husband was in every way *uxorious*, and that's the way she liked him.
Other Form(s): uxoriousness (noun)

oxymoron (ok see MOR on): self-contradictory phrase; incongruity
Part of Speech: noun
Example: If you refer to "jumbo shrimp," you employ *oxymoron*.
Other Form(s): oxymoronic (adjective)

thwart (THWORT): to frustrate; to stop
Part of Speech: verb
Example: Guards *thwarted* the attempted escape.

impugn (im PYOON): to malign; to defame
Part of Speech: verb
Example: The magazine article *impugned* him and made him a laughing stock.
Other Form(s): impugnable (adjective); impugnant (noun)

perpetuate (pur PEH choo ate): keep constant; keep from dying out
Part of Speech: verb
Example: He felt pressure to *perpetuate* the family tradition of attending Harvard.

veneer (ve NEER): façade; deceptive outward appearance
Part of Speech: noun
Example: His noble appearance was nothing more than a *veneer* that everyone saw through.

stealthy (STEL thee): sneaky; sly
Part of Speech: adjective
Example: Cat burglars are *stealthy* thieves.
Other Form(s): stealth (noun); stealthiness (noun)

wistful (WIST ful): yearning; wishful
Part of Speech: adjective
Example: She had a *wistful* look on her face when her lover left her.
Other Form(s): wistfulness (noun)

Words and Definitions *(cont.)*

——————————— Group 4 ———————————

voluminous (vuh LOO mi nus): spacious; commodious
   Part of Speech: adjective
   Example: Noblewomen wore *voluminous* dresses during the reign of Louis XV.
   Other Form(s): voluminousness (noun); voluminousity (noun)

hyperbole (hy PUR buh lee): exaggeration; overstatement
   Part of Speech: noun
   Example: She was prone to *hyperbole*, and everyone was skeptical of her glowing endorsement of the new restaurant.
   Other Form(s): hyperbolic (adjective)

platitude (PLAT i tood): a banal or trite remark; insipidity
   Part of Speech: noun
   Example: The man spoke in *platitudes* and cliches.
   Other Form(s): platitudinous (adjective); platitudinize (verb)

bereave (buh REEV): to deprive of a friend, relation, etc.
   Part of Speech: verb
   Example: Death *bereaved* the widow, and she longed for her lost husband.
   Other Form(s): bereavement (noun)

idiosyncrasy (id ee o SIN kruh see): odd mannerism; quirk
   Part of Speech: noun
   Example: His vagaries and *idiosyncrasies* were the talk of the school.
   Other Form(s): idiosyncratic (adjective)

query (KWARE ee): question; inquiry
   Part of Speech: noun
   Example: The lawyers put forth a *query*, and the witness answered it.
   Other Form(s): query (verb)

nonplus (non PLUS): to puzzle; to perplex
   Part of Speech: verb
   Example: Handel *nonplussed* the audience by having cymbals crash in his Surprise Symphony.

felicitous (fuh LIS ih tus): apt; fortunate
   Part of Speech: adjective
   Example: It was a *felicitous* stroke of luck that was completely unexpected.
   Other Form(s): felicity (noun); felicitousness (noun)

Unit 36 (cont.)

Quick Match

Group 1

A. earnest	C. complete	E. beginning	G. trite
B. chew	D. pertaining to quality	F. permeate	H. sophisticated

_____ 1. hackneyed

_____ 2. qualitative

_____ 3. masticate

_____ 4. pervade

_____ 5. zealous

_____ 6. urbane

_____ 7. inception

_____ 8. complement

Group 2

A. resounding	C. worship	E. ordeal	G. reverberating
B. hereditary	D. misuse of a word	F. trip	H. defile

_____ 1. desecrate   --

_____ 2. venerate

_____ 3. resonant

_____ 4. junket

_____ 5. plangent

_____ 6. familial

_____ 7. malapropism

_____ 8. gauntlet

Group 3

A. submissive to one's wife	C. malign	E. façade	G. yearning
B. keep from dying out	D. self-contradictory phrase	F. frustrate	H. sneaky

_____ 1. uxorious

_____ 2. oxymoron

_____ 3. thwart

_____ 4. impugn

_____ 5. perpetuate

_____ 6. veneer

_____ 7. stealthy

_____ 8. wistful

Group 4

A. deprive	C. apt	E. perplex	G. quirk
B. spacious	D. inquiry	F. overstatement	H. banal remark

_____ 1. voluminous

_____ 2. hyperbole

_____ 3. platitude

_____ 4. bereave

_____ 5. idiosyncrasy

_____ 6. query

_____ 7. nonplus

_____ 8. felicitous

Unit 36 (cont.)

Answer Key

Pre-test Yourself

Group 1
1. qualitative
2. masticate
3. pervade
4. inception
5. hackneyed
6. zealous
7. urbane
8. complement

Group 2
1. desecrate
2. resonant
3. familial
4. malapropism
5. gauntlet
6. junket
7. venerate
8. plangent

Group 3
1. oxymoron
2. veneer
3. uxorious
4. thwart
5. stealthy
6. perpetuate
7. impugn
8. wistful

Group 4
1. hyperbole
2. bereave
3. voluminous
4. query
5. felicitous
6. nonplus
7. platitude
8. idiosyncrasy

Quick Match

Group 1
1. G
2. D
3. B
4. F
5. A
6. H
7. E
8. C

Group 2
1. H
2. C
3. A
4. F
5. G
6. B
7. D
8. E

Group 3
1. A
2. D
3. F
4. C
5. B
6. E
7. H
8. G

Group 4
1. B
2. F
3. H
4. A
5. G
6. D
7. E
8. C

Index

Index (cont.)

Index (cont.)

Index *(cont.)*

Index *(cont.)*

Index (cont.)

Index *(cont.)*

Index (cont.)

Index (cont.)